Seeking the Humanity of God

Practices, Doctrines, and Catholic Theology

James J. Buckley

D1354337

A Michael Glazier Book
THE LITURGICAL PRESS
Collegeville, Minnesota

THEOLOGY AND LIFE SERIES

Volume 36

A Michael Glazier Book published by The Liturgical Press

Cover design by David Manahan, O.S.B.

Cover illustration: mosaic detail; apse; Haghia Sophia, Istanbul

1	2	3	4	5	6	7	8	9

Library of Congress Cataloging-in-Publication Data

Buckley, James Joseph, 1947–
    Seeking the humanity of God : practices, doctrines, and Catholic theology / James J. Buckley.
        p.   cm. — (Theology and life series ; v. 36)
    "A Michael Glazier book."
    Includes bibliographical references and index.
    ISBN 0-8146-5718-4
    1. Catholic Church—Doctrines—History. 2. Faith. I. Title.
II. Series.
BX1747.B83   1992
230'.2—dc20   92-12398
                                                                   CIP

To my father and mother,
John Joseph and Esther Marie

Contents

Preface

There are, experts tell us, two competing translations of the mandate of Psalm 105:4: "Seek God's face forevermore" and "Seek the One who is forever." In the first, the subject is *our* quest for God, and "forevermore" mandates constancy in *our* quest; in the second, the subject is the *God* whom we seek, and "forever" is a mark of *God's* faithfulness. Which is true or right?

Only experts in Hebrew and cognate languages can debate which is the correct translation. The rest of us must submit to their judgment on this issue. On the other hand, which translation is right will not settle the question of which mandate is right. Is this the season for recommending that we attend to the faithfulness of God or is it the season for encouragement in the face of the inconstancies of our quest? More likely, both must be said. But how and in what order? Or do we need to be warned that no amount of seeking can find the unsearchable God? These are questions on which all of us (for better or worse) have a vote—a vote we cast by the lives we lead, the beliefs we hold, and the ways we relate our lives and beliefs to those of strangers and enemies. We also cast our vote by what we read and what we write.

This book is one proposal for how to engage in theological inquiry—namely, by "seeking the humanity of God." The title and subtitle condense the subject matter of the book. Seeking the humanity of God (I shall propose) is an activity constituted

Two givers :— statics : who does it

by relating the practices and doctrines of the Christian community to those of our common humanity in ways that engage what God is doing for all humanity in Word and Spirit. Cast in the form of a practical recommendation, the thesis recommends that we seek the humanity of God in each and all the practices and teachings of our lives. The thesis is (I shall say) "context-pervasive." That is, the thesis is true and right (including useful) in each and every context; it ought, then, to inform each and every context in which we live and move and have our being. Chapter 1 unpacks four context-pervasive features of theological inquiry from the book's title. Subsequent chapters make a case for the thesis as each chapter describes a particular "practice," articulates a specific "doctrine," and proposes a theological way of relating those practices and teachings to other practices and teachings.

However, this thesis (like any other) is indeed an abstraction. Writing it out in a sentence abstracts it from the specific contexts which might give it intelligibility and applicability. Thus, although it will become clear that I think theological inquiry is a thesis-governed (or rule-governed) activity, I do not think there are theses (or rules) for seeking God that faithfully guide us, independently of our individual dispositions and affections in particular physical, social, and historical circumstances and in relation to specific topics; readers expecting clear and distinct rules for seeking God which are context-independent or topic-independent will be disappointed. Thus, my aim is not simply to argue for the thesis but to give examples of the contexts which make such arguments intelligible and applicable. We not only follow the mandate to seek the face of God in general but also and primarily in specific contexts as we worship (ch. 2) and heed the Scriptures (ch. 3), build up the Christian community (ch. 4) and move in a world of diverse religious (ch. 5) and other personal and political projects (ch. 6). In turn, the exhortation to seek the face of God is an exhortation for readers to seek the humanity of God in each and all the joys and griefs of our lives—in our worship (ch. 2) and the Scriptures (ch. 3), in our holy and sinful Church (ch. 4), in the reasons we give to a world of diverse religions and godlessness (ch. 5), and in all our quests for the new heaven and earth God is preparing in Word and Spirit (ch. 6).

Seeking the humanity of God takes a different shape depending on whether we are inquiring into Bible or worship, Church or world, or something else. As chapter 1 sketches the *context-pervasive* features of theological inquiry exemplified in subsequent chapters, so these subsequent chapters experiment on *context-specific* features of theological inquiry that cumulatively support the thesis.

Because the contexts for the thesis must be patiently described and created, it will take time for each and all the chapters to slowly but surely make the case for the thesis. Each chapter exhibits and argues for one aspect of seeking the humanity of God, simultaneously escalating potential conflicts over inquiry and contributing to their resolution. I would ask for readers' critical patience in tracking the case for the thesis. For example, the book is an essay on "Catholic" theology (says the subtitle). More specifically, it is an exercise in Roman Catholic theology. Indeed, part of the case for the thesis depends on a reading of the documents of Vatican II dispersed throughout various chapters. In particular, I propose that what Vatican II has to say about Church or world (between which some conservatives and liberals would have us choose) is subordinate to what it says about God and Jesus Christ. On the other hand, this book is not primarily about Catholics; it is about seeking the humanity of God. It is also not addressed to all Catholics—my examples and arguments are closer to some aspects of Eastern Orthodox or Lutheran, Reformed or Episcopal, Methodist or Mennonite theologies than they are to standard conservative or liberal Catholicism. I hope readers will assess it (or can learn to assess it) by whether its particular (Roman Catholic) claims are (more universally) true and right. In sum, my examples and arguments represent a particular kind of Catholic theology which chapter 1 dubs "Catholic particularity." If all were well, Catholics would assess the chapters by assenting to or dissenting from one or more of the book's claims to be true to what we Catholics do and teach—for example, "It is good that we ought to do x" or "It is true that we ought to teach y" or "It is true that we ought to be permitted to do and teach z." If all were well, students of theology would assess the chapters by assenting to or dissenting from their claims to be true to what those Catholics, to what we (or those)

Christians, to what we (or those) believers in the God of Israel, or to what human creatures ought to do and teach to be true to who we are—or to all these.

"If all were well." But all is not well. The terms—true and good, Catholic and Christian—are abstract. They are abstracted from a range of practices and beliefs which give them intelligibility and applicability. Why center on these terms and not others? Why subject ourselves to the charge of heresy and falsehood rather than protect ourselves from such incivilities by using other, softer terms? The only answers to these sorts of questions are, I think, internal to particular theologies— internal, in this case, to doing theology in relation to particular ways of reading biblical narratives and baptismal practices as well as participating in the domestic and foreign policies of a Church in a world of diverse joys and griefs. The discussions of "truth" at the end of chapter 2 and of "reason-giving" in chapters 4 and 5 are directly relevant to how this kind of theology hopes for audiences to assess it. However, even these discussions will make sense only in the context of the practices and teachings discussed earlier in these and other chapters. Just as the book's thesis will make little sense outside the cumulative construction of a context for giving it sense, so the interest in Catholic theology does not, independently of the character of the inquirer, the context of the inquiry, or the topic being addressed, yield a simple rule or rules for what Catholic theology is.

I have tried to keep in mind an audience of college students (along with the theological experts who teach them) who need to know what prompts theological inquiry, how it relates to other inquiries, and whether it is worth undertaking. I have thus written for those people, in English-speaking neighborhoods and nation states, engaged in attending to specific Scriptures, worshipping in word and sacrament, contributing to sundry common goods of the Church and their churches, sent on a mission to a world of many religions and godlessness, in solidarity with the joys and griefs of that world, saintly and sinful characters. Such people are engaged in a multiplicity of activities, including inquiring into the goodness of their practices (and the truth of their teachings) and considering what to do when such practices and teachings become depraved or dysfunctional. In other words, I presume that the reader has some intuitions about how to inquire within some of these contexts, is interested in testing those intuitions, and will respond critically and constructively to the intuitions of others on this issue.

This audience is most clearly addressed in those first sections of each chapter on what I shall call "ordinary, common sensical, and idiomatic practices." It is crucial to seeking the humanity of God that our inquiries be internal to ordinary, common sensical, and idiomatic practices such as hearing the Bible, celebrating sacraments, building local Christian communities, working and talking with strangers and enemies, becoming a person of faith and hope and love.

However, in emphasizing the "ordinary" contexts of theological inquiry, I cannot promise that all students will be familiar with all the contexts I discuss. In fact, it has been my experience that some students are more at home in one or more of the very same contexts in which other students are most alienated. The student fascinated by inquiry internal to Scripture sometimes sees no point in inquiry in relation to broader religious worlds. The student intrigued by issues of personal character or political agenda or philosophical schools is often frightened or bored by inquiry in relation to worship and sacraments.

This simultaneous enthusiasm for one context of inquiry and antipathy for another is why I have said that the audience must be students "along with the theological experts who usually teach them." Such theologians know that it is not simply students of theology but also theologians themselves who are not always at home in each and all the diverse contexts for theological inquiry. Such theologians ought, then, to be able to offer advice to students of theology from within (rather than from outside) the student's perplexities.

Note that the reason for the importance of guidance from a theologian is not that theologians have a privileged sphere in seeking the humanity of God. In fact, beginning in the first chapter, there is a polemic against those tempted to identify theological inquiry and the inquiries of theologians. The discussion of theologians (particularly in the third and final section of the last five chapters) aims to *situate* them in the context of a broader communion of saints and sinners rather than isolate them. An implication of this is that theologians are of tertiary rather than primary or secondary importance; normally we ought to give priority to exemplary Christian saints and then our pastors and finally our theologians. Such theologians issue calls to repentance from within the practices and teachings of a specific community.

Thus, I envision the use of this text to be typically not by a single reader but in a setting where theologians and those on the way to being theologians engage in debate over theological inquiry. Hence, this is not an introductory text—and not simply because of my meager writing skills, or because it presumes the reader knows something about Bible and worship, church and world. Rather people, not texts (or, at least, not texts like this), initiate us into theological issues. I thus envisage theologians who can explain to those on the way to being theologians the burdens and benefits of doing theology this way, providing background and foreground; showing those on the way to doing theology that the book is not as foolish as it may sometimes seem, nor as wise as it may sometimes appear to claim to be. I envisage readers who aspire to do justice to a partly familiar and partly alien agenda, who presume the book is addressed to them, and who respond constructively (for example, by asking whether the book is faithful to its own agenda) and critically (for example, by asking whether it speaks to the reader's agenda).

I am sure that I have not always succeeded in writing about this subject matter, with this aim and audience. Perhaps at this point the reader should simply know that I am Boston Irish and raised in the United States' Midwest, husband and father, teacher and member of a largely peaceful urban neighborhood. My upbringing was what some would call liberal Catholic. (This meant, *inter alia*, that we long favored an English liturgy and voted Democratic, at least locally.) Vatican II and the Vietnam War changed some of that. We were both too Catholic and not Catholic enough, too liberal and not liberal enough. Some of us needed something new, totally new. My theological education reflects analogous tensions—the years at Kenrick Seminary (named after a St. Louis bishop who disagreed, for a time, with what would become Vatican I's doctrine of papal infallibility) and the Graduate Theological Union at Berkeley and, finally, Yale University's Department of Religious Studies. The book surely reflects some of the joys and griefs (including idiosyncracies) of such a life. Even in this preface I have not tried to leave this "I" out of the picture; but neither do I think my experiences are of some necessary, universal, and transcendental relevance to this enterprise. (Professional theologians ought to know that I am alternately a nonbeliever and an agnostic on the question of whether there is *any* transcendental self or inquiry.)

In any case, what there are of joys in my life have been largely bestowed by parents and brothers and sisters, teachers and friends and colleagues who variously inform, criticize, and ignore my efforts to do theology. The Yale-Washington Theology Group offered competing criticisms of an early version of the book, deconstructing the myth of a "Yale School." William Buckley, Jack Buckley, Joseph DiNoia, John Farina, Stanley Hauerwas, Christopher Kauffman, George Pickering, Jane Schaberg offered helpful criticisms of a later version. David Ford, Steve Fowl, Greg Jones, Lou Pressman, Michael Root, and Bill Wilson offered detailed criticisms of each chapter. Teachers and friends and colleagues have reacted in helpful ways to specific sections—Charles Bobertz, Vigen Guroian, George Lindbeck, Paul Wiebe. I thank them, whether they are among those trying to help me do better what I aim to do, those trying to convince me to do something else, or those not knowing what to do with what I am doing. Chris and David have read not a word of this—although (or because) they have listened to my laments as I tried to write; for this and many more important reasons I am most grateful to them. They and my parents (to whom this book is dedicated) have done the most to teach me what this book is about.

James J. Buckley
May 1, 1991
The Feast of St. Joseph the Worker

Abbreviations

Biblical references are to *The Jerusalem Bible.* Garden City, N. Y.: Doubleday & Company, Inc., 1966.

CD = Karl Barth. *Church Dogmatics.* Eds. G. W. Bromiley and T. F. Torrance and trans. G. W. Bromiley, T. F. Torrance, et al. Four Volumes (1–4), with various Parts (1/1–4/4) and Halves (4/3,1, ch. 16), paragraphs (4/3,1, no. 69) and pages (4/3,1:1). Edinburgh: T. & T. Clark, Ltd., 1936–1975. I use the revised translation of 1/1 (1975).

CEJ = John Bowden, trans., *Christ: The Experience of Jesus as Lord.* New York: The Seabury Press, 1980.

Documents of Vatican II = Austin P. Flannery, O.P., ed. *Documents of Vatican II.* Grand Rapids, Mich.: William B. Eerdmans Publishing Co., 1975.
>   ALP = Decree on the Apostolate of Lay People
>   CMA = Decree on the Church's Missionary Activity
>   CMW = Pastoral Constitution on the Church in the Modern World
>   CSL = Constitution on the Sacred Liturgy.
>   DCC = Dogmatic Constitution on the Church
>   DCR = Dogmatic Constitution on Divine Revelation
>   DOE = Decree on Ecumenism
>   NCR = Declaration on the Relation of the Church to Non-Christian Religions

JBF = H. George Anderson, T. Austin Murphy, and Joseph A. Burgess, eds., *Justification by Faith. Lutherans and Catho-*

lics in Dialogue VII. Minneapolis: Augsburg Publishing House, 1985. Referred to by paragraph number.

RCI = "Rite of Christian Initiation of Adults." The International Commission on English in the Liturgy. The Rites of the Catholic Church, revised by decree of the Second Vatican Ecumenical Council and published by authority of Pope Paul VI. New York: Pueblo Publishing Co., 1976.

TI = Karl Rahner. *Theological Investigations*. Various translators. 22 Volumes. London: Darton, Longman, and Todd, 1961–1991; New York: The Seabury Press, 1974–1991.

References backward and forward in the text are made by indicating chapter and section. For example, (2.A.1) refers to chapter 2, section A, sub-section 1.

1

Theology, Theologians, and Catholic Particularity

Blaise Pascal, a seventeenth century Roman Catholic, was neither the first nor the last to charge that theology only too often amounts to "debates between theologians, not about theology."[1] This sort of attack arises out of very unusual circumstances: imagine presuming that our physicists are arguing among each other rather than about the physical world, that our physicians are holding debates between each other rather than about our health, that our philosophers converse among each other rather than about Being or our being (or whatever). Such debates surely occur in these other fields, but they were not Pascal's (or our) primary concern. The chasm Pascal found between theology and theologians was symptomatic of broader conceptual and institutional problems in theology—aptly described as problems of Catholic particularity.[2] What is Catholic particularity?

Relative to debates among Christians, Pascal wrote as a Roman Catholic against the background of a world fragmented into East and West, Roman Catholic and Protestant. The "one, holy, and catholic Church" Christians confessed in their creed had come to mean "Roman Catholic." But why tie this particular adjective (Roman) to the more universally Christian (catholic Church)? More crucially, Pascal wrote on the edge of a widening gulf between Christendom and what came to be called the modern world. This is a world where

1

Catholics and other Christians compete for catholicity with other particular individuals and groups, religious and secular. Or, to be more accurate, this is a world where many of us vie for our particular version of catholicity; claims to universality, tempting though this is to forget, are always particular. Why and how ought we to preserve or transform Catholic particularity in this world?

Theologians, Pascal thought, were not doing justice to Catholic particularity. Pascal's Jesuits had an "accommodating theology" with "something to please everyone." They were too liberal, too catholic (or not Catholic enough). Pascal's Dominicans had the right theology, but their particularity was made up of subtle theological distinctions that bore no relationship to the ordinary life and language of the broader Catholic community. They were too particular, too conservative (or not catholic enough to move outside their theological sect). Even further, in the interests of power rather than truth, Catholic accommodationists and particularists had joined in battle against a small group of ascetical reformers called Jansenists. Even the popes, who simply sought "to clear up differences between Christians," had been "caught off guard" in deciding against the Jansenists. Pascal supported these Jansenists. He was convinced that the popes would revise their judgement once they knew the facts. His own task was more local, more provincial: to ridicule and reject liberal and conservative theologians in the name of theology. Yet he did not claim to be a Jansenist or even a theologian. Pascal (or, better, his pseudonym) was one of those who claim to be catholic by having "friends in every party," despite (or because of) being "attached to no community and no individual whatever."[3]

No matter what the differences between Pascal's world and our own, we too have our liberals and conservatives, our radically ascetical reformers and church officials, as well as those unattached to any community or individual. We may find them among our family and friends. We may find them even within ourselves. How can we relate theology and theologians at a time when some wish to bring us up to date with the modern world, others call us to return to the sources of our particularity, still others claim to have more radical alternatives, and some move alone (idiosyncratically unattached to other individuals and communities)? The goal of the first part of this chapter is to offer some advice to help answer this question.

The aim of the advice is twofold. First, I aim to offer counsel about how we (you and I and others) ought to think and live in relation to this world of Catholic particularity. Because Catholic particularity is not a single thing, I offer four quite distinct counsels. The counsels are very particular. I propose no new method for doing theology, no typology of theology and theologians, no theory of how theologians fit into the Church or the world, and no grand account of the place of theologians in the evolution of the species or the revolutions of various nation states. Students of theology can readily find such discussions.[4] But it will soon become clear why I think we ought to be suspicious of any general comments *on* theology or theologians, at least for the purposes of *doing* theology. The constructive aim is simply to offer counsel that the reader might (or might not) test over against experiences he or she has in dealing with theology or theologians—whether those be experiences of censuring or ridiculing, teaching or learning from them.

But why should we consent to this counsel? Why should we care about Catholic particularity? These questions will require a book to answer. Certainly, the following pieces of advice are more particular than catholic, more Catholic than true for everyone. If these four counsels are to become catholic as well as particular, they will need to be located in broader contexts in relation to other topics. Locating the counsels in other contexts, we shall see (1.B.), sets the agenda for the rest of the book: each subsequent chapter will, in different ways, follow these four counsels. Thus, a second purpose of these counsels is to anticipate four problems that will be addressed in subsequent chapters. But, before explaining how the advice generates a book, consider these four counsels.

A. *Four Counsels*

1. *Theology is undertaken within the contexts of various* practices. *Therefore, learn to do theology within our diverse contexts; learn to locate theologians within their sundry contexts.*

Dante Alighieri's *Divine Comedy* depicts a world before

Pascal—a world when theology and theologians had clear and important contexts. This classic late medieval poem is the story of the author's journey through hell, purgatory, and heaven—a journey which begins with Dante lost in a dark wood and ends in his vision of the Trinitarian God. As the story goes forward, Dante provides a very specific location for theologians. People from the Bible, bishops and monks and canon lawyers, theologians and philosophers all join in common cause as Doctors of the Church in the fourth heaven of the *Paradiso*. But this context is one among many. There are many spheres of the heavens as well as the mount of purgatory and the pit of hell. Theologians are part of a larger story. A similar point applies to theology. We do not find Dante's "theology" prepackaged on a shelf, to be consumed or ignored as we please. Instead, we must learn it as we follow Dante's movement toward God through the contexts of the *Inferno*, *Purgatorio*, and *Paradiso*, meeting devilish and saintly individuals and groups along the way. The lesson for us is simple: we, too, need to locate theologians within contexts larger than themselves because their and our theologies are worked out as we move within such diverse contexts.

This is not a recommendation that we await a Dante-like vision of eternal life before undertaking theology—or that we locate theologians solely according to what is of eternal significance in their vocations. In this respect, Dante's theology and theologians are too otherworldly. But we can take up the implied recommendation to locate theologians in a broader world—a world where we learn to do theology within a variety of contexts. For example, pondering and enacting the sort of person I am and ought to be, I distinguish and relate my various dispositions and actions—those of a spouse and parent, son or daughter, teacher and student, poet and scientist, citizen and entrepreneur, perchance theologian. In our interpersonal relations we sort out and relate the various patterns of our co-humanity as we crisscross the loves of a man or a woman, a child or a friend, an entire household. And we practice various kinds of social relations in sundry configurations as we move from near to distant neighbors, molded by and molding various political, economic, industrial, cultural, educational, religious, and ecclesial groups—Jew and Greek, men and women, slave and free. Thus, as particular people in particular social relations, we find ourselves moving from one role to another, from community to community, from past to present to future in multilayered ways. We (or some of us) read the Bible. We celebrate liturgies. We build up a Church with particular missions to the world. We do these things in patterns of great complexity, and we somehow weave them together into a life. Similar complexities are involved as we bump against the physical cosmos—tilling the land or spying a quark or building a reactor. Our movement within and between our individual emotions and affections and diverse Christian communities, the religious and non-religious world, our neighbors and our God is constituted by sets of such practices as we enact and suffer the goods and evils of our lives.

This is one way to describe the contexts for doing theology and studying theologians. God is sought as we inquire within and between such practices, that is, those sets of ordinary, common sensical, and idiomatic activities by which we negotiate our diverse and conflicting interactions with the particular and concrete events of our lives. We "do theology" (let us say) whenever we read and write, interact with and think about God and God's relation to our world—our Scriptures and worship, our church and our relations to diverse religions and the world more generally, our individual experiences of the joys and griefs of life. Easter is thus "in ordinary," even if in extraordinary ways.[5]

Further, theologians (like the rest of us) live in a physical, social, and historical world. We need to listen for their ordinary, common-sensical, and idiomatic world as we listen to their often strange, technical, and quite unidiomatic theologies. Like the rest of us, some theologians are more at ease in one context than another—the Bible or worship, the Church or the world, our philosophies or politics or affections, and so forth. People in the Bible, bishops and monks and canon lawyers, theologians and philosophers do not usually hang out in the same contexts—at least in this world. Perhaps we ought to be prepared to spread them out over such contexts rather than locate all of them at some single place in our paradiso (or inferno). But that we need to locate theologians within specific contexts is hardly controversial advice.

All of the above is one aspect of Catholic particularity. That is, the contexts of theology and theologians are particular; such contexts include *each* occasion of human activity, occasions of joy as well as grief. The contexts are also catholic; they include *every* such occasion of human activity. A crucial question to put to our own theologies and those of other theologians is how we and they do theology within each and every one of these contexts.

Nonetheless, it is not easy to escape the charge of other-worldliness we so quickly make against Dante. "My" and "our" practices can seem as otherworldly to "others" as Dante's world seems to most of us. We may, for example, do our own (or I may do my own) theology unattached to other individuals and groups; such people form another world external to our own. It is not difficult to find cultures with diverse and opposed religions, diverse and opposed scriptures and rituals, diverse and opposed concepts of us. In the face of such other worlds, we might restrict ourselves to practices internal (rather than external) to who we are. We might aim to move in the context of our faith, isolated from other faiths. Or we might identify ordinary life with the private worlds of our jobs and family (or, for students, of those who have the same career aspirations and social tastes as they do).[6] But if we do this, we purchase one kind of particularity at the price of one kind of catholicity—the particularity of my theology in contrast to yours, our theology in contrast to theirs.

At the other extreme, we might focus exclusively on practices external (rather than internal) to who we are. Here we seek the practices everyone shares as the context for more particular practices. Perhaps (we might argue) everyone naturally pursues happiness, seeks nibbana or God, and this sets *the* context which holds together our particular contexts. But as the mention of happiness and nibbana and God suggests, it is difficult to have this kind of catholicity except at the price of one kind of particularity; claims about the practices everyone shares are made by people who move within some practices other people do not share. Others may separate internal and external practices, but Catholic particularists will seek for ways to identify and relate the diverse contexts in which we live, move, and (some say) have our being.

This first counsel can be put negatively. Neither our theologies nor our theologians are self-contextualizing. Do not undertake to do theology (or study theologians) within *one* context alone—or in *all* contexts at once. The first will make doing theology and studying theologians too facilely particular, as if theology and theologians were exhausted by how we and they move in relationship to Bible *or* worship, Church *or* world, our individual experiences *or* those with few of our experiences. The second will make doing theology and studying theologians too ambitiously catholic, as if there were one crucial context in common for all theology and theologians—perhaps whether they move internally to or externally to the worlds of Bible or worship, Church or world religions, our political or more personal experiences. All of us in fact know a great deal in practice about how to identify and relate the *diverse* contexts for theology and theologians; but we need to learn how to articulate this implicit knowledge if we are to make reflective sense of Catholic particularity.

Is this why we had ₵ ?

2. *Theology articulates* teachings *about various topics. Therefore, learn to do theology by learning to articulate teachings about these topics; learn to study theologians by studying what they teach about these topics.*

For examples of teachings on various topics, let us look not to the fourteenth (Dante) or seventeenth (Pascal) centuries but to the twentieth century. If we take the documents of the Second Vatican Council as examples of the sorts of things theology is about, we will find teachings articulated about various topics or subject matters. Thus, we find Vatican II making claims about God, the Bible, the liturgy, religious and bishops and other people in the Catholic Church, other Christian communities and the ecumenical movement, Judaism and other religions, as well as the modern world. Each of these topics constitutes a *locus*—a time and place—of divine and human activity. As we move inside and outside such *loci*, part of doing theology is teaching things about such topics, subject matters, or *loci*. How, for example, is God's activity in Jesus Christ related to our activity in using the Scriptures, participating in the liturgy, reforming the Church, discerning the truth in the religions or the presence and purpose of God in the needs and aspirations of all people? Answering this sort of question requires inquiry into how we articulate what are variously called Christian doctrines or dogmas, beliefs and action-guides—teachings which are "essential to Christian communal identity."[7]

It seems to be a matter of common sense that Catholics and other Christians implicitly and explicitly, officially and unofficially, teach certain things from the pulpit or some other podium, in classrooms and homes, in inner-Christian controversy and extra-Christian apologetic. Doing theology includes articulating such teachings; studying theologians includes studying the teachings they articulate—not only teachings about God and our community's domestic policies but also about other Christian groups and other religious and non-religious people in our foreign policies. Debates about theology can become mere debates between theologians not only by our refusing to find contexts for such debates but also by our thinking and acting as if theology were usually about itself or about theologians' reading and writing about themselves—rather than about diverse topics.

And yet, when we teach that which is essential to Christian communal identity, we are bound to generate controversy. Consider two challenges to the Catholic particularity of Christian teachings. First, Vatican II's Dogmatic Constitution on the Church teaches that God intends to raise all humanity to participate in God's life by preparing a new humanity in Israel and the Church. But Roman Catholics—lay and clergy and religious, popes and bishops, Jesuits and Dominicans and others—frequently disagree on how God is enacting this purpose. Shall we, for example, devote our energies to "all humanity" or "Israel and the Church"? Catholic (the argument might go) is too catholic a description to account for the particularity of Catholics in different roles and institutions, times and places, races and ethnic groups; it does not adequately describe the particularities of these Catholics. A similar objection could be raised about the teachings of Eastern or Russian Orthodox, Lutheran or Reformed, Anglo-Catholic or Methodist, Mennonite or Baptist, Seventh-Day Adventist or Mormon, or any individuals and groups who call themselves Christian. Do these designations, even if their use is internal to these communities, do justice to the particularities and inner tensions of these communities?

The mention of non-Catholic Christians raises a second challenge. Presume (as we have done against the first challenge) that Catholic is an apt description of the teachings of Vatican II's community. The second challenge comes from those who might argue that Catholic is too particular a description to account for what is essential to a more catholic Christian identity. What we ought to seek are not *Catholic* teachings (or the teachings of any other particular Christian community). What we ought to seek are teachings essential to *Christian* identity. Of course, those who issued the first challenge could counter-argue that Christians do not have the sort of concrete particularity that more specific churches and communities do; no one can currently speak for Christians in the way that diverse sorts of people can speak for Eastern Orthodox, Catholic, Lutheran, Reformed, and so forth. Both challenges raise the question: whence the Catholic particularity of teachings subject to challenges to both their Catholicity and their Christianness?

The problem here is not the problem of identifying and relating internal and external practices. Clearly, the teachings of Vatican II (or of other particular Christian communities) raise the problems of identifying and relating internal and external practices. That is, Vatican II's teachings arise within a particular community's contexts; they can usually be prefaced with "We teach x" rather than "I teach x," "you teach x," or "they teach x." They also aim to relate their internal practices to the practices of other individuals and groups—for example, religious and non-religious people who do not share most of the essential practices of their community. Teachings belong in such contexts. It is a great mistake to *equate* theology with articulating teachings—or to equate theologians with the teachings they articulate.

But the problem now is not identifying and relating (relatively subjective) contexts. It takes special circumstances to render questions about Catholicity and Christianness intelligible and applicable. But, not least since the German Christian (including Catholic) supporters of Hitler, it has been impossible to imagine that what Catholics and Christians ought to teach is solely determined by the faith of particular Catholics or Christians. Instead, the problem involves identifying and relating (relatively objective) topics—subject matters *distinctive* of our community's teachings and those *common to* a variety of individuals and groups.[8] If we focus only on teachings about subject matters distinctive of our Christian community (for example, Catholic teachings about Bible or worship), we will certainly have teachings about particular subject matters—perhaps so particular that they will have little to do with the beliefs and action-guides taught by other Christian communities. On the other hand, if we focus only on topics we share with other individuals and groups (for example, a common Christianness that transcends the teachings and practices of particular Christian individuals and groups), we will certainly articulate Christianly catholic beliefs—beliefs so universally Christian that we might wonder what makes them particularly Christian (for example, Catholic).

The aim of this section is not to settle the problem of identifying and relating Catholic and Christian teachings. The aim is to advise that we take it into account as we do theology and study theologians. Catholic particularists on this issue are those who claim to speak to our *common* Christian identity from the point of view of a *specific* Christian community. We learn to do this as we learn to articulate our own teachings and study the teachings of others, carefully distinguishing and relating what is Catholic (or Eastern Orthodox, Lutheran, Reformed, and so forth) and what is Christian in our teachings.

This same piece of advice can be put negatively. Do not undertake to do theology or study theologians by asking only whether their teachings are Catholic *or* Christian. Asking only whether teachings are Catholic (or particularly Christian in other ways) may force us to neglect teachings which are more commonly Christian. We may then seek to be so particular that we refuse (contrary to the teaching of Vatican II and other Christian communities) to stand within the Christian ecumenical movement. Asking only whether teachings are Christian may force us to neglect teachings which are Catholic (or particularly Christian in other ways). We may seek to be so catholic that we ignore the differences and oppositions among those who call themselves Christians. Others will choose between

Catholicity and Christianness. But Catholic particularists will learn to ask theologies and theologians what they take to be essential to Catholic as well as Christian identity. Thus, we need to learn to identify and relate various topics if we are to do justice to Catholic particularity.

3. *Theology is an activity which* aims to relate *the practices and teachings of the Christian community to the practices and teachings of other communities. Therefore, learn to do theology by seeking this* goal; *learn to study theologians by studying how well they enact this aim.*

The advice offered thus far bears only indirectly on theology itself. The first piece of advice suggests that we scrutinize the practices which form the contexts of theology; the second that we scrutinize its teachings about various topics. Those out to "do their own theology" unattached to any individuals or groups ought to remember that neither their own nor any other theology is self-contextualizing; those out to study theologians ought to remember that theology is not usually about theologians. The first two pieces of advice imply that theology and theologians are parts of a larger enterprise, a larger story.

But, we now need to say theology itself is an activity—an activity with specific goals. As there are diverse contexts and subject matters for theology and theologians, so there may be a number of goals involved in doing theology. One of the most crucial questions to ask about theology and theologians is, "Which of many possible goals is central to this theology?" Put more personally, "Which (if any) goals form the heart and soul (or the self) of our theology or this theologian?" We need to study carefully what a theologian *says* is her or his central aim; we need to study even more carefully how the theologian *actually enacts* that aim as he or she engages in theology in various contexts in relationship to diverse topics. Is the aim, more specifically, to present teachings which are Catholic or Christian or those which are "true" and "right" for everyone (that is, catholic) or both? If both, how are the two types of teachings related?

These questions are not as easy to answer as they might seem. Consider Vatican II's Pastoral Constitution on the Church in the Modern World, which teaches that "the joy and

hope, the grief and anguish of the people of our time, especially
of those who are poor or afflicted in any way, are the joy and
hope, the grief and anxiety of the followers of Christ as well"
(Preface, par. 1). Our joys and griefs are not only particularly
Catholic or Christian but also more generally catholic (that is,
common to all humanity). But such solidarity is a rare occur-
rence indeed. Even at its best (that is, prescinding from its
identity as a church of sinners), a Vatican II community embraces only fragments of individual and communal activities
throughout the cosmos. There are human activities which are
alien, strange, and foreign to this community. There are Christian activities (for example, practices in which we engage as
well as ways we teach about various subject matters) which are
foreign to this culture. There are practices and teachings many
regard as not true or right, at least for them. Whence, then, the
catholicity of teachings so foreign to so many?

The issue here is not the identity and relationships of internal and external practices (as in the first piece of advice
above). By and large, we all engage in certain practices, while
others remain external to us; but we frequently disagree over
which practices should and should not be internal or external.
Neither is the issue the relationship between subject matters
particular to the Catholic community and other Christian
communities (as in the second piece of advice). The tradition
of Catholic particularity is constituted not only by these two
problems but also by a third. Vatican II, we might say, teaches
that its practices and teaching are not only Catholic (or Christian) but also right or true. And so the issue is, "How can we
aim at proposals that are not only Catholic or Christian but
also true or right?"

Theologians in the tradition of Catholic particularity have
tried to resolve this problem by proposing various *relationships between* Christian and other practices, Christian teachings and other teachings. Some propose such relationships by
distinguishing and relating "natural" and "revealed" theology.
Others propose that Christian teachings must be "correlated
with" or "mediated by" my or our or someone's experience in
order to be true or right. A third group is wary of systematically
relating Christian and other truth-claims, whether truth be defined more objectively or subjectively; Christian and other

truth-claims, they argue, can be related only in an ad hoc fashion. There may be still other patterns for relating Catholicity and truth. The main point is that one of the most crucial questions to ask theologians is what sort of "patterns of relationships" they permit and require between Catholic or Christian and other truth-claims.[9]

Another way to explain this issue is to begin with those who deny that we ought to propose teachings that are *both* Catholic or Christian *and* true or right. For example, some Catholics or Christians often act and speak as if once we show a practice or teaching is Catholic/Christian, the theological task is accomplished; for them, to ask whether a practice or teaching is not only Catholic or Christian but also true or right is to place oneself in the sinful situation of denying the faith. Tertullian is a classic representative of this position, at least at moments when he says: "What indeed has Athens to do with Jerusalem? What concord is there between the Academy and the Church? . . . Let our 'seeking,' therefore, be in that which is our own, and from those who are our own, and concerning that which is our own,—that, and only that, which can become an object of inquiry without impairing the rule of faith."[10] Here we have another instance of particularity tyrannizing over catholicity, at least for those of us who aim to be faithful to "our own" even while we live with those who are not our own in Athens or Jerusalem, the academy or the Church.

Other Catholics or Christians act and speak as if the theological task does not even begin until we show how our proposed practices and teachings are true and right; for them, to ask whether a practice or teaching is Catholic or Christian is to place oneself in the highly anomalous situation of being concerned with matters of parochial and sectarian concern in contrast to more catholic and public concerns with our common humanity. Here we have another instance of the triumph of catholicity over particularity (or catholicity triumphing over Catholicity). If no one is answerable only to our own, neither is anyone answerable only to one city like Athens or Jerusalem or a single institution like the academy or the Church.

Are we at this point making Pascal's charge come true? Are we turning debates about the contexts and subject matters of theology into technical debates between theologians—debates about the true and the good, natural and revealed theologies, correlational and ad hoc theological strategies? Perhaps so. When a theologian (or the theologian in us) asks whether the contexts within which we move are the right contexts or whether the teachings we articulate are true teachings, this theologian may end up thinking he or she owns a perspective abstracted from any contexts or topics—perhaps the perspective of a certain kind of mystic, scholar, or God. Such thinking claims to be unencumbered by contexts and subject matters; such theological souls or selves are disembodied. Many of us who make this mistake need to be patiently taught otherwise; we may even merit the ridicule of Pascal or the infernal wrath of Dante.

But perhaps the issue of the aim of theological activity is not provincial in quite this way. Much depends on what a theologian means by Christian or true. We find that out by studying with them—or reading them carefully, arguing with them on their own terms as well as our own. We could end up discovering that when a theologian asks questions about whether teachings and practices are Catholic and true or right, he or she is engaging in an activity tightly wed to the advice offered on the contexts and topics of theology. Recall that the practical contexts of theology and theologians are particular and diverse, yet are also catholic and whole. And if this is so, the relationships theologians seek between Catholicity/Christianness and truth are representative of a range of practices by which we weave ourselves into and out of our common humanity. They stand surety for issues that arise when the Christian moves from reading the Bible to her or his morning prayer; from the Lord's Supper to parish council; from neighboring congregations to job and home, election booth and ball park—or issues that arise when a Catholic marries or befriends another Christian, when Christian works and talks with Buddhist or atheist, when we identify with the poor and afflicted. Athens, Jerusalem, and the Church do not exhaust the options. (How) can one be Christian and citizen, poet and philosopher, scientist and mother, rich and poor at the same time? Shall we say that one or more of these movements ought not to be made, or that being Catholic or Christian adds little to the way anyone engages in such activities? Or shall we say that the contexts are related as natural and revealed, that they are correlated, or that they are related in ad hoc ways?

Doing theology is aiming to propose practices and teachings that are both Catholic/Christian and true/right. We are all theologians (or on the way to being theologians) insofar as we make such proposals and test the similar proposals of others. Studying theologians is not only placing them in particular contexts in relationship to specific subject matters but also describing and assessing the patterns in which they relate the Catholicity and truth of their proposals.

Once again, we might put this advice negatively. Do not begin or end by asking whether a theology or theologian aims to make Catholic/Christian *or* true/right proposals. Restricting oneself to issues of what is generally true or right may result in ignoring the respects in which Catholic particularity ought to remain agnostic about or challenge such generalities; restricting oneself to issues of what is Catholic may result in ignoring the respects in which Catholic particularity ought to challenge any particular claims for Catholicity. We somehow need to seek ways to relate "Catholic" and "true" if we are to do justice to Catholic particularity.

4. *Theology is about the* God *of Jesus Christ. Therefore, learn to do theology in relation to this God; learn to study theologians by learning how they read and write, think and pray, and otherwise engage God.*

Like the other pieces of advice, this one might seem a mere truism. Students of theology are constantly told by dictionaries and encyclopedias that theology is "about God." Those who study theological debates will quickly learn that such debates are less over practices or teachings, theologians or theology than over God (or "God"). And yet the reminder that theology is about God can be quite deceptive when stated in general terms. It can deceive us into thinking that there is agreement about who God is so that (on the basis of this agreement) we can then debate whether God is and what God has to do with our world. But there are too many gods and too many ways of believing (or disbelieving) these gods to be satisfied with the claim that theology is about God.

For example, the typical form of the debate over God for Catholic particularity focuses on the claim that the God of the *particular* Israelite Jesus Christ is the God of *all* humanity. Jesus Christ (as Karl Barth put it) is "the humanity of God" in that this particular individual, as God, embraces our humanity.[11] From this point of view, the fourth piece of advice is not simply about one other aspect of Catholic particularity; rather, it is about the issue that sets the agenda for the applicability and intelligibility of Catholic particularity. That is, if the God of Jesus Christ (who is also the God of Israel) is the God of all humanity, Christian discipleship is a way of life that holds apart and together the diverse internal and external contexts for doing theology; we will, then, encounter the God of all humanity as we use Scripture and celebrate liturgies, as we move inside and outside a holy but sinful Church with specific missions, as we engage the myriad delights and tragedies of our individual lives. If Jesus Christ is the God of all humanity, then our teachings about diverse topics will have a way to hold apart and together claims about subject matters Catholic and Christian. If Jesus Christ is the God of all humanity, then in this One we find God, creating and redeeming, by weaving together what is Catholic/Christian and what is true/right in sundry patterns of relationships. Jesus Christ will be the way, the truth, and the life. In sum, if the God of Jesus Christ (who is also the God of Israel) is the God of all humanity, we have *the* way of engaging, interacting, and covenanting with God in each and every occasion of human activity. But is this so? How is this human being in a particular history that moves from birth and life to death and resurrection the God of all humanity? Here is the central version of the problem of Catholic particularity around which the others orbit.

Note that I have said that this is the typical form of the debate about God for Catholic particularity. There is no such thing as debates about God abstracted from considerations of context, subject matter, and the goals we have in reading and writing, thinking and speaking about God. But neither is it the case that theology is about God the way it is about practices or teachings or theological aims. God is not simply one other context or subject matter or aim for theology. The problem of seeking and identifying God is considerably more complex than the problems of seeking and identifying our practices, teachings, and aims.

For example, some might agree that the God of Jesus Christ is a particular god, much as the gods of Homer or Hesiod are the gods of their particular times and places. Theologians, then, are those who tell or construct stories of the gods who periodically appear in our world—in our scriptures and rituals, our churches and cities. These gods are like us, but in odd ways. Here we have theologies about a particular god or particular gods, but such gods are scarcely of ultimate and universal significance—although they may be of ultimate importance for you or me, for us or them.

Or consider less mythological versions of this option. God may be said to be the spiritual ground of our being (or the grounding spirit), descriptions of which (or whom) shade off into each other depending on whether we ought to locate the invisible working of this spirit in (or identify this spirit with) the depths of our consciousness, our communities, our religions, or history as a whole.[12] We might speak of "the humanity of God," but the genitive will be objective—as when we speak of "the love of God" and mean our love for God. In other words, God becomes less like a subject distinct from and extrinsic to us than a deep dimension of the context (or, if we are polytheistic, contexts) in which we move—perhaps (as some theologians say) the subject who is never object. At the extreme, seeking God will be said to be identical to seeking our humanity—in whatever particular ways we describe our humanity. Here God's particularity is purchased at the price of God's catholicity. The particularity of Jesus Christ becomes merely an instance of particularity—perhaps our particularity writ large. In this case, the advice we give about God will be very similar to the advice we give about moving within other particular contexts.

On the other hand, we might argue that the God of Jesus Christ is the God of all humanity only insofar as this God is merely an instance (perhaps the "revealed" one) of a more general (and so catholic) vision of God. We seek and find God not in each and every occasion of human activity but in an "other" world—much as we seek other "eternal and immovable and independent" entities.[13] God is less like the contexts in which we move than like those subject matters in relationship to which we move—perhaps the object who is never subject. If we speak of the humanity of God, the genitive "of" will be a subjective genitive—as when we speak of "the love of God" and mean God's love for us. Seeking God will then be totally different from seeking ways to deepen the joys and abolish the griefs of our lives. Here, we might say, God's catholicity is purchased at the price of God's particularity.

Not even these gods exhaust the alternative ways of doing theology in relationship to God; there are non-theistic religious people and non-religious people with whom we have to live and think. But these examples are enough to make the main point. If we say that theologies are about God, we must also say that they are less debates over different and opposed things to predicate of God than over different and opposed ways of identifying God. The first theological question is not, "Does God exist?" or, "Is God good, bad, or indifferent?" but, "Who is God?" For Catholic particularity, this question is identical with another: how is the God of Jesus Christ, who is also the God of Israel, the God of all humanity?

This ambiguity over "God" should not be surprising. It is important to remember that Christians once resisted the notion of "theology" as a way to describe what they taught. They also ignored or resisted the notion of "theologians" as a way to describe who they were. This may have been because they were fearful they would be confused with those who told stories of gods or those who sought a god who lived unmoved in another world.[14] We ought to keep in mind this ancient suspicion as we do theology and study theologians. None of us can or ought to engage in all the activities different individuals call theology; none of us can rightly call ourselves theologians from the perspective of all of those who call themselves theologians. Relating theology and theologians in the context of Catholic particularity includes learning this lesson.

B. *An Agenda*

So much for some advice on relating theology and theologians in the context of Catholic particularity. Again, the counsel amounts to no new method for theology, no new theory of how theologians fit or do not fit into an ecclesiological or sociological scheme. It simply aims to offer some advice about relating theology and theologians once given the problems of Catholic particularity—counsel which would have to be tightened and loosened at different spots depending on who tried to use it. This counsel is, we might say, more particular than catholic (more Catholic than catholic, more Roman Catholic than Catholic), for it does not aim to offer advice relative to gods other than the God of Jesus Christ, theologians other than those who aim at Catholicity and truth, teachings other than those Catholic and Christian subject matters of Vatican II, practices other than those in which certain of us engage. We surely need advice on these other issues, but Catholic particularists like myself are simply not in the best position to give it.

And yet the particularity of these counsels is a problem. There is no theologically neutral counsel on relating theology and theologians. We ought to be suspicious of those who advise otherwise—who act as if we can give or take advice on relating theology and theologians by standing apart from both, articulating the alternatives, and then choosing one (or none) and declaring war on the others. The examples and descriptions of practices and teachings, of theological aims at relating Catholicity and catholicity, of the God of Jesus Christ as the God of all humanity—these examples and descriptions are anything but neutral vis-á-vis theological, a-theological, and anti-theological options. Any non-trivial advice we offer on this issue is ultimately advice *internal* to particular ways of doing (or not doing) theology.

The notion of theology at work in this advice is easily summarized but it will take a whole book to explain it. In sum, *doing theology is relating the practices and teachings of the Catholic community to the practices and teachings of our common and not so common humanity in ways that engage what God is doing for all humanity in Word and Spirit.* The same point must also be stated as a practical recommendation: *Seek the humanity of God in each and every particular joy and grief of our lives—our Scriptures and worship, our holy but sinful Church, the reasons we give to a world of diverse gods and unbeliefs, and all our quests for the new heaven and earth God is cre-*

ating in Word and Spirit. That this truth-claim and action-guide is central to theology is *the thesis of this book.* We assess whatever there is of the theologian in each of us (as well as other theologians) by how truly and rightly they and we engage in this enterprise. The job of this book is to illustrate and argue for this way of engaging in theology and so provide examples of and reasons for taking up the practical recommendation.

The truth-claim and action-guide express the context-pervasive features of seeking the humanity of God, that is, the features of theological inquiry that pervade each and every context. The thesis of the book will be supported through an accumulation of context-specific inquiries, that is, investigations of inquiries in quite specific contexts. Thus, each chapter develops a sub-thesis in support of the thesis. First, I begin each chapter with an instance of "practices"—not catholic "practices in general" but Catholic practices. These are practices internal to a particular community, but they also require and permit that community to relate to the practices of other communities in specific ways. Catholic particularity is centrally constituted by our engagement in each and every such practice. The aim here is to follow the first piece of advice above by describing "samples" of "competent speakers"—or "paradigmatic ideals" of Christian *praxis.*[15] We might call this aim an inquiry into our evangelical and other practices, our ordinary and idiomatic languages, our practical wisdoms and common senses, our contexts. Even better than giving them a single label will be providing examples of such practices. There is no practice-neutral way of exemplifying, much less describing or defining, what idiomatic practices are.

Second, each chapter will then provide an instance, a sample, or example of inquiry into teachings or doctrines. The aim here is to follow the second piece of advice, suggesting ways to articulate teachings about specific topics or subject matters in particular contexts. Vatican II will prove helpful on such teachings, although not in any single way. Gradually the case will be made that Vatican II can help us articulate a Christian, ecumenical consensus on some topics—if we can learn to locate Vatican II in the right contexts and subordinate its teachings about Church and world to its teachings about Jesus Christ and God. These teachings could be wrong by failing, in different ways for different contexts and topics, to be Catholic or failing to be Christian. Here (I hope) *Roman Catholic* particularity is *identical* to *Catholic* and *Christian* particularity, at least for those sorts of Christians I discuss: Eastern Orthodox, Lutheran, Reformed, Episcopal and Roman Catholic—each from the point of view of one kind of Roman Catholic.[16]

Third, each chapter will provide an example of proposing patterns of relationships between Catholic practices and teachings and other practices and teachings. Most (but not all) of the arguments with theologians occur here, as I follow the advice of testing the ways theologians relate the Christianness and truth of their proposals in specific contexts in relation to specific subject matters. The key recommendations of these sections are not *doctrinally* essential to Catholic particularity, although I (as well as some of the theologians to whom I appeal) think they are *theologically* urgent.

Note that theologians are located against the background of broader practices and teachings. A key implication is that insofar as all of us aim to propose practices and teachings which are Catholic and true or right, all of us do theology and need to study theologians; on the other hand, theology is not usually about theologians. Further, the judgments in these sections have to do with the positions of these theologians on particular issues; I have not aimed to make overall judgments about particular theologians—much less a judgement about which (if any) theological characters belong in heaven, purgatory or hell.

Further, there is movement not only within each chapter but also between chapters. It is this movement between chapters that aims to follow the fourth piece of advice. In an earlier draft, I began with the particular figure Jesus Christ, showing how this One's particularity is a Catholic particularity by calling us to move from 1) Scripture and 2) sacraments through 3) a holy but sinful community and 4) a world of other religions and unbeliefs to 5) a world of our common and not so common humanity. This was a movement from the particular toward the universal. Catholic modified particularity (and catholic modified Catholic) more and more as the chapters accumulated. The problems for theological inquiry escalated as the chapters accumulated, as did the resources for dealing with these problems.

But many Catholic (including but not only Roman Catholic) readers had difficulty understanding why I began with Scripture (particularly given the understanding and use of Scripture in what is now Chapter 3). There are advantages (and disadvantages) to beginning with any of the practices and teachings in the following chapters; it will become clear as the chapters accumulate that I think it is a mistake to defend any single ground, source, or starting point for theology. Particularists (Catholics) are tempted to universalize the strategy of beginning with the particular authorities for our inquiry and then proceeding (on the basis of these authorities) to unfold authentic doctrine about various doctrinal *loci*, for example, the triune God, creation, sin, Christ, Church, sacraments and last things (heaven and hell). Others (catholics) are tempted to begin with the practical, experiential matrix we all supposedly share and to show how Christian symbols are grounded in that matrix.

I have tried to avoid both of these extremes—requiring the reader to seek the cumulative case at work, while permitting the reader to assent to and dissent from different chapters in different ways. Thus, for rhetorical reasons (for example, to begin with a practice bearing on theological inquiry and familiar to Catholics), I begin with one set of debates generated by one sacramental practice (Chapter 2) before moving to Jesus Christ and Scripture (Chapter 3), the common goods of the communion of saints (Chapter 4), arguments over God and religions (Chapter 5), and the broader personal and social world (Chapter 6). Exactly why I consider one chapter more catholic than another but without sacrificing particularity will emerge as the chapters proceed. The central point of the movement between chapters is that seeking the humanity of God is seeking this particular One as the One of catholic significance; grammatically put, the humanity of God is an objective genitive (our humanity) because it is a subjective genitive (God's humanity in Word and Spirit).

Still further, the thesis is about seeking the humanity of God *as* we seek and inquire into specific practices and doctrines and patterns of relationships—as we use our Bible, celebrate liturgies, enact the common goods of the Church, give reasons for the hope that is in us, and identify with and identify the joys and griefs of all humanity. Other topics are subordinate to the theme of seeking the humanity of God. As in the cases of practices, doctrines, and patterns of relationships, there is no definition of "seeking" prior to specific contexts within which we seek and inquire after specific objects. By Chapter 6, some more comprehensive things will be claimed about inquiry—comprehensive (catholic), but still occasion-specific (Catholic). Conceptual precision on this and other matters is an imitation of the precision by which the Word became flesh. But not all theologies are equally clear nor all theologians equally talented in this regard. What I mean by seeking (as well as by practices, doctrines, and patterns of relationships) will in the main have to become clear as I cumulatively offer examples and thus try to display a context for their use.

Stated negatively, seeking the humanity of God is not doing one thing—or doing just any thing. Particularists are tempted to trivialize seeking, insisting that seeking is largely a pre-Christian, even pre-human activity. Others (catholics) are tempted to let seeking and inquiry tyrannize over all we do, ignoring how diverse and depraved our quests and questions can be. We need a kind of inquiry which is neither trivial nor tyrannical. Keeping in mind the particularity of contexts prevents inquiry from becoming trivial—keeping in mind their diversity prevents inquiry from becoming tyrannical. The emphasis on particularity and diversity of theological inquiry raises questions about its catholicity and unity. Once again, such questions will be addressed as we journey through each chapter, cautiously essaying the accumulated practices and teachings. Indeed, the typical instance of seeking the humanity of God involves neither sinner nor saint but a particular kind of Christian on a particular kind of journey.

Finally, for those with ears to hear, I will continue the strategy of arguing against those who would have us choose between Catholicity and particularity—whether we find such mistakes among ordinary Christians, church officials, our fellow theologians, or other sorts of people. Sometimes Catholics are not catholic enough; sometimes catholics are not Catholic enough. Sometimes non-Catholic theologians (or non-theologians) are better representative of Catholic particularity on particular issues than Catholics are. In any case, theologies and theologians that are against nothing are also for nothing.

But it is also true that what theologies and theologians are *against* is parasitic on what they are *for*. Thus, I have tried to keep the polemical edge "indirect."[17] I realize that the rhetorical device distinguishing those who emphasize Catholicity and those who emphasize particularity does not exhaust the options. I make no claim to "mediate" between such "extremes"—at least if this means that we have some immediacy outside specific practices, doctrines, and patterns of relationships on the basis of which we can mediate. By and large, *in medio stat mediocritas*. But neither is this rhetorical device mere rhetoric. Distinguishing those who emphasize one side or other of Catholic particularity is more like an exercise in casuistry—not (I hope) the sophistical casuistry Pascal rejected but the art of casuistry that focuses on specific cases, locating them in particular contexts relative to specific topics, honing our proposals against extremes relative to a normative position.[18] These are not always extremes external to ourselves but fragmented versions of ourselves—mistakes we (and surely I) often make. Labeling theologies and theologians can be a useful exercise in some contexts—as when we offer modest advice on Catholic particularity. But we ought to be less interested in labeling theologies and theologians than in engaging in a kind of theology faithful to the God we seek in each and every joy and grief—a theology which describes each and every such practice, articulates the presumed teachings, and relates such practices and teachings to other practices and teachings because such is what God calls us to do in Word and Spirit. Rather than offer more than piecemeal advice *about* theology and theologians, we ought to *do* theology. It is time to begin doing so, once again.

2

Seek and You Shall Find

When we gather together to sing God's praises, common sense suggests that we are engaging in a set of specific activities (for example, gathering, praising). We baptize and confirm, eat and drink; we also enact marriage covenants and priestly orders, confess our sin and console our sufferers: it is thus that we respond to and mutually engage a God who provides baptism and food, covenants and orders, forgives and consoles us. We might call such activities sacraments or rituals or liturgy or ordinances—although all such characterizations only partially capture the fact that these are *activities*. In any case, the aim of this chapter is not to offer a complete description of such liturgies but to propose instead an analysis of sacraments which bears directly on theological inquiry. The thesis of the chapter (and the first sub-thesis of the book) is that *the central ritual context of theological inquiry is the Christian baptismal catechumenate*, itself a reflection of storied discipleship in the Gospels. The catechumenate (rightly practiced) is a paradigm and instance of our unfinished sojourn from and toward God. Baptism is thus the ritual context for theological inquiry as continual schooling in weaving the practices and teachings of the Christian community with those of our common humanity in a way that corresponds to what God is doing for all humanity.

Note that baptism so construed is the *sacramental* context, not the *only* context. The contexts for and topics of theological inquiry, I am beginning to illustrate and argue, are diverse. We need to take them one at a time, while keeping in mind all of them. With regard to liturgical activity, we must avoid two mistakes. On the one hand, we need to avoid reducing liturgy to other practices. For example, on one reading, the ritualized moments of biblical narratives can seem so subordinate to other moments that we might be tempted to claim that rituals *simply* confirm, repeat, or comment on the biblical narratives.[1] Such, we might say, is the position of those who think that giving sacraments their own time and place is a peculiarly Catholic enterprise, jeopardizing the particular ways Jesus Christ relates to the Bible or the broader world. However, for Catholic particularists who stand with Vatican II, liturgical celebration is "an action [*opus*] of Christ . . . and of His body. . . . "; it is "a sacred action [*actio*] surpassing all others," even if it "does not exhaust the entire activity [*actionem*] of the Church." Thus, "the aim to be considered before all else" in liturgical reform is "full and active [*actuosa*] participation."[2] How can we do justice to this sacramental activity without sacrificing our other activities?

On the other hand, we also need to avoid making too comprehensive a claim for our liturgical practices. For example, the biblical texts are so often identical with worship (for example, the Psalms) that we might be tempted to claim that there is a *single* process that embraces both so that "Scripture and liturgy" are "correlative aspects of rite."[3] Such, we might say, is the position of those who fear that giving Scripture its own time and place does not do justice to the more catholic claim that we *are* sacraments in a way that we are not scriptural texts. However, it is crucial *how* we do justice to the catholicity of our worship. The next chapter will suggest a way in which we are more like "texts" than we might think. But the point here is that there is no single process that binds Scripture and liturgy together (or our liturgical worship and our lives in the broader world). Scripture calls for liturgical enactment; liturgy is a crucial context for Scripture. But neither can be reduced to the other. Thus, for example, scriptural texts sometimes rule our liturgical movement (for example, when the Gospels are read week to week from cover to cover during the "ordinary time" of the year); and sometimes our worship rules the selection of biblical texts (for example, from Advent to Christmas and Easter). But each remains a distinct practice—although the coming reign of God might show us a single process at work that sublates the two. But, if Scripture and worship have their own particularity, how are they related to each other and to other contexts?

We must avoid reducing all our practices and teachings to liturgical ones—and we must avoid reducing liturgical activity to some other practices and teachings. The issues at stake in avoiding these extremes are large. Fortunately, we do not have to settle all the controversies involved here in order to make a contribution. For example, Christian communities of all sorts have by and large agreed that fidelity to the Scriptures calls us to baptize. Jesus' baptism, as the opening episode in a cumulative narrative moving toward the baptism of cross and resurrection, has become the model of Christian initiation.[4] Christians have, in other words, by and large agreed that here, if anywhere, we have liturgical celebration bound to the Scriptures in such a way that it takes odd, even sinful, circumstances to have to choose between word and sacrament. But distinguishing word and sacrament has at least this implication: inquiry into biblical *texts* is distinct from inquiry into *sacraments*. Inquiry into sacraments is not primarily inquiry into texts. This does not mean that there is an alienation between the two; included as a subordinate feature of such liturgical inquiry (we shall see) are a set of texts— liturgical prayers, hymns, biblical and other readings. But the anthropological data for liturgical theology is people—not people in general but specific people gathering together at particular times and places in sundry eras and so engaging in a distinctive action of Christ and Christ's body. How, then, does baptism provide an illuminating context for theological inquiry? We will proceed in three steps. First, the catechumenate will be profiled (that is, the set of practices constituting its phases and stages will be described); then I will suggest how these practices generate a doctrinal rule; finally, I shall propose that these practices and this rule require theology to weave its particular inquiry with the diverse, overlapping, and opposed inquiries of our common and not so common humanity.

A. *A Profile of Initiatory Practices*

Teaching · The *claims* we make about theological inquiry always have a *context*. In what sorts of ordinary, common sensical, and idiomatic contexts do questions about inquiry arise? One such context is the initiation of someone, particularly an adult, into our communities. Consider the sample of the catechumenate provided by the Roman Catholic "Rite of Christian Initiation of Adults."[5] We need a profile of this context in part because not all readers may be familiar with it. More importantly, even those who are familiar with Christian initiation practices may be more familiar with one part or phase of it than with the "continuum of practices" or "the whole ensemble of events" involved in the forming of Christian identity.[6]

1. *Characters and Plot*

First, note that this set of initiatory practices has what we might call (with an important qualification) a narrative shape. Like a good narrative, this initiation has a cast of characters: the candidate(s), the community, the minister, and the God appealed to at all the central points of the journey. Also, like a good narrative, it has a plot: it is a journey of candidates who arrive on the scene "to know and follow Christ" and of the community who helps them in this effort (RCI nos. 77, 81, 83–84). This plot has acts and sub-acts—or what some call four "periods" and three "stages."[7] The periods are characterized as times of investigating, inquiring, maturing—the stages as times to move forward. The rhythm of acts and sub-acts, of periods and stages, is important because, while there are crucial shifts from the beginning to the end of the catechumenate, at no stage does inquiry cease and during no period is inquiring unformed. We do not begin only as inquirers who need to move forward but also as interested inquirers who have already moved forward. We do not end as those who have moved definitively forward and upward; but as soon as we are baptized and celebrate the Eucharist, we are plunged once again into a period of mystagogic inquiry. We can say, then, that the stages lead to the periods and thus emphasize the journey as a series of novel stages; or we can say that the periods prepare for the stages and emphasize the continuities of the journey. Not only is the catechumenate called a journey but it also exhibits the starts and stops of any quest. Descriptively profiling this initiatory policy is learning to follow this narrative, particularly the prayerful interplay of ministers, community, candidate, and God as they transform the cosmos—"fire, wind, wax, bees, light and darkness, water, oil, nakedness, bread, wine, aromas, tough and graceful words and gestures"[8]—into a context befitting the shaping of Christian identity. Without such a descriptive profile we will not understand the ritual context of the kind of inquiry going on here.

2. *Stages and Phases* in medias res

The rite itself begins and proceeds and ends in the midst of things (*in medias res*). Thus, candidate, community, and minister appear on the scene to declare their intentions, to offer mutual assistance, and climactically to call on God. The official commentary fills in some background. The *first period* of the catechumenate is the time of interaction between "interested inquirers ('sympathizers')" (that is, "those who, even if they do not fully believe, show an inclination toward the Christian faith") and Christians who proclaim the living God. The *first stage* is the rite in which these interested inquirers make their intentions known to the Church and the Church admits and receives them. But we are left in the dark about what it is that makes these inquirers appear. Was it some experience? Scripture? Some of the "unseen wonders" of God's love (RCI no. 76)? Some "spirits of evil" now renounced in favor of "Christ alone" (RCI nos. 79–81)? The answer does not seem to be of primary importance for the catechumenate. The rite begins in the midst of things, leaving in the background the question of how candidate and community got there. There is (as Hans Frei put it) a relatively sharp distinction between the logic of "belief" and the logic of "coming to believe," although the catechumenate ought to make us resist joining Frei in the claim that the two are "totally different."[9]

We find a similar movement as the ritualized quest proceeds. Thus, the next sub-act is a lengthy period of initial formation into the image of Christ (*imago Christi*) (RCI no. 95). It consists primarily in continued practice in "celebrating the Word of God" (including gradual initiation into the first part of the Eucharist) and prayers for the forgiveness and blessing of the catechumens. The *second period* is the time during which the catechumens grow and mature in the dispositions enacted in the first stage as the community initiates them into its faith, its liturgy, its life of love.[10]

Thus initiated and incipiently formed, the candidates and community are prepared for the next act. This *second stage* is the rite in which the catechumens reaffirm their intentions and the community passes judgment on the catechumens.[11] God is asked to help all involved in the catechumenate (RCI no. 148)—the catechumens' teachers, their godparents, their families, the whole community, those who have not yet reached this stage, and particularly the catechumens themselves.

Candidates and community are thus readied to prepare themselves for full initiation into the community. The *third period* is "a more profound preparation for the sacrament." Here the "spiritual and catechetical preparation of the elect . . . is completed and is carried on," but this is a "spiritual recollection" more than catechesis; it is intended "to purify minds and hearts" and to enlighten "by a deeper knowledge."[12]

In the *third* and final *stage*, the candidates come forward to be baptized, confirmed, and receive the Eucharist. Thus, what I have variously called the rite of Christian initiation, baptism, catechumenate, Christian initiatory polity or policy includes rather than rivals such other sacraments.

The *fourth* and final *period* is the time "to strengthen the first steps of the neophytes"—"a time for deepening the Christian experience, for gaining spiritual fruit, and for entering more closely into the life and unity of the community of the faithful." As if to emphasize their newly granted and acquired skills, few specific practices are suggested for this post-catechumenal period: at the end, as at the beginning and in the middle, the catechumenate leaves us *in medias res.*[13]

3. *The God of the Catechumenate*

Judging from the pattern of praying throughout these phases and stages, the climax of each phase and stage is the way God is called upon during the course of the initiation rite. The aim of this first section, let us recall, is to offer a profile of a particular initiatory polity. We offer such a profile by describing *the ongoing patterns* of praying (the *lex orandi*, theologians sometimes say) and other actions which emerge from *who* (minister, community, candidate) say *what* (renunciation, praise, thanks, petition, and so forth) to *whom* and *when* in the course of the catechumenate. At each stage of this *lex orandi*, we find God beseeched in various ways. Thus, at the first stage, God is thanked and praised for calling the inquirers into the catechumenate and is asked to protect and lead them forward (RCI nos. 82, 95; cf. no. 87). As the catechumens are shaped into the "image of Christ" (RCI no. 95), God is beseeched to exorcise the candidates of sin and evil and bless their further inquiry (RCI nos. 113–118, 121–124, cf. no. 131); to guide and govern the catechumens and keep them faithful to God's calling (RCI no. 149); to help the candidates to grow and grant them "true knowledge, firm hope, and sound teaching" (RCI nos. 377, 187, 192; cf. nos. 171, 178, 381, 385); and ultimately to unseal the fount of baptism and send the Spirit (nos. 215, 230). The God of this rite is thus a God to be praised and thanked, a God before whom candidate and community confess their sin and repent, a God petitioned and beseeched.

But if we seek an identity description of this God thus climactically called upon by name, none is offered in the rite itself. We can learn who the human characters of this inquiry are—candidate and community and ministers—by learning to attend to the baptismal continuum of prayerful practices with reflection as open and critical as we would use on any novel or

poem, any theological or philosophical argument. Such is how
we attend to "the priority of persons in action" in these rituals.[14] But we cannot as directly read the character of God off
this inquiry. God simply does not appear the way the other
characters do. God, we might argue, is attested here as the
scriptural narratives are proclaimed and heard, taught and
read (2.A.2). Insofar as the catechumenate enacts response to
the baptism of Christ and disciples in their narrative context,
we can argue that baptismal inquiry is an authentic version of
storied discipleship. But the pattern of praying of the rite itself
points outside itself. The God for whom candidate and community search is a God who searches them (RCI no. 117), a
God whom this community trusts is active in many and varied
ways in their quest—but is not to be confused with this
inquiry.

We ought, then, to take seriously the warning of Cyril of Jerusalem: "Let no one enter saying: 'I say, let us see what the believers are doing: I'm going in to have a look and find out what's
going on.' Do you expect to see without being seen? Do you imagine that while you are investigating 'what's going on,' God is not
investigating your heart?"[15] From the point of view and action of
the participants, there is no way to escape from such divine investigation. Nonetheless, Cyril is to be taken seriously as a warning,
not a command. Indeed, one of *the* intelligent questions to ask of
these initiation practices is, "What's going on?" But, "What's
going on," is what *we* and *I* are doing in response to what God is
doing. However, even the observer's question, "What are *they*
doing?" may turn into God's query to them.

In any case, baptism is *this* distinctive continuum of practices (although there is no separation between what is sacra-
mentally baptismal and the rest of our world). The point here
is not to offer an exhaustive description of Christian initiation:
the rite is pervaded by a sense of freedom that makes it enor-
mously flexible.[16] Neither is the point to side-step the several
ways the rite can be criticized (for example, sexist language).
The point is to offer a profile of an initiatory polity sufficient
to describe it as the liturgical context of Christian inquiry. The
catechumenate is the "paradigmatic ideal" of the praxis of
ritual inquiry—or the *sacramental* "sample" of Christianly
"competent" inquiry (1.B).

B. *Doctrine and Inquiry*

1. *Doctrines about Doctrines*

What doctrinal rules are at stake in this assemblage of practices? It is noteworthy that the catechumens are not required to acquaint themselves with Christian doctrine before engaging in the catechumenate—and neither is the catechumenate itself primarily a matter of learning certain doctrines. On the other hand, unlike the initiates of some other religions, the catechumens are not asked "to engage in ritual action or discipline before they acquaint themselves with the supporting doctrine"[17]—and times are specifically set aside for doctrinal training. It would seem that this initiatory polity presents neither ritual action unformed by doctrine nor doctrine unformed by ritual action. Doctrinal issues arise when the minister initially asks the catechumen what he or she intends (RCI nos. 75, 318), and announces that the aim of the catechumenate is "to know and follow Christ" (RCI nos. 77, 81, 83, 84). Doctrines accumulate through each of the phases and stages of the catechumenate, climaxing in the profession of the creed at baptism itself (RCI no. 219)—a profession contextualized by a web of prayer and symbol. Implicit, then, in this inquiry is a set of rules about how doctrines or teachings are woven into the quests of catechumen and community—a set of what we might call doctrines about doctrines. Such is the focus of this section.

However, it is important to note that there are obviously all sorts of doctrines which can be teased from this (or any other) continuum of practices. The way Christians engage in this nexus of activities involves or implies teachings about the intentions and gestures of the people, the physical and social setting of the rite.[18] Yet the central issue *here* is the doctrine *about inquiry* implicit in this catechumenal quest. The central such rule, I suggest, is quite simply a claim about a particular sort of quest: "Seek and you shall find" (Matthew 7:8; Luke 11:9). I will call this "the catechumenal rule" (but see n. 6). Here are some pervasive examples of this rule at work.

2. *Presiding Doctrines*

First, how shall candidate and community "know and follow Christ"? If we recall the way this community calls upon God, we discover a pattern—a pattern of thanking and praising and blessing followed by petitions and concluding in thanks and praise. The pattern is not wooden, but it is part of what is involved in the catechumenal rule. The community thanks and praises a God whom it has found because this God has graciously found them—and petitions or seeks that this God may receive the catechumens, forgive catechumen and community, and baptize. It is this God who calls candidate and community to true knowledge and wisdom. "You [Lord Jesus]," the minister confesses for catechumen and community, "are the teacher we seek" (RCI no. 164). In the midst of everything else this God does, this God is Lord of knowledge who promises that we shall *find* in Christ and promises that we *shall* find in the Spirit. God, we might say, reveals by calling humanity to this inquiry.[19] The object of this particular quest, according to the catechumenal rule, is this particular God.

Second, how, then, do we seek and find this Christ? Another pervasive feature of this ritual quest is initiation into Scripture. The first stage of the catechumenate contains the introduction to the Scriptures, including an optional(!) presentation of the Gospels themselves (RCI no. 93). Indeed, from the very beginning, every stage and phase is informed by training in these Scriptures, particularly by using them to celebrate the Word of God (RCI nos. 91–92, 106, 185, 190, 196). These Scriptures are the most particular samples the community has of instances of finding which lead to seeking—a work of the Holy Spirit who promises we shall find.[20] Searching these Scriptures, it is promised, we will find. The paradigmatic examples of this particular quest, according to the catechumenal rule, are found in these particular texts.

Third, the catechumenate proceeds with full confidence that the God depicted in these Scriptures is at work in all its stages and phases—that the promise *is* being fulfilled in the lives of this community. We see this clearly in the confidence with which the community into which the catechumens are initiated is regarded as the context for apprenticeship in seeking

God and studying these Scriptures. The community is, of course, complex. Its cast of characters includes bishops and priests and deacons, family and friends and sponsors, teachers and catechists. The suggestion of the catechumenate is that the seeking and finding of the catechumenal rule is guided by all these groups, each in its own way. We learn to seek and find, according to the catechumenal rule, by finding our part in this community's quest. The catechumenal quest is a social one.

Fourth, the candidate comes from a world God created and which "makes known the unseen wonders of His [God's] love." (RCI no.76). It is in such a world that the candidates have "experienced your [God's] guiding presence in their lives" (RCI no. 82). As suggested above (2.A.2), the background of causes and reasons moving "interested inquirers" to the catechumenate and through post-baptismal quest is largely left unspoken; the world is a big place—indeed, as we shall see (chs. 5 and 6), many places. But the presumption of the rite is that the catechumenal rule is operative in that world also. The God of Bible and Church is also the God of the world, who promises those who seek that they shall find. God is, in the case of the candidate and elsewhere, at work in the signs of the times and the realities of the culture. Such is the broadest *context* of the catechumenal rule.

Finally, the presumption of this set of practices is that we do not normally have to *choose between* revelation and Scripture and Church and culture—between what God reveals and what candidate and community experience, between what the world reveals and what God reveals, between the world depicted in Scripture and our own world. The hope of this baptismal rite is that these resources for inquiry conspire rather than compete—conspire toward a consensus of the faithful (*consensus fidelium*)—that is, a consensus between the Spirit's action and the action of candidate and community (see Acts 15:28). However, the rite's repeated exorcisms and calls for repentance indicate that our seeking and finding are rarely achieved without conflict, error, and sin and never in a way that undercuts our belief and hope in the promises of the One who creates and preserves, liberates and reveals to us (RCI nos. 79–82, 113–18, 164, 171, 178, 217).

3. *Uses of the Catechumenal Rule*

The tension between what we might call these "presiding" instances of the catechumenal rule at work and this inquiry's confession of its sin (that is, its failure to seek or find or both) has forced most Christian communities to develop still further applications of the catechumenal rule. At their best, arguments between popes and councils, bishops and theologians, the communion of saints and individual saints, the pattern of praying and the pattern of believing (*lex orandi* and *lex credendi*) involve arguments over how to create an inquiry—a context for following the rule "seek and you shall find." The catechumenal rule does not settle the many disputes over Christians' quests that have divided East from West, Protestant from Catholic, Evangelical from Liberal Christian. Rules alone can never settle theological (or most other) conflicts—only inquiring can (at least according to the catechumenal rule).

Thus, the fact that "seek and you shall find" is a favorite rule of Luke and Matthew ought not to make us forget that "forms of this saying are known in many literatures."[21] It was even a favorite rule of other-worldly Manichees and this-worldly pragmatists.[22] But these facts ought not to frighten us from finding our own use and extension of the rule. John Wesley caught the essential drift: "'Seek,' in the way he hath ordained, in searching the Scriptures, in hearing his word, in meditating thereon, in fasting, in partaking of the Supper of the Lord, and surely 'ye shall find.'"[23] Indeed, we ought to go one step further. We seek and find by schooling in weaving together culture, church, Scripture, and the word and work of the God of this inquiry in the face of sin, error, and simple mistakes—a chore partly accomplished at each stage of the catechumenate and yet never fully accomplished before prolonged "post-baptismal catechesis or mystagogia" (RCI nos. 235–239). In sum, according to the catechumenal rule, the Christian life is permanent inquiry.

How so? This baptismal quest requires us to separate two further questions. First, what are the patterns of relationships between this inquiry (with its rules) and *other* inquiries (with their rules)? Before and during and after Christian initiation, candidate and community are distinguishing their inquiry from other inquiries—and relating it to such other inquiries. How? Why? Grant, for example, that baptismal inquiry is authentic inquiry for seeking "to know and follow Christ" (RCI nos. 77, 81, 83, 84). But how (if at all) does this inquiry *relate to* those inquiries aimed at seeking uniformities in the cosmos, philosophical accounts of things, or simply our next meal?

Second, what are the patterns of relationships between this inquiry (with its rules) and *competing* inquiries (with their rules)? Before and during and after the catechumenate, candidate and community are not simply relating their inquiry to other inquiries but also separating baptismal inquiry from competing inquiries. Why? How? Grant, for example, that this is genuine Christian inquiry (and that its rules are genuinely Christian doctrines). But are these Christianly true practices and beliefs really true? Are they preferable to *rival* inquiries and rules (for example, the rival initiation rites of a-Christian or a-religious ways of life)? Even if baptismal inquiry forms a consensus of the faithful, are not these faithful a group that in act and fact excludes other inquiries?

These questions, I would emphasize, arise in separate fashion on this inquiry's own terms. Before and during and after the catechumenal and baptismal and eucharistic inquiry, catechumens and community find their quest to know and follow Christ overlapping with as well as conflicting with other quests and questions. We need to look at whether and how following the catechumenal rule helps us in dealing with these overlaps and conflicts.

C. *Inquiry and Truths*

1. *Overlapping and Conflicting Inquiries*

a. OVERLAPPING INQUIRIES

If we begin with the first question—"What are the patterns of relationships between this inquiry (with its rules) and *other* inquiries (with their rules)?"—the answer is relatively easy. How does following the catechumenal rule help in dealing with other (that is, non-rival) inquiries? The presumption of the catechumenal rule, I previously proposed, is that this catechumenal rule is operative throughout the world as catechumens and community move into and out of the rite of Christian initiation. How far does inquiry extend? Consider the fact that many religions have rites of initiation.[24] Common sense rightly says that these initiation rites are in conflict: it would create enormous practical difficulties to participate simultaneously in the initiation rites of Jewish and Christian, Muslim and Buddhist communities. And yet there are clearly similarities between such rites: they all involve initiation into particular objects and contexts, texts and symbols, practices and teachings. Clearly, Christian baptism shares some features of these rites, at their beginning or middle or end. This may not be a great deal of overlap, particularly in view of the focus of Christian initiation on the God of Jesus Christ (in contrast, we shall see in chapter 5, to the various objects of theistic and nontheistic religions). But such oppositions are no reason for neglecting the overlaps. Such overlapping patterns of relationships may provide important clues for dialogue and interreligiously common tasks.

What does Christian initiation policy have to do with the full range of human inquiries in science and business and the humanities, in psychology and sociology, in politics and technology and our everyday affairs? Once again, common sense suggests that these quests are diverse. We are familiar with people who can inquire in exemplary fashion in their jobs if not their families, in their homes if not their neighborhoods, in their civic communities if not international politics. Some of these quests are ritualized, and some are not. In any case, just as we seek for patterns of relationships between these various contexts, so also we can seek for patterns of relationships between these contexts and the catechumenate. Insofar as we can map the various features Christian initiatory policy shares with these sorts of inquiries, we are sorting out the patterns of relationships between Christian and more generally human inquiries.

Catechumenal inquiry, then, is neither isolated from nor reduced to other religious and a-religious inquiries. The catechumenate itself calls us to map such inquiries, weaving inquiry aimed at knowing and following Christ into other sorts of inquiries precisely because the God of the catechumenal inquiry is also creator of a world subject to a variety of partly distinct and partly overlapping inquiries.

The contention here is relatively formal and leaves a great deal of unfinished work. The contention is simply that the catechumenal rule requires us to look toward inquiry itself as the central pattern of relationship between Christian and more broadly human inquiry. But it offers no *further* analysis of these overlapping inquiries or of the circumstances which call for such analyses. What are the functional analogues to the catechumenate in Judaism and Islam, Hinduism and Buddhism? How is inquiring after the God of this catechumenate similar to and different from inquiring after Yahweh, Allah, Brahman, nirvana? Still further, how is inquiry after the God of this catechumenate similar to and different from inquiry after uniformities in the cosmos, historical events, literature, our friends? How does initiation into the God of the catechumenate differ from and resemble initiation into science and business and politics? How is the way we initiate strangers into our Church related to the initiation policies of a body politic (for example, immigration and naturalization policies), a science, a business? Finally, these common sensical observations about the inquiries of religious and other ways of living do not imply that there is some general common sense we all share despite our historical and cultural, religious and ideological differences: *how* the catechumenate is comprehensive is best handled by considering the overlaps and oppositions one by one.[25] The promise of the catechumenal rule is that seeking patterns of relationships, we shall find. But on such specific issues we are seekers more than finders.

b. CONFLICTING INQUIRIES

I must put off such specifics until later chapters for the sake of addressing another important question. Up to this point, the issue at stake has been the relationships between catechetical inquiry and *other* inquiries; but clearly the catechumenate is not only similar to religious and other initiations but also opposed. I have not yet addressed how "seek and you shall find" applies to such *rival* inquiries. We do not enter the catechumenate to learn to be generally religious or to become Jewish or Buddhist or naturalized into any other particular religion—any more than we participate in (or protest against) the United States' immigration and naturalization policy in order to become a citizen in general or to become a naturalized Muscovite. Neither do we participate in the catechumenate, as candidates or community or ministers, in order to learn science or the humanities or medicine or law. Baptismal inquiry is not primarily a "species" of "inquiry in general" or "religious inquiry" in particular. The *primary* ritual matrix for theological inquiry is the catechumenate; but as we engage in this catechumenate over time—as candidates and community and ministers—we move into and out of a nexus of inquiries.

Christian initiatory polity not only is woven into other inquiries but also conflicts with other inquiries. No matter how much overlap we discover between different inquiries, we will also discover conflicts—conflicts within Christian inquiry, between various religious inquiries, between various sorts of unbelief, between the inquiries of science and politics and business. The reason for or cause of the rivalry could be either on the side of Christian inquiry or on the side of the competitor (or both). How does baptismal inquiry require us to deal with competing inquiries? How does the rule "seek and you shall find" enable us to deal with such *rival* inquiries?

We saw that the catechumenate's repeated exorcisms and calls for repentance imply that Christian finding is rarely achieved without conflict, error, and sin and never in a way that undercuts Christians' belief and hope in the promises of the One who creates and preserves, liberates and reveals. Just as there is no "logic" to such conflict or error or sin, so there is no logic to the relationships between competing inquiries. And, because there are *no patterns of relationships* between such conflicting inquiries *as conflicting* inquiries, answers to this second question will depend very much on the specific rival we have in mind; answers to this second question are occasion-specific (or ad hoc). Objections to Christian practice and doctrine can only be handled (if they can be handled) one by one. There is no single logic to these objections, no single way in which Christian or any other inquiry might be unintelligible or inapplicable. Thus, for example, insofar as a particular theory of inquiry either inadequately describes one or other kind of human inquiry or generates oppositions between Christian and other inquiries, there is conflict within or between (or both) these inquiries. But these conflicts would have no single logic. They could only be responded to one by one.

Further, the fact (as I see it) that the objections are occasion-specific does not mean that our response must be ad hoc. Job worked his way through his friends' objections (eventually doing for them what they did not and perhaps could not do for him: praying for them). What this fact does mean is that we must take seriously the way baptismal inquiry has "a paschal character" as initiation into the death and resurrection of Christ and in its movement from Lent through Easter and beyond.[26] Our enactment of baptism will be, then, the essential ritualizing of a soteriology, for example, a strategy for overcoming objections to the truth and goodness and beauty of the Christian life.

Soteriology will be the subject of chapter 4. In this chapter I am not appealing to a more general soteriology. Rather, I am appealing to the set of practices and teachings which constitute the paschal character of this catechumenate. For example, before we set about the task of reconciling oppositions, we need to make sure we are dealing with a rivalry. Further, if the rivalry turns out to be real, it must be set against the background of shared, creaturely patterns of relationships discussed above (2.C.1). These patterns may be various. We may find identities and analogies. We may even find respects in which a feature of baptismal inquiry can be reduced to some other inquiry—or vice-versa. If it is true that there is no pattern of relationship between *conflicting* inquiries *as* conflicting—the "as" is crucial—the *imago Dei* is never destroyed. The God who sets about redeeming the world does so against the background of a creation which can be redeemed. One implication is that the catechumenate itself calls us to redeem such rivalries between inquiry aimed at knowing and following Christ and other sorts of inquiries precisely because the God of the catechumenal inquiry is not only creator of a world subject to a variety of partly distinct and partly overlapping inquiries but also redeemer of that world in Word and Spirit. The primary (if not only) point of what theologians sometimes call apologetics is not to make the gospel generally intelligible or applicable but "to amplify the power to see God in all things"[27]—a God who overcomes our falsehood by suffering our lies and so promising universal reconciliation.

Finally, the primary competing inquiry with which this baptismal inquiry is concerned is distortion of the catechumenate itself. I mentioned that the cause of any rivalry could be either on the side of Christian inquiry or on the side of the competitor (or both). Here we touch on the ancient problem of Christian liars (I John 2:4; 4:20). The temptation here is to avoid real conflicts (that is, the conflicts caused by Christian falsehood) in favor of more superficial rivalries (that is, the falsehoods of other inquiries): Job's friends did it with him, the disciples with Jesus, we with each other and ourselves.

The catechumenal rule requires Christians in particular never to rule out the possibility that what they think is authentic Christian practice and teaching is not. This means that Christians may periodically need to call a moratorium on seeking patterns of relationships between themselves and their culture precisely because they have betrayed their own identity. But the moratorium is always strategic. Thus, the catechumenal rule requires us to seek in expectation of finding (but without having found) a full range of patterns of relationships between inquiries of different sorts; and it requires us not to seek any systematic map of rival inquiries, but to subject all falsehood (particularly our own) to the judgment of Jesus Christ.

2. *The Case of Truth and Truths*

The catechumenal rule needs to be tested in subsequent chapters on a number of topics before we will know how inclusive its reign can be. However, it will also be useful to abstract the issue of truth (1.A.3) from baptism and compare the way different theologians handle this issue. This will teach us little new about the central thesis, but it will provide a small test-case relevant to the academy.

In describing this section as a small test-case relevant to the academy, I need to exorcise a possible misunderstanding. People (students and teachers) educated in a modern academy ought to be "teachers of the uninstructed" in two senses.[28] First, we ought to be able to do what I have thus far aimed to do: redescribe the catechumenate, unpack the logic of its teachings, speak to how it might be similar to and different from the practices and teachings of other inquiries. As we do this, we should sometimes stand *outside of* (or in front of) those we instruct. We should offer something new, strange, unknown. But second, the same people who are catechizers of the uninstructed are so only *from within* the uninstructed, only insofar as they are also and primarily one of the uninstructed. That is, the examples of inquiry given thus far have been diverse in kind and comprehensive in scope; they have ranged from mundane quests for a friend or a meal to highly technical quests for uniformities in the cosmos. But no individual or community can seek (much less find) in all these ways. No one can be son and daughter, married and celibate at the same time; few of us can be poet and philosopher, entrepreneur and citizen at the same time. Each of us is, then, among the uninstructed on many issues.

It is very difficult to be teachers of the uninstructed in both senses at the same time, and I am sure I will not entirely succeed in what follows. On the one hand, I will consider three competing ways in which theologians talk about the relationship between Christian and other truth-claims; I will give advocates of these positions the labels "natural theologians," "correlationalists," and "ad hoc-ists." The foreign labels suggest that there is something new for the uninstructed to learn here. The risk of such labels, of course, is that these positions will seem to embody only debates among theologians rather than debates about theology. This is the reason we must, on the other hand, keep in mind the way questions about truth might be raised by different individuals during the course of the catechumenate. Such questions are not exclusively or even primarily the questions of theologians. In fact, after describing the three theological positions below, I will go on to show that locating the debates among theologians within the context of the catechumenate can provide a foothold for understanding and joining in the debate over patterns of relationships between diverse truths.

a. THREE PATTERNS OF RELATIONSHIPS BETWEEN TRUTHS

Understanding theological arguments over patterns of *relationships between* truths requires that we also understand why theologians also debate the *definition* of truth as well as how we can *test* for truth.[29] Consider the following different ways of defining truth, providing a test for truths, and sorting out patterns of relationships between truths.

First, natural theologians follow the catechumenal rule in beginning with the question of overlapping inquiries. However, natural theologians then proceed to sort out what Christian inquiry shares with the standards of rationality of other inquiries (including the ways we know God by the natural light of reason) and then to describe how Christian faith renders the probable judgments of reason more certain. Christian faith, they say, both perfects and exceeds the rationalities of other inquiries. Their interest is in mapping the patterns of relationships between the objects of belief presumed or implied by the baptismal inquiry and the objects of belief of other inquiries. A typical strategy is to find one or more controversial things we all admit we know (because our knowledge of these things "corresponds to reality") and base or found the other things we know on these things; we might, then, call the former our natural knowledge and the latter revealed knowledge. The notion of truth at work here is sometimes called a correspondence theory of truth and its adherents sometimes called foundationalists.[30] In sum, for one kind of natural theologians, truth *is* correspondence between mind and reality; truth is *tested* by arguing for the rationality of the objects of our belief; and truths are *related* to each other as natural and revealed.

Second, correlationalists suggest that any answer to the first question (that is, "What are the patterns of relationships between catechumanal inquiry and other inquiries?") presumes catechumanal inquiry is authentic inquiry; because this presumption is challenged by myriad religious and a-religious inquiries, granting priority to the first question presumes we have found a way that undercuts our ability to seek further.

Therefore, we do well to begin by focusing on conflicting inquiries, critically correlating the Christian catechumenate and other inquiries. Since the object of theological inquiry is in dispute, we need to turn to its subject. The interest of correlationalists is in mapping the patterns of relationships between the experiences of the catechumenate and more common human experiences: a typical strategy is to interpret Christian and other knowledge and belief against their experiential backgrounds, criticize both Christian and more broadly human experience, and then correlate the two by showing how the Christian and more broadly human experience meet at their respective boundaries or limits. It is important that although correlationalists agree that questions of truth and knowledge depend on some prior context, they disagree on what that prior context is (for example, who I am, the group for which and because of which I seek to know, the historical era in which I live, or the evils we wish to preserve or abolish). More complex methods of correlation aim to embrace a variety of distinct but overlapping models of truth.[31] In sum, for a correlationalist, truth *is* constituted and *tested* by its relationship to our experiential matrix; truths are *related* by showing how they meet at their boundaries or limits.

Third, we might argue that to focus on rival inquiries is to grant a priority to the apologetical task which will inevitably undercut the unique character of specifically Christian inquiry. It presumes we can seek without having already found. Better to proceed in occasion-specific (*ad hoc*) fashion, beginning with the first question and answering it by thick descriptions of specific inquiries rather than by methodologies which presume to cover inquiry generally. Such ad hoc-ists would not be primarily interested in either the objects or the subjects of Christian initiatory policy but in mapping the patterns of relationships between the communal shape of the catechumenate and other intersubjective inquiries, between the scriptural narratives and the diverse and contradictory forms of human experience. On issues of truth, then, ad hoc-ists would focus on no one theory of truth while being open to the usefulness of any theory of truth for different occasions. George Lindbeck, for example, implies that Christian *doctrine* requires no way for us to close the gap between "intrasystematic truth" (roughly, the pragmatic definitions of truth so dear to some correlationalists) and "ontological truth" (roughly, the correspondence theory of truth so dear to natural theologians); the implication seems to be that when truth is determined by the coherence of utterances with their "total relevant context" (intrasystematic truth) *and* this context includes correspondence to "God's being and will" (ontological truth), God's free love must be the sole (not solitary) binder of intrasystematic and ontological truth. It may well be, then, that truth is an eschatological concept. That is, the correspondence between God's life and ours may lie entirely in the future and our present life may thus be constituted by a lack of correspondence between our life and God's—perhaps even an absence of correspondence between our minds and other things (*inadequatio rei et intellectus*).[32] On the other hand, Lindbeck's own Christian theology *permits* theologians to press questions of intelligibility on the model of that "prolonged catechetical instruction in which they [early converts to the Christian community] practiced new modes of behavior and learned the stories of Israel and their fulfillment in Christ."[33] In sum, the ad hoc-ist is suspicious of general theories of truth or tests for truth; *definitions* of truth, *tests* for truth, and patterns of *relationships between* truths are highly occasion-specific.

b. Dealing with Alternatives

From the viewpoint of the catechumenal rule, natural theologies, methods of correlation, and ad hoc strategies are competing ways of following the rule "seek and you shall find" in relationship to inquiries which are different from or rivals to Christian inquiry, or both. There are no good doctrinal (in contrast to theological) objections to any of these theologies from the point of view of the catechumenal rule, *as long as* they are located in relation to Christian baptismal inquiry. The issue at stake here is not doctrinal but theological; it has to do not with teachings distinctive of Christian identity but with the way we relate such teachings to the teachings of other ways of life and language. My summary stand is that I think that what the ad hoc-ists permit (taking Christian initiation as the paradigmatic inquiry), the catechumenate and its rule require—and in requiring it, move ad hoc theologies closer to the other two positions without sacrificing the priority of ad hoc concerns. The following is, I think, what the practices and teachings of the catechumenate require of us.

First, the catechumenate and its rule agree with natural theologians that truth is "correspondence." However, "correspondence between mind and reality" is not quite the right description, at least if "mind" refers to an isolated individual and "reality" implies that there is one thing. The theological correspondence is not primarily a correspondence between an autonomous mind and a monistic reality but (as ad hoc-ists insist) between the communally circumstanced individual and God. Thus, the catechumenate and its rule side with ad hoc-ists in their insistence that what is sought in inquiry is *covenantal correspondence* with the being and will of God; we know "x" (whether "x" be a belief or a practice) is true or right if "x" conforms to the mind of the Christ who (Christian initiatory policy confesses) is the only true Teacher. The correspondence between our mind and *all* reality, sought by natural theologians, is more promise than reality; neither is there yet the fit between "the Christian fact" and "common human experience" sought by correlationalists. When natural theology or the method of correlation makes this part of its case, the kingdom will have come.

Second, the catechumenate and its rule agree with natural theologians and correlationalists that Christians are called to map *comprehensive* patterns of relationships between truths and rights. Covenantal correspondence *is* promise, and natural theologians as well as correlationalists are right to call for a systematic quest of those patterns of relationships which make the promise come true. Both natural theologians and correlationalists are interested in the full range of patterns of relationships between Christian and other inquiries. The catechumenal rule implies that we can know God by the natural light of reason (see 5.C.2.a) and that we rightly hope for full-fledged correlation between Christian and more broadly human experience. In claiming we are doctrinally and not only theologically *required* to seek for patterns of relationships between Christian and other inquiries, the catechumenal rule stands closer to natural theologians and correlationalists than to ad hoc-ists. Ad hoc-ists are not always clear on this score, exploiting philosophical and other studies of theological issues but always insisting that this use is ad hoc.[34] The result is that while not ruling out the quest for patterns of relationships in principle, ad hoc-ists usually will not apply this rule more broadly; in other words, while they do not violate the catechumenal rule, neither do they give it its full extension. With ad hoc-ists, the catechumenal rule does not rule out a firm distinction between intrasystematic truth and ontological truth. "Seek and you shall find" has to do with a God of loving freedom, not with any theory or practice (or *praxis*) of truth. But this God calls us on a quest to find relationships between the intrasystematic and ontological truth—a quest which *must* include the full range of tools provided by the Christian initiation rite.

Third, although Christians ought to seek comprehensive patterns of relationships between truths, the Christian community (in contrast to individuals and groups within the Church) ought not to teach all these truths. We need to discriminate between teachings of the whole community and teachings of particular individuals and groups among us. How can we test for such truths? On the issue of tests for truths, the catechumenal rule sides with ad hoc-ists in insisting that these tests are frequently occasion-specific. For example, suppose we agree that truth is correspondence to the being and will of God, creator and redeemer, and suppose we grant that this particular correspondence requires that we seek comprehensive patterns of relationships between our diverse practices and teachings. How can we test for this truth of a particular teaching or the rightness of a particular practice?

We have seen that the catechumenate implies several such tests for truths—tests internal to the catechumenate. We would need to know how the teaching or practice relates to Scripture. We would need to know what the community as a whole (living and dead) as well as particular ministries within that community (saints, pastors, theologians) says about the practice or teaching. We would need to know what the teaching or practice has to do with what the catechumenate calls the unseen wonders of God's love in the world. We would need to know which teachings best identify what they teach and are coherent with other teachings. On grounds internal to the catechumenate, there is no *single* way to test for the truth of a teaching or the rightness of a practice; there are *several* tests (including their rational coherence and experiential effectiveness), and *how* we apply such tests will be context-dependent or occasion-specific.

For example, we may find natural theology of value in addressing an Aristotle or a Thomas Jefferson or any culture which significantly overlaps with a theist's world; but it may prove to be of secondary helpfulness or even distort dialogue with the Buddhist, the Marxist, or the nihilist. We may find the method of correlation helpful at the limits of science or ethics or the everyday world and the New Testament of but little use for mapping the non-limit patterns of relationships which constitute most of our ordinary lives. The occasion-specific character of our quest for testing (not defining) truths and patterns of relationships between truths is particularly important in view of the multiple ways that the catechumenate and other inquiries can overlap as well as conflict (2.C.1). In its hesitancy to make generalizations prior to investigation of other inquiries one by one, the catechumenal rule is more ad hoc than either natural theology or the method of correlation.

Probing and testing the practices and teachings of the catechumenate is, ad hoc theologies remind us, best done in relationship to specific practices and teachings. In other words, once we define truth the way we have done and once we insist that this truth calls us to map comprehensive patterns of relationships between various truths by taking up teachings and practices one by one, we can best inquire into debates over the tests of truths by taking up specific practices and teachings. Such is the task of subsequent chapters.

The catechumenal rule, then, enjoins sympathy with the natural and ad hoc theologians in subordinating apologetical to more positively constructive questions, with the natural theologians' and correlationalists' desire to provide a comprehensive map of the patterns of relationship in question, and with the ad hoc-ists' wariness of imposing a single test for truths or patterns of relationship on what is surely a complex weave of inquiries. A *general* theory of truths and their tests is not (yet) *essential* to Christian communal identity, but Christian theologians need to seek such a theory to weave theological and other inquiries.

In terms of one of the issues raised in chapter 1, the aim of theology (1.A.3) ought not to be restricted either to a Catholic or particularist focus on the Catholicity or Christianness of our practices and teachings—or to a catholic or universalist focus on the truth and rightness of our teachings and practices. But neither ought we to systematically correlate Christianness and truth, overplaying our catholicity; nor ought we to teach that their relationship is *systematically* ad hoc, overplaying our particularity. Instead, if any belief or action-guide is an authentic doctrine of this community, it is true or right—although not every truth-claim or right-claim *is* an authentic doctrine of this community. Whether a particular truth-claim or right-claim is an authentic doctrine of this community will depend on the pattern of relationships it bears to this community's practices and teachings.[35]

Criticisms of alternatives are always incomplete. I have barely touched upon the diverse, conflicting notions of truths and rights as well as upon the ways we have of testing and relating such truths and rights to each other. Further, even *if* these criticisms of Swinburne and Tracy and Lindbeck are correct, we could render the three counter-proposals more potent by considering other versions of their claims. Aquinas's natural theology is woven into a system of sacramental virtues that makes it more formidable than most other natural theologies. Karl Rahner's weave of common human experience and Christianity undercuts efforts to call him systematically correlationalist. And Barth's argument that intrasystematic truth cannot not be ontological truth in the case of God's truth (revelation) alone depends on a powerful reading of Anselm's so-called ontological argument. I will discuss some of these positions in subsequent chapters, once we have in hand more tools for dealing with them. For now, the catechumenal rule provides no guarantee in advance that these positions can be refuted—although I think that the most potent challenges Aquinas, Rahner, or Barth could offer would have less to do with the proposal here than with how this proposal relates to issues in subsequent chapters. The catechumenal rule provides only the hope that if we seek we shall find.

Conclusion

I have proposed that because baptismal inquiry is the presiding ritual context of Christian inquiry which drives and is driven by the catechumenal rule, the Christian life is a permanent catechumenate constituted by continuing schooling in weaving the inquiry into Christ with inquiries into our world in a way that conforms to what God is doing with our world.

Where does this leave us? We can challenge, deepen, or move forward this view of theological inquiry. It could be challenged by eliminating all ritual contexts or proposing a different ritual context for Christian inquiry, by creating or discovering a different rule for Christian inquiry, by showing that Christian inquiry is either isolated from or reducible to other kinds of inquiry, or by all these. Even to challenge the account is to take up one of its key recommendations: if you would live in and think about, understand or explain this community, attend to the way the catechumenate provides the ritual context for this community's inquiry.

Further, this view of theological inquiry could be deepened by considering how other sacraments are included within, built into, or inscribed in the catechumenate. More justice needs to be done to the way the catechumenate embraces the sacraments of baptism, confirmation, and the Lord's Supper. Even further, more justice needs to be done to the way baptismal practices embrace other rituals. Such supporting rituals initiate not merely the *whole* communal life but *particular* interpersonal (marriage) and social (orders) forms of such life—as well as rituals which nurture or renew not merely the *joys* of our interpersonal and social lives but the massive threats to the person and social agency in *sin* (reconciliation) and *suffering* (anointing).[36] And if the patterns of praying and acting are set in an unfinished narrative, in doing all these things, we are moving toward a new humanity in various ways. For example, we are initiating and confirming a common life which embraces and transcends our economic, political, and other human goods. We are nurturing a starving humanity with prayerful food and drink. We are loving each other in our marriages and justly ordering our common life. We are forgiving our enemies and facing the resultant suffering with hope and trust in the Spirit's promise of a new heaven and a new earth.

But there are two major reasons to reserve such tasks for another time in order to move the inquiry forward. First, our inquiry must become more particular. The aim of the cate-chumenate (we saw at B.1) is "to know and follow Christ." But who is this particular individual, Jesus Christ? The Gospels tell the story of One who was baptized (like us) without baptizing (unlike us). But what is at stake in this story? The next chapter will answer this latter question. The point might also be put this way. Jesus' baptism in Scripture is only the opening of a narrative which leads through a life of word and deed and suffering in the service of God and humanity. There is no story of Jesus without baptism (or the Supper or other liturgies), but neither do such liturgies constitute "the whole story." What then is this whole story? This question will be addressed in chapter 3.

Second, our inquiry must become more catholic. Our profile of the catechumenate could scarcely avoid describing not only this sacrament but also the broader life of this community and its world. Liturgies form a distinctive context for Christian life and theological reflection, but we understand these particular gatherings only when we see how they are related to a commu-nity dispersed at other times. The catechumenate itself re-quires us to move on to Church and world as contexts for seeking the humanity of God. Specifically, there is a problem with the axiom "seek and you shall find" which has thus far re-mained hidden. This baptismal liturgy is strikingly optimistic about the journey which it displays. There are stops and starts to the catechumenal quest. There are confessions of sin and pleas for repentance. But the practices here do indeed form a continuum, an assemblage that might seem to belie the broken nature of our quests—including the shoddy ways we enact bap-tism itself. In terms of the catechumenal rule, baptism might imply a finding without the labor of seeking—as well as with-out coming to terms with those who seek without finding and those who neither seek nor find. Such problems ought not to fool us into ignoring the joys of a baptizing community, no matter how fragile those joys are. But they do require us to probe Christ crucified and inquire into the perverse practices and false teachings of a still broader context. This is the subject matter of chapter 4.

In sum, we need to move on to other chapters, practices, and teachings so that our inquiry can become both more particular and more catholic.

3

Quests for Jesus Christ

Jesus Christ, according to classic Christian confession, is truly God and truly human, named Jesus "because he is the One who is to save his people from their sins" (Matt 1:21). This Jesus Christ is the *particular One* Christians glorify, follow, think about—the One about whom Christians make their most distinctive claims. We persistently repent of our failures to be named after Christ in thought and deed and word; but we know our failures were and are and will be exposed and judged, forgiven and redeemed by this One. Answering the question, "Who is Jesus Christ?" is an essential part of Christian self-description.

Further, Christians have confessed that this particular One is of universal (catholic) importance for each and every moment of their lives. If Jesus Christ is of such universal importance, then there are numerous practical *contexts* for inquiring into Jesus Christ. For example, we have already seen that the aim of the catechumenate is "to know and follow Christ." But much could also be learned by inquiring into other patterns of praying—particularly into the Eucharist, where we find Christ present in the reading and preaching of the word, the eating and drinking of the body and blood of Christ. Or we could turn to those we take to be exemplary Christians in the communion of saints, those who have given up everything to gain eternal life. Or we could turn to the sphere of human religiosity, probing the respects in which Jesus Christ is of ultimate importance in a world where similar claims are made for other messiahs or prophets, avatars or enlightened ones. Or we could turn to the field and profession and discipline of history, analyzing the facts and creating a tale of Jesus of Nazareth in much the same way we would seek any past figure.

These two observations condense the central issue in Christology (that is, inquiry into Jesus Christ): how, if at all, can we hold together the facts that this Jesus Christ is a *particular* figure who is different from any context and that this figure has a catholic *context* (personal, communal, sacramental, historical, political, and so forth)?[1] But we have already seen a foreshadowing of a crucial part of this question in the previous chapter. There we saw that the catechumenate is modeled on Jesus Christ's baptism and aimed at knowing and following Christ. But I also suggested that Jesus' baptism was the opening episode in a cumulative narrative that moves toward the baptism of cross and resurrection. As baptism provides one way to begin the story of Jesus, so baptism could also provide one way to begin our story; as the story of Jesus' baptism is incomplete without the rest of the story, so also our own baptismal catechumenate. The analogy between Jesus' baptism and our own obviously presumes an appeal to a very particular set of texts. This raises the question: what is the relationship between inquiry into Jesus Christ and inquiry into scriptural *texts*? As we shall soon see, seeking the relationships between Jesus Christ and these texts raises some very peculiar problems that require their own time and space and chapter.

However, I must issue a warning. Catholics as well as catholics (ch. 1) ought to be suspicious of this chapter. That is, Catholics (those who confess "the holy catholic church" of the ancient creeds) ought to fear that any distinct attention to the Scriptures will isolate these texts from the whole of the Church's life—our worship, our pastors and people, and other parts of the Church's common life. This has been one of the standard fears Anglo-, Eastern, and Roman Catholics have of the communities of some of the sixteenth-century reformations of the Catholic Church, namely, that their use of and teachings about Scripture inevitably isolate Scripture from the broader life of the Church. On the other hand, catholics (for example, those who permit appeal only to texts all persons agree are important) ought to fear that any distinct attention to these texts will isolate them from our individual or more common human experiences, especially those joys and griefs that seem to render inquiry into these texts archaic or trivial. This chapter will seem, on the surface, alien to the fears of both groups.

However, I hope to show that such fears are, if not groundless, unsupported by the particular character of these texts. Catholics as well as catholics are correct in holding that there is no such thing as Scripture in isolation from the range of activities and teachings that constitute our lives—whether we live those lives in more particular (Catholic) or universal (catholic) fashion. We attend to the Scriptures for particular purposes; we take them out of their liturgical and religious and more worldly contexts to address these purposes. For other purposes, the abstraction may be trivial, or even perverse. In what follows, I shall inquire into these texts informed by the tradition of Catholic particularity (1.A); this will be clearest when I discuss Vatican II (3.B) as well as some arguments of theologians over the bearing of these texts on our world (3.C). This chapter (like the first) is an example of how theological inquiry, even as it focuses on particular contexts and subject matters, must keep other contexts and topics in mind.

But the central thesis of the chapter (and the second subthesis of the book) has to do with the possibility and limits of seeking Jesus Christ by exploring the world of this Bible. The thesis is that *the Gospel narratives relate scriptural texts, contexts, and subject matter in a way that aptly distinguishes and relates inquiry into Jesus Christ and inquiry into Scripture.* Seeking the humanity of God *in these texts* is a unique activity with its own time and place, which also calls for further inquiries. This thesis will be supported, first and indirectly, by our providing a crucial example of inquiry into these texts, then by a (Christological) teaching or rule which is implied in this activity, and finally and most directly by our suggesting how such practices and teachings imply a particular set of patterns of relationships between Jesus Christ and these texts.

A. *The Biblical Idiom*

1. *Jesus Christ and the Bible*

The notion that we are schooled in knowing and following Jesus Christ through texts (that is, the Scriptures) will strike some readers as odd—and others as obvious and common sensical. The oddness arises from the dissimilarities, the obviousness from the similarities between inquiry into Jesus Christ and inquiry into these Scriptures. That is, Jesus Christ is a singular *character* whose story is told in the Gospels; the Scriptures, on the other hand, are a *book*—rather, a library of holy books (Sacred Scriptures). The storied Christ *acts*, does things—teaches and heals, lives and dies, rises and promises to come again; the Bible does not do anything, *does not act*. The texts are not self-authoring, self-using, or self-interpreting; people do things with or use texts—and texts act, function, or do things in the metaphorical sense in which we speak of impersonal things doing things. How, then, can inquiry into these (or any) impersonal texts teach us anything significant about Jesus Christ, God, or ourselves?

In the face of some texts, we may wish we would have occasion to follow St. Clare's advice to devote ourselves to activities other than learning to read texts.[2] However, for readers of this book, it is too late to follow this advice. In any case, in and with disagreements over the nature and use of the Scriptures, Christians have agreed that the scriptural texts are somehow distinctive of and essential to Christian identity. Inquiry into these texts would seem to be a necessary condition of any inquiry into Jesus Christ.

If we press the dissimilarities between the character of Jesus Christ and these texts, we will dissociate Christological inquiry and inquiry into these texts: we may even be tempted to turn from these texts to their subject matter (for example, an immediate encounter with Christ) or their human contexts (for example, an encounter mediated by our experience, our liturgy or community, our church officials or historical researchers). On the other hand, if we press the similarities, we may replace inquiry into Christ and the Scriptures with a more pure inquiry into these texts, perhaps even with bibliolatry (that is, worship of the Bible).

These dissimilarities and similarities imply that there is both unity and difference between Jesus Christ and the Scriptures—and therefore between inquiring into Jesus Christ and inquiring into these texts. We inquire into Jesus Christ by moving through (not around) this book; yet the distance between Christ and the Scriptures seems to block this movement. Seeking the humanity of God through these texts is in some respects a species of a broader quest—yet it is also a species of inquiry which raises unique problems.

These conceptual issues are reflected in the ordinary ways Christians treat the Bible, even though it is hard to say which temptation is more prominent for our ordinary, common-sensical, and idiomatic lives. On the one hand, it is not difficult to find testimonies of people, past and present, to the value of the Scriptures in their lives; on the other hand, these often extravagant testimonies are not consistent with the difficulties many Christians have reading these texts to themselves or hearing them read by others.[3] What this suggests is that we Christians are struggling with—and may be seriously confused over—the issue of similarities and dissimilarities between Jesus Christ and these texts. Whether Christian common sense with regard to Scripture is primarily struggling with or confused on this issue probably depends upon which local parishes and congregations in which nation-states we focus. Wise theologians aim to learn from and instruct those who are struggling, always wary that their learning and teaching may be part of the confusion rather than its resolution.

2. *Following a Narrative*

A common-sense way of relating inquiry into Jesus Christ and into the biblical texts is to use biblical *narratives*, for it is precisely the central (if not the only) role of these narrative *texts* to depict the *agent* Jesus Christ. But we need to be careful at this point. It is clear that different individuals and groups currently have different and opposed answers to the question, "Why narrative?"[4] But this does not mean that the issues raised by more general discussions of narrative are unimportant. Indeed, by chapter's end I will suggest how arguments over narratives are an important new way to state some old issues. For now, however, we need to attend to the way biblical narratives contribute to relating inquiry into Jesus Christ and into these texts.

In sum, the difference between inquiry into these texts and inquiry into Jesus Christ is that the texts merely *witness*—or depict, render, or mirror—Jesus Christ. On the other hand, the similarity between inquiry into these texts and inquiry into Jesus Christ is that these narratives are the *texts* that depict this particular *character.* It is the link between these texts and what is going on in these texts which accounts for the priority many Christians give to the Gospels:[5] the Gospels are narratives of Jesus Christ and of this Christ's interactions with God and people—individuals and communities, small and large groups, friends and enemies and strangers—and the whole cosmos. Training in the biblical idiom involves learning these stories of Jesus—his life and words and deeds, passion and death, resurrection and promised return, and particularly the transitions within and between all these.

Four features of these narratives are particularly crucial for inquiry into Jesus Christ.[6] First, the Gospels are centrally about *a particular individual.* These narratives are about One with a singular and unsubstitutable identity. Particularity in this case is the particularity of this person.[7] Following these narratives is following One with a specific proper name: Jesus. This is no simple chore: not only are the Gospels very different from each other but also each Gospel is internally complex. Like the disciples, we may search for Jesus Christ—only to discover that when we find him, this Christ moves on to neighboring towns (Mark 1:35-38). Who is this Jesus Christ?

Second, this figure is depicted in *interaction with* God and various geographically and socially circumstanced people. These narratives are centrally, but not exclusively, about the particular figure Jesus Christ. For example, although God rarely appears in the gospel narratives, the tale of Jesus is inseparable from characterizations of God the Father and the Spirit. We also find in these narratives the figures of

Elizabeth and Zechariah, Mary and Joseph, Peter and John, the disciples and crowds, the strangers, the friends and enemies of Christ. The portrayal of these individuals and groups is diverse to the point of contradiction. The Mary hailed in Luke as favored by God (Luke 1:28, 30) is elsewhere portrayed in ambiguous fashion (Mark 3:20-35). The Peter who confesses true Christian faith (Matthew 16:16-17) is also the sinner who misunderstands and is rebuked by Jesus (Mark 8:33; 9:5-6; 14:66-72; John 13:6-11; 18:10-11).[9] But the depictions of these individuals and groups are clearly subordinate to the central character, Jesus. What we learn from the gospel portrayal of Jesus Christ interacting with these other characters is that this One's identity is tied to what he seeks on behalf of God and us (*pro Deo* and *pro nobis*). Or, in other words, what this One seeks is not his own identity but the will of his Father and the salvation of these people as the will of this Father. How so?

Third, the interaction is *cumulative*, Christ moving from the background (for example, infancy narratives) to the foreground (for example, Christ's teachings and miracles), the disciples and crowds moving toward and away from this center of action. The storied shape of this text (including chronological sequence) is neither extrinsic nor incidental to the identity of the Christ, the God, or the people witnessed in these narratives. Seeking what is going on in these texts requires following this narrative from beginning to end, from Jesus' words and deeds to his death and resurrection and beyond.

Fourth, the characters of Jesus Christ and God and these people are decisively shaped in the powerlessness of the crucifixion and the vindication of the resurrection. The Christ who seeks the will of the Father in the salvation of these people finds that will through his death and finds these people through their betrayal. The disciples and crowds end up seeking the condemnation, through trial and inquisition, of the One who seeks their salvation. In the end, they find what they least expect: they find God in the crucifixion and this human being risen. "Why," they are asked, "do you seek the living among the dead?" (Luke 24:5). The disciples do not even recognize Jesus when he walks and stands among them but only when he blesses the bread, gives himself to be touched, and eats (Luke 24:16, 30, 36, 39). When found, he vanishes and withdraws, sending them "what the Father has promised" (Luke 24:49).

3. *Ending a Narrative*

What is going on in these texts is subject to a number of descriptions: our justification and sanctification, liberation and vocation. Some—thinking perhaps of those parables in which the Son of Man comes "to seek out and save what was lost" (Luke 19:10), the shepherd seeks and finds the lost sheep (Luke 15:4-7), the woman seeks and finds the lost coin (Luke 15:8-10), the prodigal son who is lost is found (Luke 15:24)—even find Jesus as the One "through whom you [God] have sought us when we did not seek you, and sought us that we might seek you."[10] But here we are less interested in how these narratives depict quests than in how inquiry into Jesus Christ is bound to inquiry into these texts.

In this regard, the crucial issue is learning to hold together these four features of the gospel narratives. For example, how is this particular One of universal significance? How does powerlessness yield salvation? At no time are such questions more appropriate than when we ask for the respects in which these narratives do and do not end.[11] What could be more simple? The narrative ends. Jesus is risen. The reader is called to believe. But this is not the way the story goes. Granted, at first the narrative seems to end for Christ: he is risen. Here we have the "essentials" of the identity of this One. Christians expect to meet this same One, written of here, when they celebrate their sacraments, build up the community, clothe the naked and feed the hungry, and seek Christ's final parousia. But the resurrection itself is not narrated. It is not as if the question, "Why do you seek the living among the dead?" is rhetorical. We do not usually seek the living among the dead, any more than we seek power among the powerless. And yet Christ's story does not end in that Jesus Christ promises his continued presence and coming again. Jesus Christ's narrative ends in one sense, but not in another.

On the other hand, initially the narrative does not seem to

end for the people involved. Not all are chosen to see him risen (Acts 10:40-41). Even those chosen are called to form a community of Jew and Greek, slave and free, men and women—reading, praying, ordering ministries, sent on religious and political missions. We can hardly have complete narratives of these people without depictions of how they respond to their own betrayal and forgiveness. But in another sense their tale ends: there are victories of the Spirit in the successes of Jerusalem and Corinth and Rome, in Peter and Paul, in the martyrs of the Apocalypse. The scriptural canon moves on to the story of the Acts of the Apostles and the letters of Paul and others. Again, the story of these people ends in one sense, but not in another.

In sum, the precise respects in which the narrative ends for Christ are seemingly the respects in which it is open for God and people—and vice-versa. The fact that the narrative ends is firm warrant for the way Christians bind inquiry into Jesus Christ to these texts; the respects in which it does not end drives us to reflect on and apply these texts. A central problem for inquiry into these texts is holding both sides of this ending together.

The problem can be addressed in two main ways. First, we must re-read these stories, seeking their practical wisdom in smaller segments, a verb or verse of an individual Gospel. For example, roughly speaking, Matthew and John emphasize the way the narrative ends, while Mark and Luke emphasize the way the narrative does not end. Understanding why and how this is so would involve rehearsing the details of these stories—following these characters in their circumstances, heeding the warnings, and celebrating the promises at work. This is a never-ending chore, enacted as Christians make use of the Bible for personal and liturgical devotion, for education and moral decision-making, and for all the particular joys and griefs of their lives. It is an inquiry we will need to keep in mind as we move forward in this and subsequent chapters.

But this is not just any kind of story-learning, for these stories seemingly imply particular sorts of *claims*. A second strategy is to show how such claims or teachings are internal to these narratives. We need to articulate the ways these narratives end and do not end and so show how the claims or *teachings* about Jesus Christ and our world are *internal to* these *narratives*. This is what, following our second piece of advice to search for teachings (1.A.2), we need to do now.

Parenthetically, there is another option which would lead us in an opposed direction. Instead of appealing to a distinction *within* (*internal* to) the gospel narratives (that is, a distinction between the way the narrative ends and does not end), we might analyze the relationships *between* (*external* to) the gospel narratives and our world. For example, we might turn to the relationships between the "story" and our liturgical experience of *Christus praesens*,[12] or between this story and some other feature of our personal and political world. This option has the advantage of insisting that the gospel narrative implies a truth-claim about our world and not simply the world of the biblical narratives; it has the disadvantage of presuming too quickly that we must move *outside* the biblical narrative to fill this supposed gap. The role of liturgical contexts was explored in the previous chapter; the role of other contexts will be the topic of subsequent chapters. For now we need to probe the rules internal to these narratives for reading the narrative as a whole.

B. *Jesus is Alpha and Omega*

1. *Teacher and Teachings*

Articulating teachings about Jesus Christ, it might be thought, is quite separate from following the gospel narratives of Jesus Christ. The early Christological controversies climaxed in the Chalcedonian definition of Christ as "in two natures . . . one person"; but the Chalcedonian consensus left Christians in the East divided into Nestorians, Monophysites, and Chalcedonians, producing an abiding schism in Christianity. Later Christological controversies in the West produced considerable theological diversity on the work of Christ on our behalf—diversity which climaxed in the split in the West between Roman Catholics and Lutherans, Reformed and other

Protestants, and eventually Enlightened and other Christians. Catholic particularists can hardly hear and read these narratives without remembering the debates they have generated over the centuries. But what, we rightly ask, do such arguments have to do with following the gospel narratives?

An initial clue to the role of teachings is provided by the way the gospel narratives locate Jesus' teachings. Matthew's Gospel condenses the anomaly: teaching is the principal activity of Jesus' ministry (as in Mark and Luke)—and yet only strangers and opponents address Jesus as teacher. Further, as the Gospels narrate Christ's passion and death, there is less and less "teaching." Such literary anomalies are intertwined with the ways that historically Jesus' teachings were sometimes similar to and sometimes different from those of diverse first century groups: Essenes, Zealots, Pharisees, apocalypticists, and prophets. No wonder that theological appeals to Jesus as teacher in the history of Christianity have been qualified by other descriptions: priest and king and prophet, Word and Son of God, Messiah and Lord and God.[13]

This oddity is a reminder of how crucial it is to hold together teachings and Teacher with the multiplicity of words and deeds, actions and passions of this Christ. These teachings are inseparable from the teacher, and this One's identity as teacher is inseparable from other descriptions of Jesus Christ. It is also a warning against separating teachings about this Christ from the community who teaches and the One about whom they teach, making these teachings *merely* a species of Socratic dialogue, eternal forms, factual propositions, or other sorts of truth-claims. On the other hand, Jesus was and is and will be Teacher, and what we teach about this One is a crucial part of Christian identity. It is important to recall that it is *we* who teach (1.A.1, 2). We do not follow these narratives without a network of teachings that are shaped by and shape our reading of these narratives. This chapter aims to *focus on* the relationship between inquiry into Jesus Christ and into these texts, not to isolate that relationship. As we probe the relationship between the Gospels and these teachings, we need to keep in mind both the limits and the importance of focusing on the teachings of or about Christ.

2. *Vatican II's Alpha and Omega*

At first sight, Vatican II's Pastoral Constitution on the Church in the Modern World seems to be an odd exemplar of teachings about Jesus Christ. Chapter 1 suggested problems this Constitution raises (1.A.3): how can we accommodate ourselves to (and even identify with) the modern world without sacrificing that which is most distinctive of our identity? And yet, this Constitution is a good sample of teaching about Jesus Christ because of its remarkable Christocentric structure.[14] The *thesis* of the Constitution is that the joys and griefs of the people of our time, especially those who are poor, are the joys and griefs of the followers of Christ and nothing that is genuinely human "fails to find an echo" in their hearts (CMW no. 1). The Constitution supports this thesis by specifying its relationships to the dignity of the individual (CMW pt. 1, ch. 1), the community of humankind (CMW pt. 1, ch. 2), and human activity throughout the cosmos (CMW pt. 1, ch. 3) before specifying the role of the Church in relation to this modern world (CMW pt.1, ch. 4). The *climactic warrant* of each of these four chapters is a description of Jesus Christ in relationship to the topic of that chapter: in the case of individual as well as communal activity throughout the cosmos, Jesus Christ is the One who "perfects" human activity. As Word of God, Christ is the "most perfect embodiment" of the dignity of the individual (CMW no. 22), the One in whom our "communitarian character is perfected" (CMW no. 32), who teaches us that God is love and love is "the fundamental law of human perfection" (CMW no. 38), who "was made flesh, so that as perfect human he could save all people and sum up all things in himself" (CMW no. 45). The ultimate confession is simply an appeal to this Christ's self-attestation: "I am the alpha and the omega, the first and the last, the beginning and the end" (Rev 22:13, quoted in CMW no. 45). The joys and griefs of individuals and groups actively transforming the universe are the joys and griefs of the Christ who transforms and perfects each individual, all human communities, all human activity throughout the cosmos and who stands and moves as the alpha and the omega of human as well as ecclesial life.

What is crucial for our purposes here is that the support for the Constitution's thesis is ultimately a set of teachings about who Jesus Christ is. What makes these teachings remarkable is the congruence between the Christological paragraphs (CMW nos. 22, 32, 38, 45; cf. no. 10) and the features of the gospel narratives noted above. Thus, first, the Christological paragraphs make it clear that they speak of a particular individual, Jesus Christ. Part 1, chapter 1 of the Constitution specifically focuses on the way this One's irreducible individuality perfects our own—the grandeur of our existence as embodied, intelligent, and free; the misery of our internal divisions even unto death; the paradoxes of our atheistic denials of each individual's divine vocation.

Second, this Christ is located in relation to all individuals and groups, actively transforming the cosmos—all individuals in their grandeur and misery, particularly in their call to communion with God and in their atheism (CMW pt. 1, ch. 1); men and women, families and societies, friends and enemies (CMW pt. 1, ch. 2); our individual and communal activities as creatures and sinners saved by Christ and called to shape a community of love (CMW pt. 1, ch. 3). Part 1, chapter 2 of the Constitution focuses on the way this One's identity is constituted by the way he shares human fellowship—from the wedding at Cana to his meals with sinners (CMW no. 32).

Third, this Christ is sketched cumulatively. It is only as we hold together the One who is the new Adam in solidarity with the whole human community in his transformation of the cosmos into a new heaven and new earth by calling a people to be his sacrament that we know the Christ here depicted. Part 1, chapter 3 of the Constitution focuses in particular on the way our individual and social identities are perfected in this One's activity over the course of time.

Fourth, Christ is Lord of all individuals, all human community, all human activity throughout the cosmos—*and therefore* Lord of Christians (CMW no. 40). The relationship between Church and world is "mutual" (for example, the Church both offers something to or aids the world and receives or benefits or adapts to this world) precisely because of the Christ, who is Lord of both (CMW nos. 40, 45). Just as the risen Christ is Lord of all humanity and therefore the One who calls specifically Christian disciples, so also in Vatican II Christ sets about "perfecting" our individuality, our social interactions, and our activity throughout the cosmos by calling a Church to solidarity with that world.

The aim here is not to do justice to all that Vatican II teaches about Jesus Christ[15] but to provide a good example of how seeking such teachings contributes to holding together inquiry into Jesus Christ and into these biblical narratives. On this score, Vatican II yields a Christological rule: Jesus Christ is alpha and omega by perfecting our individual and social activity throughout the cosmos in his incarnation and life, action and passion, resurrection and promised return. And this teaching implies a rule for reading the Gospels: always read the Gospels by following this particular figure who interacts with God and neighbor over the course of time, from life through death to resurrection. In still other words, a central function of Christological teachings, doctrines, dogmas, rules, or beliefs is to make a claim about the key respects in which the gospel narratives end by holding together the four features of the gospel narratives (3.A.2).[16]

3. *Problems Teaching Jesus Christ*

And yet it is precisely the systematic teaching of this perfecting activity that raises a question about these teachings. Vatican II is not always clear on what it means to say that Christ's identity "perfects" our own. In ordinary language, "to perfect" is fully to accomplish a task, to bring it to completion, to bring it to perfection. Thus, in confessing that Jesus Christ perfects our personal and social activities throughout the cosmos, this document from Vatican II highlights the "completion" of "Christian" identity in Christ. "Jesus Christ is our alpha and omega," we might say, provides a rule for the respects in which the gospel narratives *end.* But what we might call the patterns of relationship between Jesus Christ and our individuality, our interactions, our activity throughout the cosmos are taught and confessed (merely dogmatically asserted, some might say) but not here elaborated.

Indeed, it might be possible to read the history of post-Vatican II Roman Catholicism as a debate over how (or, perhaps, whether) this teaching can do justice to our individual experiences of rebirth or authenticity, our social identities as members of sundry churches or nations, our human activity throughout the cosmos, or our *praxis* on behalf of the oppressed. This teaching about Jesus Christ, it might be argued, articulates the incoherence between a set of claims about all humanity (individually and together in our activity throughout the cosmos) and a set of claims about the particular figure Jesus Christ. The combination of such teachings is precisely what renders the document's key thesis—that the joys and griefs of humanity are our joys and griefs—dangerously utopian. Insofar as the teachings are inclusive of our common humanity (that is, all people), they threaten to underplay the many aspects of our common humanity which are alien, strange, and foreign to the disciples of Christ; insofar as the teachings are focused on Jesus Christ, they seem to exclude our common humanity.

But, if we locate Vatican II's teaching against the background of the gospel narratives, there is another way to read this teaching. In this view, teachings about Jesus Christ ought not to aim at saying everything about Jesus Christ but only that which is essential to this One's identity. For example, because Jesus Christ embraces the joys and griefs of humanity, the disciples of Christ are called to do to do the same. It is therefore by looking for the shape this Christ takes in the naked, the hungry, the imprisoned that Christians follow Vatican II's mandate. The point of the Constitution is that the thesis is the case only insofar as these Christians are disciples of Christ. In other words, while the Pastoral Constitution on the Church in the Modern World might rightly be called the Church's foreign policy (1.A.3), it is not the foreign policy of this Christ, for the claim of the Constitution is that nothing is foreign to this Christ. In the measure that the followers of Christ live up to this (and in that measure alone), will it be true that "nothing that is human fails to find an echo in their hearts" (CMW no. 1).

In more general terms, both the logic and criticism of this teaching of Vatican II are best revealed by locating this teaching against the background of the gospel narratives. As the teachings of Christ are contextualized by the Teacher, so the teachings of Vatican II are contextualized by the gospel narratives. As the gospel narratives both end and do not end, so also the teachings of Vatican II. These teachings contribute to holding together inquiry into Jesus Christ and inquiry into the gospel narratives by teaching that the biblical world is our world precisely because Jesus Christ is alpha and omega in and of both. Inquiry into more detailed patterns of relationships between who Jesus Christ is on our behalf becomes a distinct task we have yet to pursue.

The same point can be made this way. I am largely in agreement with what the 1985 Roman Catholic Synod of Bishops claimed about the documents of Vatican II. And yet the bishops are overly concerned to guard the *internal* coherence of Vatican II, emphasizing that difficulties with Vatican II are due to "an incomplete understanding and application of the Council," while not ruling out "other causes."[17] The emphasis here is on one such "other cause." Difficulties with Vatican II are not primarily difficulties internal to the documents but difficulties locating the documents of Vatican II in the context of Christian practices—here, the practice of following the gospel narratives. My argument has not been that the authors of Vatican II's Pastoral Constitution on the Church in the Modern World aimed to relate their teachings about Jesus Christ only to the central features of the biblical narratives noted above, although the authors would clearly claim that such a coherence was a necessary if not sufficient condition for the adequacy of their teaching. Instead, the argument has been that Vatican II's teaching on Jesus Christ articulates a rule for holding together inquiry into Jesus Christ and inquiry into the Bible—a rule which requires us to seek more detailed patterns of relationship between this storied Christ and the practices and teachings of our common and not-so-common humanity.

C. *Realists, Functionalists, and Texts as Practices*

The Gospels are narratives of Jesus Christ (3.A). This Jesus Christ is alpha and omega (3.B). Thus far the main point has been that this teaching (3.B) provides a rule for reading these narratives (3.A). And yet I have left a major question unresolved. What shall we do about those features of the narrative which do not end as well as those aspects of our teaching which are unresolved? Answering this question will require discussion not only of gospel narratives and conciliar teachings but also of a set of arguments about theologians.

It may help to clarify the issue at stake by comparing it to a question often taken to be the central question involved in inquiry into Scripture: should we take Scripture literally? This is a question about what theologians have sometimes called Scripture's "literal sense" (*sensus literalis*). However, the question itself can (literally) be asked and answered in a number of ways. For example, for those in England and the United States, the question has been shaped by controversies over Darwin's *The Origin of Species* and the Fundamentalist controversies; these controversies were debates over the relationship between what the Bible says about the world and what evolutionary biologists tell us about the world on grounds quite *external* to the Bible. But students in these countries also need to account for the fact that their controversies have not been central in all modern (much less pre-modern) nation states. In Germany, for example, the controversies over Darwin and Fundamentalism have not played a major role in discussions of Scripture; instead, the discussion has focused on the Bible as a written source with its own history. Here questions about the literal sense have been less about issues that arise outside the biblical text than within that text.[18] Still further, for Christians in local communities in South Africa or South America, questions about the literal sense have to do less with evolution or history or literary criticism than with (for example) how we ought "literally" to work for justice while loving our enemies. Others might say that to take the texts literally is to be individually "born again." In these contexts, to take the texts literally would not be primarily to *believe* what is said in the texts but to *live* as these texts require.

Clearly the question, "Ought we to take Scripture literally?" means different things in different contexts. The literal sense of Scripture is not one, single thing. Answering the question would thus require that we rehearse different ways of taking the literal sense of Scripture, showing which of these ways is consistent or inconsistent with the others. We might even conclude that the notion of the *sensus literalis* has become so confused that it is no longer a helpful notion.

Because of this ambiguity over what it might mean to take Scripture literally, I think it will be more helpful to subordinate questions about the literal sense to the question, "What is the relationship between inquiry into Jesus Christ and inquiry into these texts?" Consider a general formulation of our problem. The storied Christ is One who acts and suffers over the course of time in relationship to us (*pro nobis*). But how can we describe the patterns of relationship Jesus Christ has in fidelity *both* to this Christ's particularity *and* this Christ's relationship to us? As Rowan Williams puts it, "Christ is with the believer and beyond the believer at the same time: we are in Christ and yet face to face with him."[19] That is, as a particular individual, Jesus Christ is different from us, external to us, or *extra nos*. Yet, because Jesus Christ's particularity is constituted by this One's relationship to us, we must also say that Jesus Christ is of universal (catholic) significance, internal to us, or *in nobis*. How can we hold together and apart those respects in which this Jesus Christ is external and internal to us, in himself for us and for us in himself? In still other words, how can we glorify, follow, and think of this One not only as a particular individual but also as a particular individual of catholic significance?

We have already seen one example of an answer to this question in the previous chapter: Jesus' baptism is not ours, yet our catechumenate corresponds to his baptism *as* the initiation of his life and death and resurrection. The Christological issue will also be at stake in the discussion of patterns of relationships in each subsequent chapter. For purposes of this chapter, the patterns of relationship in which we are interested are very peculiar, for they have to do not only with relationships between Jesus Christ and us but also with patterns of relationships between inquiry into Jesus Christ and into these biblical texts.

Consider a problem for Catholic particularity raised by our appeal to the gospel narratives. I have thus far proposed that the gospel narratives provide an essential context for relating inquiry into Jesus Christ and inquiry into the biblical texts, yielding the teaching that Jesus Christ is alpha and omega. But as I previously suggested (3.A.2), the appeal to narrative raises a problem for Catholic particularity. If, on the one hand, we focus on the particularity of these texts in relationship to their central subject matter (Jesus Christ), the presiding test of these narratives will be their realistic portrayal of this subject matter. Let us call this position "narrative realism." The central chore of narrative realists is to seek relationships between such narrative texts and what we might call their *subject matter*. The central way to test how well we do this chore will be how well the student of these texts can describe what these texts say about Jesus Christ. The central problem of narrative realism is whether we can read and pray these texts without a fideistic intuition of their subject matter.

On the other hand, we might judge that this problem with narrative realism is insuperable. Narrative realism (the counter-argument goes) purchases particularity at the price of catholicity. The way to purchase catholicity is to show how these texts function within specific *contexts*—whether those contexts be liturgy or the Church, the narrative quality of human subjectivity, *praxis*, or human agency more generally. We might call this position "narrative functionalism," for here the ultimate test of narrative would be pragmatic or functional.[20] The central chore of narrative functionalists is to spell out the relationships between these texts and their contexts. The central way to test how well students of Scripture do this chore is by testing how well we can *use* the texts in diverse circumstances—to pray and preach; to make decisions individually and as a community; to speak to children and adults, Christians and non-Christians. The central problem with this pragmatic or functional strategy is that it may justify any use of the narrative in any context. The narrative realist's counter-argument to narrative functionalism is that narrative functionalists purchase the catholicity of these narratives at the price of their particularity. At the extreme, inquiry into the Bible is subordinated to (if not reduced to) inquiry into these contexts.

In sum, I am suggesting that we take this debate between narrative realists (with their focus on Jesus Christ as the *subject matter* of the gospel narratives) and narrative functionalists (with their focus on the diverse *practical contexts* of biblical narratives) as the focus of our inquiry. This will not answer all the questions involved in narrative uses of Scripture (much less the *sensus literalis*). But I hope it will clarify at least some of the issues at stake.[21]

1. *Subject Matter, Texts, and Contexts*

a. SUBJECT MATTER AND TEXT

What are the patterns of relationships between Jesus Christ and Scripture? Relationships are not identities; there is no identity between Jesus Christ and these narratives. Christians have typically insisted that these texts be reverenced, not worshipped. Yet the fact that the narratives *end* is firm warrant for the way Christians have related inquiry into Jesus Christ and inquiry into these texts. A classic description of this intimacy is the claim that these texts themselves are "the body of Christ"[22]—the written shape the Word takes on (or the Spirit gives to Christ) over the early decades of Christian life. One advantage of this description is that it suggests how the patterns of relationships between Jesus Christ and these texts are inseparable from their relationships to the Eucharist and the whole life of the Church.

Indeed, it is even tempting to agree with Hans Urs von Balthasar that Scripture and Eucharist and Church are so closely related that they "can *only* be different aspects of the same thing."[23] This, I think, is a mistake, albeit a profound one. It is a profound mistake because it highlights the Catholic contention that there is usually no need to separate Scripture from its liturgical and other contexts. But it is a mistake because it collapses the distinctive joys and griefs of the biblical texts into other contexts. Perhaps there will be a day when Bible and sacrament and Church will be "aspects of the same thing." Indeed, perhaps we ought to have hope that (like the teaching of some of the Jewish Kabbalists) God will one day annul or re-arrange these texts to make their subject matter more perspicuous.[24] But we live in the era prior to such eschatological events. For now at least, the identity of the particular individual Jesus Christ is related to the particularity of these texts in ways that this One is not related to sacraments or the Christian communal life. The particularity of their subject matter requires us to heed the particularity of these Scriptures as texts outside us *in a way* that neither sacraments nor Church is outside us (*extra nos*). For now at least, we have these texts to struggle with, enjoy, and follow.

In sum, narrative realists are correct in that inquiry into *these* narratives is inseparable from inquiry into *this* subject matter (that is, Jesus Christ) so that if there is a conflict between subject matter and text, we need to be reminded of the subject matter. That is, we ought to stand with those interpreters for whom (as Hans Frei puts it) "the *Sache* [subject matter] had been more important than the words if one found a state of affairs in which there was a conflict. Where a person, for instance, thought that by affirming verbal propositions [for example, Jesus Christ is alpha and omega] or the stories in the Bible as true [for example, these stories depict the true identity of Jesus Christ] he had done his religious duty by Scripture, he was apt to be reminded that he had not yet come to the subject matter. But such ways involved misunderstanding Scripture; they were not the normative situation."[25] The fact that these are narratives of *Jesus Christ* is more important than the fact that these are *narratives* which perform a variety of functions.

How might we work out more precisely the range of patterns of relationship between Jesus Christ and the Scriptures (between subject matter and text, between Head and body)? The answer to this question is an ingredient of a doctrine of God. And developing a doctrine of God would require remembering the Hebrew Scriptures. For example, think of the way the book of Exodus depicts the relationship between Yahweh and Israel's seminal texts. Yahweh tells Moses to write (Exod 17:14; 34:28)—and Moses writes (Exod 24:4; 34:28). Yet Yahweh says, "I have written. . . ." (Exod 24:12; 34:1)—and the narrator confirms this (Exod 31:18; 32:16). Still further, Moses breaks up this writing (Exod 32:19), and re-writes (Exod 34:28). Some find room here for arguments over how many of the words are inspired; others reject the myth of a book-writing God. But what we need to do is carefully study such tales rather than presume we know in advance what they say. Exodus, for example, offers no narrative of God writing. Who, we are forced to ask, is the God whose fidelity is signified by these written texts? What is the relationship between these texts as

"body of Christ" and "Word of God"? Pursuing the relationship between inquiry into Jesus Christ and inquiry into these
texts requires engaging in inquiry into God. Such will be a central issue in subsequent chapters, particularly the final two.
But there are other issues to pursue before we walk on this holy
ground of inquiry into God.

b. SUBJECT MATTER AND CONTEXT

What are the relationships between Jesus Christ and the
context of these texts? The story, we have seen, does not end in
that Jesus Christ promises continued presence and coming
again. It does not end in that the scriptural canon moves on to
the story of the Acts of the Apostles and the letters of Paul and
others. It does not end in that these texts call for the continued
life of the Christian community—Jew and Greek, slave and
free, male and female—reading, praying, ordering its ministries, sent on religious and political mission. It does not end insofar as we are called to seek and find our individual vocations
in the new aeon. In sum, the story does not end insofar as we
need to map the patterns of relationships between the storied
Christ and the world which is the context of these texts. Such is
an implication of the universal significance of Jesus Christ. Insofar as the story does not end, we cannot identify Christ or
ourselves with these texts: they are only the *body* of Christ.
They only witness, mirror, depict this Christ. This text itself
calls for us to say how this is so in specific contexts: liturgical,
ecclesial, religious, and more worldly.

To this extent, narrative functionalists are correct. Part of
the test of biblical narrative is pragmatic—at least in this
sense: it includes appeal to the relationships not only between
subject matter and text but between these texts and the range
of practices which form the contexts for these texts. As
Nicholas Lash puts it, Christian practice "consists in the *performance* of texts which are construed as 'rendering,' bearing
witness to, one whose words and deeds, discourse and suffering 'rendered' the truth of God in human history."[26] According
to this view, we hold together the subject matter and context of
these texts by giving a priority to "performing the Scriptures"
much as we might perform a symphony or a play. The recom-

mendation that we perform the Scriptures does not mean we need to turn away from the scriptural texts to an encounter with God or Christ "unmediated" by them—as if any difficulty with these texts could be remedied by having us celebrate liturgies, join a church, dialogue with the religious or more secular world or as if there is any context, practice, or performance which guarantees that these texts will be used correctly. We must somehow maintain multiple patterns of relationships between the subject matter of these texts and their contexts.

However, the risk of the pragmatic or performative test of biblical narrative is that the performance of the text—the use of the text in a variety of contexts—will be granted a systematic priority over the subject matter of the text. That is, the risk is that priority will be given to catholicity of performance (our use of the text in a universal variety of contexts) over particularity of subject matter (Jesus Christ). But if this happens, the catholicity of Jesus Christ triumphs over the particularity of Jesus Christ.[27]

In contrast, I suggest not only that inquiry into Jesus Christ and inquiry into these texts are bound to each other but that each (alone and together) is unintelligible without inquiry into other contexts—the public and private lives of Christian communities locally, nationally, and internationally. If the relationship between subject matter and texts forces us to unfold a theology (that is, a doctrine of God), the relationships between subject matter and contexts compel us to develop an anthropology (that is, a doctrine of human beings). This would be not primarily about human beings in general but primarily about human beings-in-act in a variety of specific contexts—contexts to which these texts relate in very different ways. What those contexts are and how they are related to the storied Christ is the subject matter of the subsequent chapters.

c. TEXT AND CONTEXTS

Thus far I have proposed that narrative realists can embrace the claims of narrative functionalists in a way that functionalists cannot embrace the claims of realists. But all is not well with narrative realism. One of the most perplexing claims made by narrative realists is that the world of the Bible "embraces" our experience or "absorbs" our world; as Ronald Thiemann puts it, "the text does create its own context" in various ways—by identifying Jesus Christ, the God of prevenient love, and Christian discipleship; by promising a new world to us and inviting us to be disciples.[28] Such claims are perplexing because they amount to anthropomorphizing this text—speaking as if these texts do things. But texts (not even these particular texts) do not act, whether to render Christ, identify God, shape our identities, or otherwise "function." Narrative realism thus far seems compatible with churches and communions that find a particularity to these texts that sets them outside these texts' contexts, giving them a self-interpreting perspicuity. It does not seem compatible with churches which insist such texts are at home within particular contexts. Stated in intra-Christian terms, narrative realism seems to be more of a Protestant (and more Reformed than Lutheran) than Catholic (Roman or Eastern or Anglo-) position. It is for some such reasons that even Catholics otherwise sympathetic to narrative realism might hesitate to endorse it.

However, I do not think we need to play a Reformation narrative realism off a Catholic narrative functionalism if we notice that inquiry into the patterns of relationships between texts and contexts is distinct from the previous inquiries (that is, inquiries into the relationships between subject matter and text or context). If there are the patterns of relationships between Jesus Christ and text and context suggested above, we must say that these texts metaphorically create their context in this sense: they are not things which act (or perform or function) but examples of how our identities are formed only in relation to what others have done in these texts. They are, we might say, activities, practices, even performances—but primarily the performances of others rather than ourselves. Some depict our present world, others the world of our past relatives, and still others a world that is not yet here. In still other words, these texts embrace, absorb, and even create us insofar as we are part of their tradition. Granted, this tradition is not constituted by these texts alone—and we are not governed by Scripture isolated from everything else (*solitaria Scriptura*); and it will only be on very special occasions (for example, when it is time to pray and preach and teach the Bible) that we will follow only these texts—and we are seldom governed by Scripture alone (*sola Scriptura*). But the subject matter of these texts gives them a particularity that deserves its own time and place. There is, once again, no single way these texts are related to their contexts. However, if these texts are practices, we can understand why they naturally elicit the question: what is *going on* in these texts? We catch on to the answer to this question not primarily by quoting a text or seeking a revelatory experience but by seeking to engage it, the way we catch on to any action. This engagement, we shall see, is a cumulative life-project, so that the best exegesis will be one that enacts the rule of love.

On the other hand, it is also true that contexts shape these texts and therefore our engagement with them. Two crucial points need to be made if the influence of contexts on texts is not to undercut the priority of these texts for theological purposes. First, uses of Scripture in theological *arguments* are almost always "indirect."[29] There is no way to make an adequate case for narrative readings of Scripture (or, indeed, for any use of these texts) without cumulative appeal to their internal shape as well as to uses of these texts in their social and ecclesial setting, in our worship and catechesis, in their relations to religious and secular analogues (in novels and elsewhere). But this does not mean that the contexts of these texts ought to systematically dominate them—whether that context be the inner dynamics of the act of faith or a more general "anthropological starting point."[30] It simply means that making a reasoned case for these texts will take intellectual patience—and that such case-making is situated in a variety of practical contexts.

Second, the contexts of these texts extend from archaeology to form criticism, from their uses in tradition to their uses in the contemporary life of synagogue and church and world, from biology to theology. These texts do not simply permit but actually require that relationships with all these contexts be sought. This does not mean that such relationships will always be found—or that the results of historical or literary inquiries (for example) will always bear on theological inquiry. Just as many of the results of theological inquiry may be irrelevant to the historian *as* historian, so many of the results of historical inquiry may be irrelevant to the theologian *as* theologian.

Further, the theologian has no guarantee that investigations of such contexts will not yield descriptions and even explanations that would require us to abandon the claims Christians make for these texts and even the texts themselves. But if subject matter and texts and contexts are ranked and related the way suggested here, such backsliding will be a complex event. Christians are called to see, think, and act like "a letter from Christ, drawn up by us and written not with ink but with the Spirit of the living God, not on stone tablets but on the tablets of your living hearts" (2 Cor 3:3). We inquire into these texts as we become such "texts." Therefore, an abandonment of these texts would constitute that absurd self-transformation we Christians could only describe as sin.

Thus, this subject matter and text and context are related in various patterns by the God whose self-impartation in Word and Spirit requires us to pursue still other topics and texts and patterns of relationships. This is centrally because the Word who became flesh is also the One about whom it has been said that "if all were written down, the world itself, I suppose, would not hold all the books that would have to be written" (John 21:25). Seeking the humanity of God through these texts is thus a theologically *sui generis* task. Inquiry into these texts requires a distinctive place in discussions of theological inquiry. But it is also of a piece with our quest for this humanity in other times and places.

2. *Ugly Ditches*

From one point of view, the patterns of relationships with which we ought to be concerned are quite different from those that have been discussed in this section so far (3.C). According to this opposed view, the crucial issue would be that Christological readings of Scripture and teachings are impractical or unintelligible or both. Thus, by the beginning of the nineteenth century, the issue of Christological dogma paled before other challenges.[31] Indeed, the very contexts for asking, "What shall we teach about Jesus Christ?" became more fragmented. In particular, we lost what Albert Schweitzer called the "thread of connection" between Jesus of Nazareth's supposed character and circumstances, consciousness and words and deeds, life and death, resurrection and promised return in relation to Jew and Gentile, slave and free, man and woman.[32] Even if we grant that knowledge of Christ is had through these texts, to what features of these texts shall we appeal? Shall we seek Christ by inquiring into the social and political circumstances of Christ or his "consciousness," the parables or beatitudes or apocalyptic sayings, the miracles or more ordinary deeds, or something else? And even if we agree to inquire into all of these, what is the thread that holds them together?

I do not wish to deny that some non-Christians often know better than Christians that Jesus Christ is the center of *Christian* (if not, they say, their own) lives—the reason some non-Christians come to call them "Christians" (Acts 11:26). Such people would be surprised to engage some self-avowed Christians, only to find that Jesus Christ was not of central importance for them. They might be amazed or angered at the confession that Jesus is Lord; since many past and present characters will be more interesting to them than Jesus Christ, they may be less interested in who Jesus is than in developing an account of the odd fact that others confess this one Lord and Messiah (for example, some theories of myth). Such arguments usually presume that the key patterns of relationship are not like those indicated above but rather are the *oppositions* between Christian practices and teachings and those of other religious and non-religious individuals and groups. Or, in still other words, instead of patterns of relationships, we must spy or debate each other across ugly ditches.[33] If so (this argument goes), any such patterns need to be established, re-established, or otherwise constructed in the face of an unbelieving world.

The problems here are real—and various kinds of theologians offer various responses to challenges to the actuality and possibility of a Christocentric revelation. But it is a large error to mistake such apologetics (that is, the defense of Christian practices and teachings) for the primary goal of mapping patterns of relationships—for two reasons. First and more importantly, questions about patterns of relationships arise *internally* to describing the identity of Jesus Christ and Christian discipleship. That is, they arise because Jesus Christ is who he is on our behalf. We may say that the problematic ugly ditch from a Christian point of view is the gap between what Jesus Christ is for us and what we Christians are (including the way we so frequently cannot find the thread of connection in these narratives). But in any case, the demand for inquiry into patterns of relationships arises out of the internal logic of the faith before it arises from external challenges. If the external criticisms cannot be avoided, neither ought they to be confused with what the gospel narratives require.

Second, if the ugly ditch exists, where would we find the common ground to permit or require debate or dialogue on this issue? I am not denying that Christians and non-Christians share much common ground, many practices as well as truth-claims and rights-claims. But what common ground do we share that is patterned enough to give a *single* context for Christological apologetics—whether it be some actuality or possibility or narrative we all supposedly share? Is it plausible that there is a single systematic response to the objections to Jesus Christ of Thomas Jefferson and William James, Marx and Nietzsche and Freud, Islam and Buddhism, our relatives and friends? Indeed, my hope is that the notion of multiple patterns of relationships will help us locate objections in a more piecemeal fashion, addressing problems for Christology raised by our individual and social identities, our activity throughout the cosmos and our Scriptures one by one rather than under a single rubric. Subsequent chapters bear on how this might be done.

Conclusion

This chapter has explored the relationships between inquiry into Jesus Christ and inquiry into Scripture. The central claim has been that these two inquiries are related by learning to read the Gospels as narratives which attest the particular figure Jesus Christ in what he does and says and suffers over the course of time on behalf of friends and strangers and enemies. To engage in this way of reading the Gospels is to teach that Jesus Christ is the alpha and omega of our lives individually and together, from the creation of this heaven and earth to the creation of the new heaven and earth. Thus, to read Scripture under this doctrinal rule is to take these texts as practices—particular (even peculiar) practices by virtue of their subject matter and their diverse contexts. Seeking "what is going on" in these texts is one form of seeking the humanity of God—a form that raises problems we do not find elsewhere, while requiring us to seek elsewhere also.

Note, then, that this chapter has been about *inquiry*—or better, the way two inquiries are internally related to each other so as to raise the question of how they relate to still further inquiries. However, the chapter's subject matter is neither Jesus Christ nor the Bible but inquiry into Jesus and the Bible. A Christology would have to say much more about the conceptual and practical issues involved in holding apart and together the person and natures, work and states, *extra nos* and *pro nobis* of Jesus Christ's identity; a theology of Scripture would have to say much more about the Scriptures' growth and canonization and use past and present, about the *sola scriptura* and tradition, fundamentalism and historical criticism.[34] Both these *loci*—Christology and bibliology—are important. But so is inquiry into them and their relations. Indeed, it is as impossible to conceive of this Christ or these Scriptures without this inquiry (for example, a Christ or Bible which set us on no quest or about which we have no questions) as it is to conceive of this inquiry in some pure form unrelated to this inquiry into this Christ or these Scriptures. This is not to say that there are not other inquiries distinct from and opposed to these: there *clearly* are. It is to say that these other inquiries are not absolutely unrelated to these. It is time to develop what it means to seek the humanity of God beyond the Scriptures and sacraments, without leaving the previous chapters behind. The potential for conflicts will escalate in subsequent chapters—but so will the resources for the resolution of such conflicts.

4

Saints, Sinners, and Soterialisms

The biblical narratives are (we have seen) not only about Jesus Christ but also about various individuals and groups, disciples and crowds, friends and strangers (3.A.2). Such narratives provide samples of and a context for seeking salvation. That is, we find narratives of divine and human freedoms engaged, thwarted by human freedom, and saved by God's freedom in the stories of Genesis and Exodus, Judges and Kings, Mark and John. Charting the ways the plot is enacted and the characters depicted in such diverse narratives is a central theological chore—particularly the way salvation involves both God's justice and mercy in the cross and resurrection. Biblical stories, symbols, and wisdom all focus on (among other things) such "soterial" action.[1] Further, from chapter 2 we know we can find other examples of and contexts for seeking salvation in our liturgies. The baptismal catechumenate is soterial (paschal)—from its exorcisms and anointings through the confessions of sin at the Lord's Supper (2.A). Roman Catholic and some other Christian churches have quite distinct rituals of reconciliation in rites of penance for our sinners and rites of anointing for our sufferers.

Still further, diverse cultures that are optimistic and pessimistic, hopeful and undecided in the face of particular griefs (for example, an incurable disease, the death of a parent or daughter or son, a retarded child or brother or sister, a natural disaster) provide yet further samples and another context for seeking salvation.[2] In such concrete cases, we seek to move from some evil to some good by some means. But the concrete cases remind us that "we" are not just anyone but particular parents and children, brothers and sisters, doctors and patients. We struggle not usually with "evil" but "evils." Even in these particular cases, evils do not usually evoke general claims but particular soterial actions and reactions—complicity and resignation, revulsion and opposition, suffering and sometimes victory. Our strategies for seeking salvation are more apparent in the particular ways we relate to large scale genocides and small scale self-hatreds than in our general claims about how we move from evils to good by various means. The particularities of "we," "evils" and "goods" and "means" suggest to others that seeking or finding salvation is an absurd quest in a fragmented world.

In any case, we could turn for examples of seeking or inquiring into salvation to Scripture or liturgy (as in chapters 2 and 3)—or to more common cases (as in chapters 5 and 6). But it will more fruitfully advance our inquiry to consider another context more catholic than Scriptural texts or liturgical rites—and less catholic (or more Catholic) than a plethora of joys and griefs from human experience more generally.

Recall that we are moving slowly but surely through the diverse contexts for seeking the humanity of God, gradually making the case that we seek the God of Jesus Christ as we relate such contexts (and their teachings) to each other in ways that engage what God is doing for all humanity. Advancing our inquiry includes moving on to other contexts without permitting any single context to monopolize our inquiry.

The Christian community itself is another context for our particular inquiry. This community is no less than its Scriptural texts and liturgies; but it is also more, for the Christian community is constituted not only by word and sacrament but also by still other practices and teachings.

Again, as in the case of the move from sacraments to scriptural texts (3.C, introduction), there are problems in moving from biblical narratives to the whole of the Church's life—problems which can make the inquiry of this chapter more difficult and even perilous than the inquiries of previous chapters. On the one hand, we need a community particular enough to confess its own limits and its own sins before it can speak with authority to a world capable of the noblest and foulest sorts of soterial activities. We cannot leave behind our Scriptures and life of worship. On the other hand, problems of soterial action (I hope to show) are broader than problems of word and sacraments, and we need a community catholic enough to nurture diverse practices and teachings.

In fact, it is precisely our failure to be such a community that makes this Church a good context for issues of soteriology (that is, inquiry into salvation or soterial action). Christians are not reconciled among themselves, that is, they do not have a great deal of skill in standing and moving in relationship to fellow Christians, monastic and lay, East and West, Catholic and Protestant, Evangelical and Liberal. Catholics, it seems, are more particular than catholic; Christian is a catholic qualifier of communities divided over the particulars of the common life. What can it mean to seek and find salvation in this *communal* context—a context where we disagree on who are our sinners and saints, as well as on the transition from one to the other? The point of this chapter is to answer this question.

The first section (4.A) suggests how this communal context escalates the possibility of conflicting inquiries, while the second section (4.B) suggests ways of resolving such conflicts. The thesis of the chapter (and the third sub-thesis of the book) is that *we engage in theological inquiry in the context of a holy yet sinful community whose hope is Jesus Christ because this community is the hope of Jesus Christ.* By chapter's end it will be clear how the engagement of these two hopes—Christ's and ours, in that order, but neither alone—is the centerpiece for engaging the joys and griefs of all humanity.

A. *Holy and Sinful Practices*

1. *Vatican II as Pastorally Descriptive*

One way to describe a Christian community seeking reconciliation is through Vatican II's Dogmatic Constitution on the Church.[3] I will take sections of the Constitution not primarily as proposing doctrines about the Church but as describing a range of purposeful practices which are cause and effect of the Council's dogmatic claims. That is, it is common wisdom that if we take the documents of Vatican II as a set of teachings, it is not easy to make the case that such teachings are internally consistent.[4] The use of Vatican II in chapter 3 implied that one way to seek consistency in the teachings of Vatican II is to locate them in relation to particular practices (for example, scriptural narratives). This chapter exhibits a different strategy. Not all (or even the bulk) of Vatican II's documents propose teachings. Vatican II was, a saying goes, primarily a "pastoral" council. Part of what this means (I suggest) is that we need to attend to the way the documents frequently aim less to teach than to describe from within the contexts of their teachings. Such, I think, is what is going on in Vatican II's Constitution on the Church—as follows.

The subject matter of the Constitution is the "nature and universal mission" of this Church (DCC no. 1)—not simply what the Church is or does *ad intra* or *ad extra*, but all of these. What is this nature and mission? Initially it seems obscurantist to begin with "The Mystery of the Church" (DCC, ch. 1) until we note that "mystery" is used here in a peculiar sense. "Mystery" is a predicate of "purposes" (cf. Eph 1:9); and when the document speaks of the mystery "of the Church," the genitive is objective (God is this community's mystery) and subjective (The Church is a mystery). That is, the mystery of the Church is the role this community plays in God's purposes—and therefore the purposes and designs this community ought to have. These are, be it noted, communal, common, or collective purposes. We want to know what it is (in and with and sometimes against God's purposes for us individually and together) that gives this community common goods and purposes. What are these purposes?

God's purposes as Father and Son and Spirit are to raise all humanity to share in God's own life by preparing a new humanity in Israel and the Church (DCC no. 2). This community is therefore the pilgrim people of God whose supreme goal and good and purpose is this God. And because all humanity individually and together is this God's common good, this community's purposes include all this Church's members in their life of virtue and priestly worship, prophetic and charismatic gifts, faith and love, royal and kingly mission toward a universal kingdom at the service of this God, this Church, and all humanity (DCC nos. 9–16).

How, we rightly ask, do the common goods of *all* humanity (non-members) relate to the common goods of *many* of humanity (members)? How does the common good of all the members *all the time* in its historical communion relate to its common goods at *special times* (in preaching and sacraments)? How do the common goods of the all and the many relate to the common good of *some* members—its bishops and laity and religious locally, nationally, and internationally? How do these common human purposes relate to God's *single* purpose for the all, the many, the some? Vatican II is optimistic that we do not have to choose among these diverse purposes. These "descriptions" or "models" of the Church complement each other.[5] If the Church is a community whose common good is a particular God (and therefore all humanity, all this community's members, and particularly those with special needs and gifts at the service of this God and this people), there will be no need for this community to purchase one of its many common goods—its God, all humanity, its own members—at the expense of others. To seek paradigms of Christian identity or samples of competent Christian speech and action (1.A.1) is to seek the individuals and groups who enact these diverse purposes.

2. Problems with Vatican II

The primary problem is not that we have treasure in such diverse earthen vessels, but that the earthen vessels are often broken, depraved, sinful.[6] None of us would have a difficult time giving examples of this Church as a church of sinners. But consider the following disagreements among Christians—disagreements which have contributed to turning us into opposed communities.

If we ask how the common goods of the all and the many relate to the common good of *some* members (for example, its bishops and laity and religious locally, nationally, and internationally), we find Christians divided by the diverse ways they distribute offices, charisms, and other communal roles to ordained and non-ordained, clergy and religious and lay. For example, traditionally Roman Catholics have found the work of God in Rome's Petrine ministry, Anglicans and some Lutherans in the episcopate, Presbyterians in the presbyterate, Baptists in the local congregation—while other Christians are either agnostic on such issues or anti-papal, -episcopal, -clerical, -congregational.

If we ask how the common goods of Christians gathered together at *particular times and places* to celebrate word and sacrament relate to other goods, we find not only disagreements about the truth-claims we ought hold about such gatherings but also diverse and opposed gatherings. For many Eastern Orthodox, as well as some Anglicans and Roman Catholics, the liturgical pattern of praying is the time and place of communal activity, *the* common good that creates and saves us. Other Christians are suspicious that the recurring character of such rituals generates mindless and mindful hypocrisy. Eastern Orthodox, Roman Catholics, Anglicans, and other Christians gather roughly once a week to celebrate the Lord's Supper; others celebrate this Lord's Supper less frequently, some rarely. Many Christians gather for specific rites of marriage and orders, reconciliation and anointing, washing of feet and revivals (or novenas); other Christians gather at particular times primarily to organize parish finances or play bingo.

Or if we ask about the common goods Christians share across time, we find Christians trained in different tales of the traditions—emphasizing perhaps the first ecumenical councils or the later Western councils, the Reformation debates or post-Reformation saints and sinners. If we ask how these common goods of Christians relate to the common goods of humanity, we find Christians fragmented into liberal and conservative, sexist and racist, capitalist and socialist. Most crucially, oppositions between these common goods suggest that the God these communities confess may be manifold rather than one. Arguments over the Trinity, the God of wrath and mercy, the God who acts in particular ways in our individual lives, and the God who grounds cosmic processes may not be arguments over the same God (1.A.4). The conclusion seems obvious: unless we restrict ourselves to fields of action smaller than a community (for example, the Scriptures or sacraments), there are no good samples of Christian community, no paradigms of Christianly competent speech and action.

3. *A Sinful Church of Sinners*

This odd conclusion might make more sense if we restate it in terms internal to this community. The problem is this: in what sense can the Christian community truly confess that it is "a sinful Church of sinners"?[7] Press the diverse purposes sketched by Vatican II, and we might say we have "a Church of sinners" without "a sinful Church." That is, teaching that this community is a Church of sinners would be claiming that the *individual* members of this community persistently distort and refuse to take up the aims and purposes of their charter; such a claim is a logical inference of the teaching that this is a people not yet at its ultimate goal (Church, chs. 5, 7). However, the Christian community is not a sinful Church (the argument might go) because it is a holy Church, transformed by God's grace into the immaculate (perhaps even immaculately conceived) body of Christ in its Scriptures or sacraments, the objectivity or subjectivity of its saints.

Many Christians would delight to discover a Church of sinners which was not a sinful Church. However, these same Christians might also wonder where they should look to find such a group. They would sooner press the way these purposes conflict, concluding that we do indeed have a sinful Church. A claim that this community is a sinful Church is a claim that the practices and teachings of this community itself (and not just of its individual members) are depraved and unauthentic: not only individuals but the Church as a whole misses God's mark in matters biblical and liturgical, ecclesial and ecumenical, inter-religious and more commonly human. To such Christians, teaching that the Church is a sinful Church seems to be a piece of common sense modeled on the infidelities of Israel and the disciples, pastors and theologians, rich and poor. The point here may not be that God is not at work transforming this community from sinner to communion of saints but that these soterial moments go on simultaneously with massive sin. We might argue that only if we take the sinful Church to be a rule of faith can we understand why the creed confesses this to be a holy community: a sinful Church must insist that it is by the grace of God alone that this sinful Church is a holy Church. This is a Church of sinners and even a sinful Church not because its purposes are many but because it fails to faithfully engage the God who is its sole purpose.

However, from the point of view of those who deny that we are a sinful Church, the problem with this affirmation is that, applied with rigor to the multi-purposed Church of Vatican II, teaching that the whole Church is a sinful Church would be to teach that there are no *good* examples of Catholic practice and teaching; it would be to teach that Christ is active and present in neither its Scripture, its liturgy, its whole communal life, nor its mission to the religions and the world (cf. DCR no. 21; CSL no. 7). The result would be a community which could only act sinfully—and which, therefore, would have to be treated with perpetual suspicion. The difficulties for theologians, students of religion, and more ordinary folk would be enormous. Where would theologians turn to criticize this community on its own terms? Where would students of religions turn for examples of this community? Why would anyone be interested in being in a wholly sinful Church? Why would God choose them?

This debate, I would emphasize, is intra-Catholic as well as intra-Christian. Among all Christian Churches there are different sensibilities between those for whom it is essential that we constantly sin in matters of practice—and those for whom such sin occurs against the background of a genuinely holy Church. The documents of Vatican II are unclear on this score. The most we can claim is probably that the documents of Vatican II *permit* adherents to claim that the Church is not only a Church of sinners but also a sinful Church. The position might be read as a middle way between strong claims about the holiness of the Church and claims about the sinfulness of the Church—or it might be read as a compromise which has the worst of both worlds.

How can this "hippopotamus Church" (T.S. Eliot) in any way be a soterial community (one, holy, catholic, and apostolic)? How can a sinful church of sinners be more than part of the problem *from* which we need salvation rather than a context *for* salvation? What is anomalous about this situation is not only these disagreements over church order and worship, traditions and mission to the world in themselves. Rather, what is anomalous is also that such disagreements are examples of a more basic disagreement over what constitutes soterial *activity*. Without consensus on soterial activity, Christians can have only disagreement on other matters of the nature and mission of this Church. Soteriology is the central clue for these other disputes. It is, then, only as Christians develop consensus on soteriological practice and doctrine that oppositions on other matters can be overcome. Are there any rules embedded in sinful Christian practice that we do or ought to follow, need to or can follow?

B. *Christ is Our Hope*

How can we seek the humanity of God in such a sinful yet holy context? A good model of a quest for Christian doctrine on this issue is the soteriological volume of one of the Lutheran-Catholic dialogues.[8] These Lutherans and Catholics (1) aim to engage in a "common search," rather than, say, a compromise, (2) by (a) each side sympathetically examining the formulations of their dialogue partners, (b) both sides together formulating a statement of agreements and disagreements and (c) proposing to their Churches their reasons for thinking that "disagreements over justification that were once irresolvable may not now be church-dividing" (JBF nos. 3, 5, 165). Each phase requires comment.

1. *Oppositions and Common Ground*

Given the historical depth of the disagreement between the two Churches, how can they claim to be engaged in a "common search" (JBF, preface)? Their common ground is a focus on the central claim of specifically Christian soteriology:

"We emphatically agree that the good news of what God has

done for us in Jesus Christ is the source and center of all
Christian life and of the existence and work of the church"
(JBF no. 4).

The issue for these Christians is not whether Jesus Christ is
"source and center of all Christian life" but how this is so when
we come to speak of "justification." Yet this focus for their
common search leads to their central common discovery.

In view of this agreement we have found it helpful to keep in
mind in our reflections an affirmation which both Catholics
and Lutherans can wholeheartedly accept: *our entire hope of
justification and sanctification rests on Christ Jesus and on
the gospel whereby the good news of God's merciful action in
Christ is made known; we do not place our ultimate trust in
anything other than God's promise and saving work in Christ.*
(JBF nos. 4, 157)

The central teaching is thus quite simple: Christ is our hope,
the hope of the righteous and unrighteous, saints and sinners.
The burden of the document, then, is to describe the *transition*
from this common ground on Jesus Christ to this common
ground on justification. Making this transition is the point of
the document's three key steps.

2. *Ecumenical Reasoning*

a. A NARRATIVE OF THE QUESTION

Thus, first, the sympathetic examination of the formulations of the dialogue partners largely takes place through the
discovery of a new way of narrating "The History of the Question" (JBF ch. 1). In the story's first act (that is, before the time
of the Reformations), "Eastern theologians described salvation in terms of a return to God of a creation that had gone
forth from God"—a deification at once cosmic and human,
formulated in terms at once biblical and Neo-platonic "in contrast to the prominence of fate and inevitability in some pagan
and gnostic thought." Western theologians, on the other hand,
described salvation as a justifying transformation made neces-

sary by human sinfulness and made possible by the predestin-
ing grace of God alone—in contrast to a Pelagianism which
denied the priority of God's over humans' action. Western
medieval theology distinguished various forms of grace (for
example, operating and cooperating, prevenient and subsequent) and merit (for example, congruous and condign), climaxing in the theological claim that God "does not deny grace
to those who do what is in them" (JBF nos. 6–20).

In the second act, the Reformers, seeking to deal with the
"works-righteousness" and "terrified consciences" caused (or
occasioned) by aspects of late medieval theology, changed the
issue from justification by grace alone (*sola gratia*) to justification by faith alone (*sola fide*), asserting that the Christian is "simultaneously a righteous person and sinner" (JBF nos. 21–28).
In the third act, Post-Reformation controversies were a tale of
the solidification of the oppositions between Western medieval and Reformation soteriologies as well as the abandonment
of Lutheran-Catholic dialogue in favor of various disputes
within Lutheranism and Catholicism.

The final act is the twentieth century, partly a continuation
of the earlier separatism, but with the difference that Catholics
and Lutherans have become increasingly self-critical (as a result of the renewal of the uses of Scripture and celebrations of
liturgy as well as of the developments in ecclesiology and
eschatology) and that some theologians "no longer viewed justification as essential Christian doctrine" (JBF nos. 71, 86).

This narrative is a two-edged sword. On the one hand, just as
the teachings of Jesus are contextualized by a particular narrative (3.B.1), so also are the teachings of these Churches. A skill
at offering a history of these teachings is built into the very
concept of teaching what these Churches teach. Understanding the historical context of another church's teachings is a key
way to avoid premature ecumenical polemics (for example,
using war-like rhetoric when faced with an opposition of teachings). On the other hand, it might be tempting to think that oppositions between these Christian teachings are overcome
once we understand the opposition in historical context. If a
narrative of a teaching helps us avoid being polemical, it may
tempt us to be prematurely irenic (for example, declaring doctrinal peace where there is no peace). But the participants do

not claim that the oppositions between them are overcome simply by understanding what each side teaches in historical context. In fact, the way the document is written seems to suggest that there is a *single* history of a *single* question which, taking various forms in different historical eras, sets a context for subsequent teachings. But what is "*the* question" of which this is "*the* history"? Why not read the diverse descriptions— "deification," "justification," "grace"—as incomparable answers to incomparable questions rather than similar answers to a single question? Can the unity-in-difference of narratives embracing Eastern Orthodox and Roman Catholics and Lutherans in their diverse histories yield unity on teachings? Clearly, offering a narrative of this teaching is a necessary but not sufficient condition of overcoming oppositions between Christian teachings on this issue. What else is necessary?

b. COMPARATIVE DOGMATICS[9]

Second, the participants formulate a statement of agreements and disagreements focused on "contrasting concerns and patterns of thought." The contrasting concerns have to do with different ways of taking their engagement by *God*. Lutherans "focus on safeguarding the absolute priority of God's redeeming word in Jesus Christ" and Catholics focus on "acknowledging the efficacy of God's saving work in the renewal and sanctification of the created order" (JBF no. 95). The contrasting patterns of thought have to do with different ways of conceiving *their* engagement by God. Lutherans think of sinners standing *coram Deo* (before God), focusing on the discontinuous and even paradoxical ways we ought to speak before the face of God; Catholics think of creatures and sinners progressively transformed by God's infusion of saving grace. Here the issues involved in the sinful Church of sinners above are repeated in vocabulary specific to two Churches. Lutherans, who emphasize the justifying action of God revealing our sinfulness, will insist that the Christian community is *simultaneously* just and sinful (JBF no. 102) while Catholics will emphasize that the indwelling Spirit *transforms* sinners into a genuine communion of saints whose "loving commitment issues in good works" (JBF no. 105). These two views are called the (Lutheran) "simultaneity model" and the (Catholic) "transformationist model" (JBF no. 154). Stated in terms of the previous section (4.A.3), the difference breaks down the *opposition* between the sinful Church and the Church of sinners into a *contrast* between their teachings about God and themselves. The patterns "may in part be complementary and, even if at times in unavoidable tension, not necessarily divisive" (JBF no. 94).[10]

More particular agreements and disagreements are analyzed against the background of these contrasts by summarizing Lutheran and Catholic stands as well as the "fears" each side has about the other's position. For example, for Lutherans, justification is "the forensic act whereby God declares the sinner just" with the result that good works follow, whereas Catholics focus on justification as one description of the interaction between God's pouring forth of the Holy Spirit into our hearts and our response in faith, hope, and love. Such Catholics (Eastern Orthodox, Episcopal, or Roman) fear that Lutherans disregard the benefits of God's love, and Lutherans fear that Catholics might "throw believers back on their resources" (JBF nos. 98–101). This pattern is applied to several other particulars (JBF nos. 98–120): we are dealing with contrasts (not oppositions)—but contrasts which leave as much room for fear as hope. Note that specific affections like fear and hope are built into these teachings: (dis)agreements are a matter of mind and heart. One way to find an ecumenically divisive disagreement is by seeking which teachings of others we *fear*. One way to heal such disagreements is to provide good reasons for teaching that hope outweighs the fears. Just as "the history of the question" was a necessary but not sufficient condition for overcoming opposed teachings, so also a comparison of contrasting answers to the question is a necessary but not sufficient condition for warranting their agreement. Skill in comparing and contrasting teachings is a part of teaching what these Churches teach. But a final step is clearly needed.

c. WEIGHING CONVERGENCE AND DIVERGENCE

Thus, third, if this dialogue avoids polemics and irenics, it is also not satisfied with comparisons which merely list agreements and disagreements, hopes and fears. The aim of the participants is to construct a formula on which both sides agree but which preserves what each side regards as indispensable and so to describe why "disagreements over justification that were once irresolvable may not now be church-dividing" (JBF nos. 5, 4).

This stage sketches two "perspectives for reconstruction." First, the participants' appeals to "biblical data" provide the framework for both sides to *criticize* their own positions *from within*. "From within" here refers not to the "within" constituted by any or all of the practices and teachings of their Churches but to the biblical charter which stands as judge over their practices and teachings (3.C). The appeals are unfortunately quite technical, focused on historical analysis of concepts and images of justification. But their net effect is to suggest how these Scriptures partly overlap with Catholic and Lutheran understandings of justification—as well as to call for each to qualify their positions (JBF no. 123). A central example of such internal self-criticism is the claim that it was Paul's "eschatological outlook" which enabled him to hold together what Catholics and Lutherans often tore asunder. That is, "justification . . . is an eschatological reality which stretches from the past through the present and into the future" (JBF no. 136). A central implication of the appeal to Scripture is that the re-discovery of biblical eschatology has transformed the context for dealing with church-dividing differences on justification. It is only as holy and sinful practices, saints and sinners, the sinful Church and the Church of sinners, the simultaneity model and the transformation model are set in motion by a still outstanding (eschatological) goal that we can confess (as Vatican II says) "a genuine but imperfect holiness" (JBF no. 74).

Second, their consensus is unpacked by describing the respects in which Lutherans and Catholics do and do not converge practically and doctrinally. On the one hand, the participants claim that there are *practical* convergences on the interpretation of Scripture, liturgical renewal, continual reformation of their communions, cooperation in the service of human needs, and the appropriation of intellectual developments in non-theological fields (JBF nos. 150–152). Further, there is a *doctrinal* convergence on "the criterion" (or teaching) of justification by faith (4.B.1), including its various "elements." For instance, the authors commonly confess that creation is good, all are ruled by sin, and God is about the task of overcoming evil by opposing and suffering it and calling humanity to a life of faith and hope and love focused on the kingdom (JBF nos. 155–156).

On the other hand, there is a "lesser" or "incomplete" convergence on the "application" or "use of the criterion," including diverse ways of describing justification required "by the needs of gospel proclamation in each age" (JBF nos. 158–159). Disagreements over purgatory, the papacy, the saints, and the different ways of "describing" (or "conceptualizing," "picturing," "interpreting") God's saving action are examples of disagreements over "which beliefs, practices, and structures pass the test"—a doctrinal test on which both sides agree: Christ is our hope.

These practical and doctrinal convergences, the authors imply, outweigh these practical and doctrinal divergences. This warrants the recommendation to the Churches that they study this document and "increasingly proclaim together the one, undivided gospel of God's saving mercy in Jesus Christ" (JBF nos. 165, 4,).

3. *Practices and Teachings*

The three stages of ecumenical reasoning (4.B.2) suggest a strategy for common inquiry in a holy yet sinful Church: once given an opposition and common ground, offer a narrative of the opposition, sort out the contrasting concerns at stake in the controversy, and explain why the resulting agreements outweigh the disagreements (or vice-versa). But there are two major ways to challenge this ecumenical reasoning.

First, serious Christians (one challenge goes) *obviously* agree that Christ is our hope, else why call themselves Christians? But the notion that such Christian common sense overcomes centuries of disagreement is implausible. Teaching that Christ is our hope is either a truism that has nothing to do with disagreements between Christian Churches or an important truth that renders disagreements between Christian Churches trivial. But, at least for ordinary folk, this teaching does not overcome disagreements on soteriological practice or teaching. It displaces or ignores such disagreements.

This challenge, we ought to admit, *might be* true. Whether it *is* true depends on whether counter-arguments can be offered to the three stages of ecumenical reasoning (4.B.2) which form the transition from common ground on Jesus Christ to common ground on justification (4.B.1). I do not mean primarily the counter-arguments by historical theologians to the narrative, by dogmatic theologians to the contrasting concerns, by theologians and bishops to the weighing of convergences and divergences (although these counter-arguments are important). I mean primarily the counter-arguments that will be displayed in the lives of Christians as they do or do not "receive" such teachings—where "reception" includes becoming the sort of people who know each others' stories, articulate the contrasting teachings at work in these narratives, and truthfully repent of their failures to live up to their common hope.

The second challenge will require a more lengthy response in the remainder of the chapter. The document's candid contrast between greater and lesser convergence (this challenge might say) suggests that this proposed teaching stands in some jeopardy. The document articulates a "Christian" confession as well as a specifically "Lutheran" and "Catholic" one. But is it "true"? Granted, the authors may not ask this question. For them, just as the confession is labeled Christian as well as Lutheran and Catholic, so it might be labeled Christian as well as true.[11] But there are two circumstances in which a contrast between "Christian" and "true" make sense.

One situation is that in which confessors of common elements of a soteriology seek *resources* for exploring, applying, developing, expanding, and deepening their teaching. Thus, insofar as we confess that "our *entire* hope of justification and sanctification rests on Christ Jesus" and "we do not place our *ultimate trust* in anything other than God's promise and saving work in Christ" (see the key confession in 4.B.1), we raise questions like, "How does this 'ultimate trust' relate to penultimate (or even trivial) trusts or how does our 'entire hope' relate to those partial hopes we have (or do not have) about our next meal or night's sleep, our health or mortal ills, our spouses or children, our jobs or our nations?" Such penultimate or partial hopes are not necessarily *rivals* to Christian hope but rather *resources* for unpacking and testing such hope. How so?[12]

Another situation is one in which adherents of *rival soteriologies* meet for conversation, collaboration, or combat. It would not be surprising to find adherents of competing quests for reconciliation claiming that this soteriology was Christian but not true. For example, how can we claim Jesus saves by justifying through faith in a world where justification is, in small or large ways, unintelligible or inapplicable?

We will shortly see a number of religious and non-religious examples of such rival soteriologies. This second challenge raises the issue of "rivals" and "resources" again (see also 2.C), but now with the implication that what we *count as* resources and rivals depends on how we confess soterial action. The doctrine that Christ is our hope is both an end and beginning, both an "already" and a "not yet," proposed with confidence and tentativeness. It is an end because agreement on this essential teaching provides the crucial rule for pursuing remaining conflicts—a beginning because agreement on essential teaching leaves other issues unresolved. The opposition between a sinful Church and a Church of sinners becomes the contrast between simultaneity and transformation models held together by the common teaching that Jesus Christ is our hope; and this contrast leaves still other issues to be explored. How?

C. *We Are Christ's Hope*

Inquiry into the issues left open by the teaching that Christ is our hope is primarily inquiry into the common ground on which the Lutheran-Catholic dialogue began: Jesus Christ. Here we need to address an issue that was left in the background in the previous chapter (3.A.2, 3.B.3). Jesus Christ is a particular individual who in interaction with God and neighbor over the course of time enacts salvation on our behalf. Given the diverse ways the narrative ends and does not end, what (we asked) are the patterns of relationships between this Christ and our world (3.C, introduction)?

This question is particularly crucial with regard to Jesus' soterial action in death and resurrection. In the crucifixion Jesus enacts solidarity with humanity in power and powerlessness even unto death—and in the resurrection Jesus Christ is victor over death on our behalf. But the transition between the cross and resurrection "is not and doubtless cannot be described."[13] Even further, it is precisely at this point that the patterns of relationships between Jesus Christ and our lives seem radically problematic, for we cannot save each other by such a wondrous exchange.[14] Here, above all, our righteousness is "alien" and this One is external to us. In both cases— the transition from Jesus' death to resurrection and the transition from this crucified and risen One to our lives—we are tempted to find relationships where none exist. At the extreme, we read the story of Christ's death as if it were not real; we act as if we must somehow remain alive for this One to save us. Saints find massive patterns of relationships in imitation of God's transforming action in poverty, chastity, obedience, and non-violence; sinners find a radical distinction between what God does for them and what they can do for each other. Or is it sinners who seek patterns of relationship imitative of and so internal to Jesus Christ and saints who seek patterns of relationship more distant from or external to Jesus Christ?

Michael Root is, I believe, correct in proposing that the patterns of relationships we seek with resources and rivals will be "storied relations" (between patterns in Christ's narrative and patterns in our lives) whose crucial problem is the "non-narrated interlude" between burial and empty tomb—Christ's and (the Spirit promises) ours.[15] Here I will propose that spanning the gulf between saints and sinners does not depend primarily on the (ecclesiological) teaching that *Christ is our hope*; instead, the non-narrated interlude between God's cruciform activity and God's transforming action is overcome by seeking soteriological patterns of relationships which depend on the (anthropological) teaching that *we are Christ's hope*.

What does this teaching involve? Most importantly, it means that we (provisional representatives of all humanity) hope for the reconciliation of all humanity by tracking the way opposed and diverse soteriologies are (primarily) resources for and (secondarily) rivals to our own. This theological mouthful needs exemplification. The strategy will be to explore three different ways Christian theologians seek and find patterns of relationships between our soteriologies. I will call inquiry into such relationships between soteriologies "soterialisms."

1. *Orthodox and Christian Soterialisms*

Christians confess that Jesus Christ is the One who saves us from our sin. "Jesus," the Gospel of Matthew says, *means* "the one who is to save his people from their sins" (Matt 1:21). The Christian Scriptures and rituals are rich in stories and images, prayers and teachings which depict Jesus Christ as savior. Christians, we have seen, offer different and partly opposed teachings about salvation: Eastern Orthodox speak of deification, classic Western soteriologies of atonement, and more recent theologies focus on liberation and reconciliation. But if recent ecumenical discussions are on the right track, all Christians agree that Jesus is what this name says, namely, the One who saves his people from their sin and is therefore reconciler. Christ is our hope.

How might we handle other soteriologies? One strategy is to take all soteriologies as rivals. Soteriology (one version of this argument might go) is a matter of grace or revelation or faith, not nature or experience or reason. It is in Jesus Christ, the Bible, liturgy, or the Church or all of these that we find true salvation—to the exclusion of other contexts. As rivals and challengers and opponents, other soteriologies are to be opposed and overcome. This is not to say, of course, that adherents of these rival soteriologies are *only* rivals. They are (perhaps even primarily) God's good creatures, called to eternal life with God. It is not their status as creatures that is problematic but their status as reconciled; it is not necessarily their psychologies and sociologies and philosophies but their soteriologies that embody falsehood. But in any case, the line (this argument goes) between creation and redemption, nature and grace, is firm. These conceptual distinctions will be embedded in institutional separations between "religious" and "lay," between those who live lives of poverty and chastity and obedience and those who follow Jesus Christ at much more of a distance in the world, between sects and churches, or even between us saints and those sinners. Jesus Christ (such Christians confess) is indeed our hope and we are Christ's hope— but the "our" here is we Christians (or, better, the saintly Christians among us). I will call this conceptual and institutional strategy "orthodox soterialism." It is a sort of Catholic particularity, but more particular than catholic.

Admittedly, this dualism is more Western than Eastern— and few Western theologians today maintain the position in a form unalloyed with other options. The Eastern Orthodox theologian Vladimir Lossky, for example, criticizes Western theology for focusing on redemption as a juridical relation, proposing instead that "[t]he redeeming work of the Son is related to our nature. The deifying work of the Holy Spirit concerns our persons. But the two are inseparable."[16] *All* humanity is redeemed in Christ, while our unique personhood is being deified by the Spirit in ways that will not be perfected until our personal existence embraces our nature (that is, all humanity). We can almost hear Lossky lament about the Lutheran-Catholic dialogues: "We are not primarily a Church of sinners (much less a sinful Church) abiding in a tension between simultaneity and transformation under Jesus Christ. We are a holy people, redeemed in Christ and befriended in the Spirit, and so caught up in God's Trinitarian nature and persons."

Lossky provides some genuine clues for mapping patterns of relationships between soteriologies. First, the patterns of relationship at stake are those *God* creates and saves in Word and Spirit. In the idiom of previous sections, Lossky is centering on the mystery of the Church, the one common good which holds together the common goods of all, many, and some of us and so holds together saints and sinners. The God who is the mystery of the Church is the single common good who holds together our other common goods, bearing the sins of the world in the Word, and so our "ultimate trust" whose Spirit is transforming our world into God's, a new heaven and earth. It is because God holds *us* as *God's own* common good and purpose that we are enabled to hold God as our own common good and therefore direct our sundry purposes to their eschatological goal.[17] The community whose sovereign good is this God is being shaped into the body of Christ but is not yet what Augustine called the "whole Christ" (*totus Christus*) and becomes so only as it is trained to recognize how the Spirit is shaping the hungry and the thirsty, the stranger and the naked, the sick and the imprisoned into the new humanity (Matt 25:31-46; Eph 2:15).

Further, Lossky reminds us that we seek patterns of relationships both as individuals and as a community. We seek not simply patterns of relationships within our individual lives or our community but patterns of relationships by which we all live. The question for this community would not be whether there are the diverse goods mentioned above (4.A) but how such diverse goals are to be held together in different circumstances—when this people is a set of enslaved or wandering tribes, when it is a kingdom or exiled, when it sits together to be instructed by its Lord, or when it sinfully flees when its Martyr or martyrs are accused of political crimes. In short, the problem is how this community can model itself on the diverse biblical narratives of the journey of Israel and the nations in the Torah, of the disciples and the crowds in the Gospels, of the communion of saints and sinners in the traditions of church and world.

But there are also serious problems with Lossky's proposal—problems which led Lossky to insist that the divide between Eastern and Western Christendom on matters of practice and dogma is insuperable. In sum, it is not easy to discern what concrete patterns of relationships emerge from Lossky's proposal. Take, for example, the dispute between "monks and humanists" in the Eastern Church—monastic theology sometimes *equating* the Christian and the monastic life and humanist theology promoting philosophical and political *dialogue* with Hellenism.[18] Lossky seems to come down on the side of the monks. Eastern monasticism, as "union with God in complete renunciation of the life of the present world," is "the highest degree" of "the free turning of our will toward God"—even though there are also "many examples of spiritual perfection acquired by simple laymen and married people living in the world."[19] Eastern monasticism is the highest degree, we might presume, because its life of prayer and worship and work most fully attests Jesus Christ, particularly the risen Christ we see transfigured on Mount Tabor. What, then, about the trivial and massive sins of our monasteries? Even more crucially, what about discipleship on the plain or the lake, in Gethsemane or on the way to Emmaus? Here we have a kind of Christological and institutional particularity that leaves us wondering about its universality.

Or, to take a conceptual example, Lossky recommends we "resolutely renounce the sense of the word 'person' which belongs to sociology and to most philosophers" and which implies that "each person exists . . . by excluding others." Whereas "what we habitually call a human person is not truly a person but an individual, a part of the common nature," what Lossky means by person is our existence in relation, "to" or "towards" the other.[20] I am not here interested in the important metaphysical questions raised by the distinction between "individuals" and "natures" and "persons." Rather, the point is that Lossky's proposal that we distance ourselves from our use of terms like "person" in academic and ordinary life requires a conceptual asceticism analogous to the practical asceticism of the monastic life. What, then, about our lives in this world? This is precisely the question with which Western theologies have struggled. The dualisms we generated between Roman Catholic religious and lay patterns of relationships, between a Lutheran simultaneity model and Catholic transformation model, between sects of the radical reformations and churches of the magisterial reformations, between grace and nature are the abiding institutional and conceptual marks of our failure. But the problems are real, at least for us "Westerners."

Lossky's formulations are careful. He finds lay saints. He carefully maps some similarities and differences between his and other uses of "person" and "nature"—even the renunciation of ordinary language for theological purposes requires knowledge of such academic and other uses. I do not wish to make Lossky the target of those who are anti-monastic; those who are satisfied with a dualism between monastic and married life; or those who find no difficulties with our ordinary, common sensical, and idiomatic uses of "person," "nature," and "individual." Indeed, Lossky's proposal that Jesus' activity on our behalf in the Spirit calls for our *imitatio Christi* demonstrates a courageous consistency, not unlike Pascal's (ch. 1), rare among lay theologians. If God so calls, there is no better way to attest select features of the gospel narratives—certain kinds of prayer and work, poverty and chastity and obedience—than monastic life at its best.[21] The question is whether such consistency ought to lead us to look ultimately (if not only) to the monastery for our saints. My major point is that unless Lossky can deal with humanists as well as monks, with ordinary uses of "person" as well as his own, *his* claim that *we* are redeemed in the Word and deified in the Spirit has little concrete content.

In sum, Lossky is a good critic of orthodox soterialisms that generated Western dualisms. His is also a good example of a Christian soterialism insisting that we seek patterns of relationships *internal* to what God is doing in Word and Spirit. But how do *we* seek such relationships not only in our monasteries but also in the other joys and griefs of our lives?

2. General and Christian Soterialisms

We can easily find even more radical challenges to proposals like Lossky's. His stand, this argument might go, is *prima facie* implausible. The problem of specifically Christian soterialisms is that they are specific and therefore not of more universal applicability or intelligibility. That our person and natures are redeemed and deified in Word and Spirit is an alien claim in an alien vocabulary. Clearly (other Christians argue), salvation can be more universally described as the *process* by which *we* move or are moved from some *evil* to some *good* by some *means* (for example, by doing or ignoring evil or both, suffering or overcoming evil or both, returning good for evil or bringing good out of evil or both). This (it is presumed) is a general description of salvation. Granted (the argument might go), each of the highlighted concepts (process, we, evil, good, means) generates diverse soteriologies. For example, we might read diverse religions as partly overlapping and partly opposed ways of salvation, each living out different ways some or all move from samsara or sin or other evil to nirvana or eternal life or some other good by nurturing various attitudes and actions, ritual and moral. But the soteriological process does not have to be religious. The process might be a human movement from radical evil to good within the limits of reason alone (Kant), a cosmic process in which species evolve from one stage to another by means of natural selection (some Darwinists), a political process in which we move from alienation by revolutionary praxis (Marx), a psychological process in which we move from repressions to true self-knowledge by means of psychoanalysis (Freud), and so forth. But what I will call "general soterialism" argues that such differences are not as important as their common ground in claiming that salvation is the process by which we move from some evil to some good by some means.[22]

A Christian theologian who was not a general soterialist might nonetheless argue that general soterialisms are not *only* rivals to Christian soterialism. They are also resources, assets, and goods which must be related to creation and to salvation. A frequent strategy for relating such soteriologies is to correlate Christian and more general soterialisms. For example, Edward Schillebeeckx aims at "a mutually critical correlation" between "the great Jewish-Christian movement and . . . new experiences of both Christians and non-Christians."[23] His goal is not to propose that the claim that Jesus saves is simply one version of a general process of salvation but to bring these two sources into dialogue and confrontation by showing the relationship between Jesus Christ and "mankind in search of a way of life which will overcome suffering" (CEJ p. 672). This is what it means to aim to correlate specifically Christian and more general soteriologies.

Roughly, he first surveys the "New Testament theology of the experience of grace" while claiming that this theology cannot be "directly" applied to our experiences (CEJ p. 22). He then describes our world as a world responsible for its own future and "in search of a way of life which will overcome suffering" (CEJ pp. 654, 672). But his final stage is a complex weave of claims accepted and rejected from the first two stages. "God does not want mankind to suffer but wills to *overcome* suffering where it occurs in our history"—in nature and culture, individuals and society, time and space (CEJ pp. 730, 734f., 743). Christian salvation is concerned with all these "coordinates." It rejects claims that salvation concerns only one of them, teaching that the synthesis of all of them is partly accom-

plished and partly not accomplished and that "complete salvation" is therefore impossible to completely define in the present (CEJ pp. 743, 790). We experience this, Schillebeeckx says,
in an encounter with God mediated in a variety of ways (CEJ
p. 809). In particular, God has done this in Jesus Christ, "despite" his death (CEJ p. 729), and in those Christian communities which "are part of the full identity of Jesus Christ" (CEJ p.
802)—communities which attest this "by a fragmentary practice of reconciliation" (CEJ pp. 835, 25).

On this score, the central strength of Schillebeeckx's account
is its insistence that doing soteriology includes discerning saving activities going on in our world—in our individual and social lives, in our own and other times and places, in culture and
nature, in Christian communities and other religious and non-
religious communities. Unlike Lossky, these are clearly diverse
and concrete patterns of relationships between God's soterial
activity and ours—patterns embracing the monastic life
within the context of a broader life in the world.[24] Soteriology is
a pervasively practical ("experiential," Lossky says) matter. As
the lay Lossky ironically tilted toward the monastery, so the
Dominican Schillebeeckx tilts toward the world—a world
where Christian discipleship sometimes takes the form of poverty and chastity and obedience and at other times almsgiving
and marriage and freedom. Any simultaneity of justice and sin
is subordinate to the clear affirmation that God is transforming the world in which we live in a variety of ways, including
the ways all humanity is seeking salvation. Schillebeeckx
would agree that we live in a sinful Church of sinners, but the
world as a whole is not sinful enough to undercut our common
quest to overcome suffering. In other words, Schillebeeckx's
correlationalist strategy ends up holding together the transformationist and simultaneity strategies we saw in the previous
section. But priority is given to the former, and both are
mapped on the world as well as the Church.

Indeed, Schillebeeckx's universalist strategy raises questions. In the story of Jesus, the Word overcomes suffering *by*
undergoing it on our behalf. But do our lives attest this blessed
exchange? How do *we* overcome suffering by undergoing it in
our individual and professional and social lives? How do the
diverse coordinates of our lives attest a *dying* which leads to

living? I find no answer to this question in Schillebeeckx. "The death of Jesus," Schillebeeckx says, "was a suffering through and for others as the unconditional endorsement of a practice of doing good and opposing evil and suffering."[25] This is true—and there is no need to reject this overlap between Christian and more general soterialisms: we oppose evil on behalf of others in all the coordinates Schillebeeckx mentions (nature and culture, individuals and society, time and space). Surely, we might say, we are followers of Christ insofar as our lives attest one or another feature of Christ's life. But if our "search for a way to overcome suffering" is not a discipleship of the cross and resurrection, can the correlation be more than an echo of a whisper?

As we wondered whether Lossky does not pay the price of subordinating most of our lives to lives in the monastery, so we wonder now whether Schillebeeckx does not pay the price of focusing on the abstractions of soterial action we share with the world. How can a focus on what we share with worldly ways of overcoming suffering attest to the Lamb of God who takes away this world's sin?

Parenthetically, it is unclear where Schillebeeckx stands on the ecumenical issues involved in soteriology (4.B). It would be surprising if he took the position that disputes among Christian soterialists are so particular that they cannot be related to our more common quests to deal with suffering. As Lossky is critical of orthodox soterialism, so Schillebeeckx is critical of general soterialism. He is "in dialogue with" general soterialisms rather than permitting such soterialisms systematically to set the agenda for Christians. In short, he is a correlationalist. Perhaps Schillebeeckx presumes that the issues dealt with in the Lutheran-Catholic dialogue on justification are a sixteenth-century version of the modern search for a way to overcome suffering. Something similar applies to the way he locates his Dominican spirituality in the context of humanity's quest for a way to overcome suffering. I have suggested that this universal human quest does not attest the specificity of salvation by Christ in the way that religious vows in the Catholic community do, although this general human quest does partly overlap with what Christians mean by reconciliation and salvation. But perhaps Schillebeeckx presumes a community, like the Dominicans, which institutionally embodies an *imitatio Christi* and which therefore can have less fear of collapsing Christian into a more general soterialism.

If this is so, I would say that such presumptions can no longer remain presumptions in our world. They must be spelled out quite explicitly if the patterns of relationships we live in our institutions and think in our theologies are to be fair to Church and world. Perhaps this point will be clearer once we look at a third option.

3. *Relativist and Christian Soterialisms*

We might issue an even stronger challenge to Schillebeeckx's proposal. Since only Christians claim that Jesus is salvation in incarnation and life, death and resurrection, would it not be more accurate to speak of opposition and rivalry at *this* point (if not other points), rather than a relation (or correlation)? Stated on Schillebeeckx's terms, can Schillebeeckx make good on his *general* soterial claims? On the basis of an analysis of sundry religious and non-religious systems, Schillebeeckx contends that humankind is "in search of a way of life which will overcome suffering." But what about groups who challenge the generality of such claims?

For example, some claim that because evil is a part of life, salvation is not possible—or that because evil does not exist, salvation is not needed or necessary. Such anti-soterialisms must remain for Schillebeeckx an "*exception*"[26] to the (less exceptional) human quest for salvation; if this exception became the rule, it would undercut his more general claim that humanity is in search of a way that will overcome suffering, as well as his more particular claims about Jesus Christ. Or to take a more plausible challenge to general soterialisms, some might claim that there is no cross-cultural description of the origin and nature and goal of evil or any other component of salvation. In this view, talk of salvation is relative to particular individuals and groups, historical eras and cultures; the mistake of Christian and other soterialists (whether religious or not) is to speak and behave as if salvation had some universal intelligibility and applicability. Both religious (Christian or Jewish,

Buddhist or Humanist) and non-religious (Darwinian or Marxist, Freudian or Kantian) soteriologies, this argument goes, err in not recognizing the relativity of both the concrete (for example, the figure Jesus Christ) and the abstract (for example, claims about good and evil) features of reconciliation. We might call this challenge relativist soterialism.

"Relativism" is a technical term used in a variety of ways. There are metaphysical, epistemological, historical, and other forms of relativism. From a viewpoint internal to a sinful Church of sinners, soterial relativism is the relativism with maximal power to make a difference. Pressed to define it, I would say that soterial relativism denies that any soteriology provides a correct description of soterial action for *all* times and places, individuals and groups—all the while affirming that some soteriologies do provide a correct description of soterial action for *some* times and places, individuals and groups.[27] But an example of relativist soterialism might be more helpful than a definition. Consider one reading of William James. Perhaps, James suggested, a God who "produces real effects" (for example, saves) exists; if so, "tragedy is only provisional and partial." Then again, perhaps there are only fragments of salvation and we end up with "a sort of polytheism," with "this world partly saved and partly lost." In either case, "the *chance* of salvation is enough."[28] A few wars after James, worldly wisdom ruled out the theistic or polytheistic hypothesis: we do not even need a chance for salvation but only for small victories, perhaps not amounting to any human (much less religious or Christian) "whole"—all the while remaining open to the joy of a possible universal reconciliation (or the despair of no reconciliation). Here soteriology is not deconstructed but simply decentralized, made more modest, and realistic. Salvation comes piecemeal, perhaps in particular battles for civil rights or in a world without war, perhaps only in periodic sighs of self-forgiveness.

To return to Schillebeeckx, despite his insistence that salvation is still "fragmentary," he comes down more on the side of what the Lutheran-Catholic dialogues called the (Catholic) transformationist model than the (Lutheran) simultaneity model. If all humankind is seeking to overcome suffering, salvation is more than fragmentary. For Schillebeeckx, humanity is in search of ways to overcome suffering, even if all have not equally found such ways. Thus, for Schillebeeckx, general soterialisms are resources and anti-soterialisms are rivals. Yet (the counter-argument goes) once we can make the case that a question has been raised and a search begun, the inquiry is half way home. Given various nihilistic and relativistic soteriologies, how can we sustain the claim that all human beings seek salvation? Why presume all humanity seeks salvation when the concrete particulars of how they do it are so diverse and opposed?

Such problems with the method of correlation yield another option which challenges all the soteriologies seen thus far. We might choose to make a virtue of soterial relativism (to redeem it) not by holding a relativistic version of Christian soterialism but by drawing the truth out of all relativisms by showing how they are reconciled by Christ. Christian soterialism reconciles soterial relativism (and only secondarily general soterialisms). Take, for example, one reading of Karl Barth. At first Barth seems to be merely a particularly powerful version of orthodox soterialism. He rejects any theological strategy which either makes or threatens to make Christian soteriology a version of a more general soterialism. Jesus Christ is not a particular instance of a general process of salvation (or, for that matter, of a general salvation history). We have, Barth insists, "no analogy on the basis of which the nature and being of God as Reconciler can be accessible to us" (*CD* 2/1:77). Thus, Jesus Christ is reconciler—for example, the judge judged for us on the cross and acquitted in the resurrection. Some other descriptions— for example, justification, sanctification, vocation—are subthematic descriptions of this reconciliation. There are other metaphors for salvation—financial (Jesus Christ redeemer), military (Jesus Christ victor), and cultic (Jesus Christ priest and victim). But, says Barth, these are not as frequent in the Bible, ought to be used only in a subsidiary way, are "now rather remote from us," or are otherwise not "advisable." (CD 4/1:274–75). Nonetheless, one thing is clear. All these descriptions and images are primarily about Jesus Christ, the One crucified and risen in a unity which has a definite sequence (CD 4/1:297–98).[29]

However, one difference between Barth and orthodox soterialism is that Barth explicitly affirms that there are witnesses to Christ's reconciliation in Bible, Church, and "secular parables of the kingdom" in our world at large (CD 4/3,1:123).[30] "We are those for whom Jesus Christ is" (that is, we are justified) because Jesus Christ is "in transition" from "the One who has come and is present" to "the One who is present and has still to come" (CD 4/1:133). We are, then, Christ's hope—where the "we" is the Christian community ruled by the Scriptures in a world this Christian community provisionally represents. There are witnesses, analogies, parables of this reconciliation in our Scriptures, our Church, and our world. Barth then rejects any general process or history of salvation in favor of the salvation who is Jesus Christ—and the Bible, Church, and secular witnesses to this Christ's self-attestation.

In this view, soterial relativisms are rivals to salvation in Christ (just as they are for orthodox soterialisms). Unlike orthodox soterialisms, salvation in Christ means that *rivals become resources* for soteriology. They become such as we (by grace) make critical yet also positive, positive yet also critical use of them (CD 4/3,1:153). Like theologians in dialogue with general soterialisms, Barth seeks patterns of relationships between Christian and other soteriologies; unlike such theologians, Barth admits no single pattern (for example, correlation). Every such pattern is subordinated to (not correlated with) the claim that Jesus Christ is reconciliation, and all such patterns are "usually extraordinary" or ad hoc. Like Schillebeeckx, Barth holds together Catholic transformationist and Lutheran simultaneity models—although, as in the case of Schillebeeckx, it is very difficult to tell when Barth is making claims he regards as essential to Christian communal identity and when he is making claims he would regard as important but non-essential. But for Barth, unlike Schillebeeckx, the only clear transformation is Jesus Christ and (by grace) Christian community and individuals. There are other transformations, but these are occasion-specific (ad hoc) events.

The anthropological novelty of this position is that even if soterial relativists are correct, Barth's position is unaffected: Christ reconciles our worlds, whether they have any capacity for it or not. In other words, where for correlationalists general soterialisms are resources and relativist soterialisms are rivals, for people like Barth general soterialisms are (primarily if not secondarily) rivals and relativist soterialisms are (primarily if not secondarily) resources. Relativist solerialisms may be resources because *they make no universal claim to reconcile all things in the resurrection of the dead and eternal life.* The reconciliations in our personal and interpersonal lives, in our professional lives as health care workers and politicians, as lawyers and soldiers are genuine but partial reconciliations.[31] The soterial relativist says they may or may not be part of a larger whole. Christians can then learn from these partial reconciliations, mapping patterns of relationships with surgical precision rather than generalizing. Indeed, one might make a case that this has been the traditional practice (if not theology) of classic Christianity: Christians have experimented with the ideologies and institutions of our world; they have often been mistaken in the patterns of relationships they mapped with various philosophies and nation-states, and (at their best) have repented of such sins, even if centuries after the fact. But they have still sought and found such patterns in more than extraordinary ways.

But as we have Barth query Schillebeeckx's presumption that humankind is "in search of salvation," so Schillebeeckx might query the implicit anthropological relativism of Barth.[32] For Barth, secular parables are those lights of creation of which God makes critical yet also positive and positive yet also critical use and which theology uses as extraordinary witnesses to Jesus Christ's self-attestation (CD 4/3,1:115, 118, 153). Indeed, so extraordinary are these secular parables that the theologian can only give particular examples—"this or that person or event or enterprise or book"—"in a particular context" (CD 4/3,1:135). But, Schillebeeckx implies, there are some reconciliations going on in our world of which we can make positive use without making critical use—and these parables of the kingdom, far from being extraordinary, fall into a pattern which we can confess is the doing of the Spirit. The examples we give will always be bound to particular contexts, but those contexts are many. Take the example of the monastic and religious life. Although Barth says that the monastery "was never the den of arrogance and tyranny that the majority of average Protestants imagine," its endeavor to institutionalize an

imitatio of the relationship between God and humanity is
"very dubious and very dangerous," granting that a genuine
fellowship of saints can "take place . . . even in the sphere of
this kind of institution" (CD 4/2:11–19). It is important that
Barth's objection is not doctrinal (that is, he does not rule out
monasteries from the Christian Church). Nonetheless, we find
here excessive caution in the face of a Church and world which
needs the testimony (Lossky and Schillebeeckx have argued) of
something like religious orders as well as other forms of
ministry.

4. *Theological Pluralism within the Ecumenical Church*

The argument between theologians like Lossky and Schillebeeckx and Barth is complex. It involves their overlapping and
opposed teachings on creation and evil and salvation, set
against the background of once-opposed traditions and even
different cultures. There can be no sheer election or rejection
of one of these options. Every election (Barth might say) has a
rejecting shadow side—and every rejection is in an elective
light. (How) can we tilt in the direction of Barth or Schillebeeckx or Lossky without ruling the other positions out on
doctrinal grounds? In other words, (how) can all three be participants in the same Christian community without denying
their theological differences?

Recall their common ground. Lossky and Schillebeeckx and
Barth agree that Jesus Christ saves. All agree that this transforms our world in a specific teleology from a good creation
through an absurd sin to a promised salvation. All agree that
seeking salvation requires theology to deal with soteriologies
which are both rivals and resources. All three agree that Jesus
Christ is our hope insofar as we are Christ's hope. In still other
words, all three agree that we are in our way the humanity of
God insofar as Jesus Christ is in his way the humanity of God,
even unto death.

But in between and beyond the sinful Church and the
Church of sinners, simultaneity and transformation, between
monks and laity, between correlation and ad hoc events, there

is another alternative. The life we know and live is pervaded by good and evil, sense and nonsense, joys and griefs bound inextricably together and redeemed in Jesus Christ. Yet transformations (of sinners into saints) do break through the simultaneity (of sinners and saints) in enough of a pattern to say God is working true justice, sanctifying, creating anew, redeeming, accepting our sacrifices, conquering despite our wars and violence. These images are made good as they condense what is going on in our churches and hospitals and courts of law, our military battles and economic exchanges, our schools and liturgies. We find such transformations in the Scriptures, sacraments like baptism and the Lord's Supper, those Christians who are genuine disciples of Christ in their private and public lives, and also wherever we find righteousness is wrought. When we move to engage and otherwise discern the reconciling work of Christ in our world, our basic strategy does not shift to the occasion-specific or ad hoc (2.C). Here is the strength of Schillebeeckx's position and the weakness of Barth's.

But we do not need to spy this justification in the whole of history or history as a whole, in the whole of our lives or our lives as a whole in order to engage particular evils. In fact, such claims are to be treated with suspicion in view of the mass murders and pathologies of our everyday lives. What we have in particular instances of word and sacrament, Church and world are concrete instances of God's saving action. Our time is better spent not seeking a single way to map patterns of relationships but sorting out the soteriological spheres one by one, attending to the broader context Christian reconciliation provides for our endeavors to heal the sick, defend the poor, teach the ignorant, and otherwise bear each others' burdens (Gal 6:2). Here is the strength of Barth's position and the weakness of Schillebeeckx's.

In still other words, it is not as if we are left with simultaneity without transformation (Luther). It is not as if we have transformation without simultaneity (Lossky). It is not as if we have simultaneity against the background of transformation (Schillebeeckx)—or occasional transformations against the background of simultaneity (Barth). None of these large scale claims alone or all of them together capture the key point:

"Jesus reconciles" implies that God opposes and suffers and so overcomes evil in a way that calls us to oppose and suffer and overcome evil in each and every one of our relations—with our God, our friends and enemies and selves, as well as our cosmos.

The point is similar to one Karl Rahner makes about thinking of Mary as Virgin and Mother. "One finds oneself forced to maintain dialectically opposed positions at one and the same time: a really new beginning, in the midst of the old, which is being truly and patiently taken over in the flesh and the spirit—this is the criterion of the salvific economy of Christ in general. It is difficult, if not impossible, to balance out both sides correctly." It is "difficult" to find a balance or equilibrium because sin and suffering and evil permit no such relaxation; our efforts to fill the silence between Good Friday and Easter, to say when we ought to die that others might live, to bear each others' burdens without counting the cost are indeed limited. Indeed, they are so limited that we must resist any single way of characterizing the solution (including and perhaps particularly the notion that the chore is one of maintaining "dialectically opposed positions").[33] However, it is "not impossible" because we live under the promise of the Spirit. Soteriological inquiry is not only limited but also and primarily open—open for seeking and finding cases of the Spirit at work bringing good out of evil in our lives. But its openness is an openness to highly relative reconciliations—the fragile joys of a pilgrim community.

Thus, if this multilateral conversation over competing ways to map patterns of relationships between soteriologies is correct, we can truthfully say that on this issue Lossky and Schillebeeckx and Barth are participants in the same Christian community without denying their clear differences. Christians need to take into account orthodox, general, and relativist soterialisms. We need to refuse to identify Christian soteriology with any of these, while also refusing to isolate Christian soteriology from any of these. In this view, the issue is not *whether* we ought to map diverse patterns of relationships between diverse soteriologies but *how far* these patterns of relationships can extend into the world. That, we shall see, is the topic of the final two chapters.

Conclusion

We seek salvation in the context of a community of saints and sinners whose hope is Jesus Christ because we are the hope of Jesus Christ. Note that this claim does not resolve complex issues of the relationship between what theologians sometimes call Christology and anthropology, ecclesiology and eschatology. All such "-logies" are complex sets of narratives and symbols and truth-claims variously defined. If pressed to put the issues in terms of the lexicon of such abstractions, we might say that soteriology requires an anthropology and cosmology (or doctrine of creation) to describe what makes salvation possible; a hamartialogy (or doctrine of sin) to unpack the absurdity of sin, suffering, and other evils which make salvation necessary; an ecclesiology (or doctrine of the Church) to rule the multi-layered common goods of the common life; and an eschatology (or doctrine of last things) to guide our unfinished movement from nature through grace to glory; a spirituality to train each of us in our unique contributions to Christian living; a theo-logy to describe the God who saves. Each of these *loci*, in other words, are a phase of unpacking soterial action. My focus on soterial action implies that soteriology is the clue to these *loci* rather than the reverse, but we still have to face these other issues.

Similarly, although I mentioned the diverse patterns of relationships lived and thought by what Roman Catholics awkwardly call religious and lay forms of the Christian life, I make no pretensions to having resolved the issue of institutionalizing these and other forms of Christian life.[34] I have been primarily interested in such religious and lay activity as components of each and every Christian life. Religious imitation and lay discipleship are (among other things) features of every soterial activity. And both are conceptually and institutionally coherent only in the context of a community of saints and sinners sent on a mission, a community of people whose hope is Christ because they are Christ's hope. Thus, the crucial issue is not sinful and holy practices or teachings or patterns of relationships between rivals and resources. The crucial issue is living and thinking about patterns of relationships which overcome rivalries against the background of resources by witnessing, in every one of our own actions, to Jesus Christ's soterial action. Thus, soteriology remains central, all the while claiming that the unresolved problems are what constitute it as an inquiry (in contrast, say, to a set of settled questions).

There are, in particular, two unresolved problems that arise out of this network of soterial practices and teachings. First, the God who is "the mystery of the Church" is the single common good who holds together our other common goods in the Word bearing the sins of the world and so is our "ultimate trust" whose Spirit is transforming our world into God's new heaven and earth. But what is it to seek this God? How can we do so in a world of competing ultimate trusts? This is the subject of the next chapter. Second, the Christian community has no identity outside its missions to *the world*. But how do we seek and find in such a world patterns of relationships that do justice to the comprehensive promise of Jesus Christ while dealing with the relativities of this world? This will be the subject of the final chapter.

5

Seeking the Face of God

Theology, it is sometimes said, is "the study of God." This definition is doubly dangerous, for it can leave both God and us "faceless." That is, calling theology the study of God is dangerous if it suggests that we can engage in theology without having anything else to do with God. But study of (or inquiry into) God, I have been proposing, involves describing particular practices, like hearing and reading biblical texts or celebrating liturgies or reforming a holy but sinful community, articulating the doctrines or teachings that govern such practices, and relating those practices and teachings to other practices and teachings—relating texts and subject matters and contexts, truth-claims of different sorts, soteriologies of different kinds. We inquire into God within these (and, we shall soon see, other) contexts. We inquire into God as individuals within such particular physical, social, and historical contexts. Theology is not simply the study of God but people with faces zealously seeking the face of God.

More to the point of this chapter, calling theology the study of God can also leave God faceless—in two different ways. First, "the face of God" is an analogy suggesting both God's otherness to us (for example, God's face is God's, not ours) and God's relationship to us (for example, we shall one day see God "face to face" [1 Cor 13:12]).[1] Second, calling theology the study of God can jeopardize both features of God's face. For example, we may presume that we already know the face of

God. If we are already on such intimate terms with God, we may then be tempted to think that we do not need to waste time asking, "Who is God?" It would be better (this argument might go) to move on to more practical questions like, "How shall we meet and know, seek and find God?" Here we have a subtle transition from seeking the face of God (for example, asking, "Who is God?") to seeking something about our own faces (for example, asking, "How shall *we* or *I* seek and find God?"). In other words, a claim to be intimate with God can be a denial of the God whose face is *other than* our own.

On the other hand, if we are familiar with the many forms of religion and unbelief that constitute our world, we may not find the face of God at all. Here we are tempted to substitute the question, "How can we seek the face of God in a world which disagrees over the intelligibility or practicality of such a quest?" for questions about God. In this case we miss not the otherness of the face of God but the *openness to* others that marks God's face. In sum, calling theology the study of God can neglect the particularities of the face of a God who is both other to and engaged with our world.

The aim of this chapter is to probe what it might mean to seek the face of God in our world, while avoiding the mutually reinforcing temptations of those who know too much or too little about this face. Those who know too much will dismiss the question, "Who is God?" in favor of questions like, "How can we seek the face of God?"; those who know too little will dismiss these questions in favor of questions like, "How can we seek the face of God in a world which disagrees over the intelligibility or practicality of such a quest?" I will suggest a way we can order and relate (rather than dismiss) such questions.

The central thesis of this chapter (and the fourth sub-thesis of the book) is that *seeking the face of God is a project we undertake in contexts domestic and foreign, governed by the rule that the God of unrestricted importance is with us for each and every occasion of our lives.* But it will take three (now familiar) steps to explicate this thesis. First, the diverse ordinary, common sensical, and idiomatic contexts in which we call upon, name, and describe God display what I shall call the "cosmological" context of seeking the face of God. Describing this context will consolidate the particular appeals to God from previous chapters; it will also suggest why seeking the face of God requires a more catholic context than we have seen thus far. Second, seeking the face of God includes teaching that God is with us: "The Lord is with us" (*Dominus nobiscum*) guides cosmological argumentation. Third, seeking the face of God for each and every occasion of our lives requires making the case that God is of unrestricted importance for our lives before diverse gods, diverse religions, diverse forms of godlessness.

A. *Cosmological Contexts for Seeking God*

1. *Domestic Contexts*

Although previous chapters were not centrally about God, they did suggest how we—or some of us—seek the face of God in a variety of contexts. For example, we seek *God* as we seek to follow, listen to, and read the Scriptures. In fact, the main force of calling these texts our "Scriptures" is that here God is sought and found. For example, God is the central character in many of the biblical narratives. We find out who this character is by seeking what God does over the course of time in relation to Israel and the nations, Jesus and the disciples and the crowds. This quest is not a simple one. It requires tracking the ways God is characterized in narrative and other genres, including the ways God is rendered as the God of our lives. But if the case can be made, we can begin to understand why Christians have claimed that these texts are the Word of God: if what we find going on in these words is centrally the portrayal—perhaps not a complete portrayal but the necessary outline of any such complete portrayal—of who God is in relation to our world, then here we find the Spirit at work.[2]

Thus, we seek God in what this God and others are doing in these texts and in our world. "In our world" binds our quest for what is going on in Scripture to our quest for God in other contexts. Normal circumstances do not require us to choose between scriptural and other contexts for calling upon and describing God, between these texts and the texts we are called to be (2 Cor 3:2). In fact, those of us in communities which use the Scriptures in worship throughout the year are given a further context for seeking the face of *God* in our worship. Such liturgies are recurring patterns of prayerful interaction at particular times and places. What is crucial for this chapter is that these are contexts for praising and beseeching, engaging and thinking *God*. We baptize and confirm, eat and drink, enact marriage covenants and priestly orders, confess our sins and console our sufferers. In so doing, we respond to and mutually engage a God who initiates us into community and feeds us along the way, covenants with us so we can live with each other interpersonally and socially, reconciles us so we can forgive each other evils, and promises healing of sickness and death. Persistently to celebrate such sacraments is to proclaim a God who does these things in these ways.

Such Biblical and liturgical contexts for God are parts of a still broader set of activities which constitute our Church. These are activities focused on the common goods of all humanity (particularly the poor or those in any way afflicted), of many of us (now and over the course of time), and of only some of us (in our various local, national, and international roles). All of these common goods are focused on the *God* who (we confess) is our one common good and purpose. We seek God as we help others seek their vocations and seek our own; as we confess our own failures and suffer those of others; as we struggle with the hopes and doubts of our children, our fellow parishioners, our neighbors, and ourselves. Once again, what is crucial here is that these are contexts for engaging and thinking a particular God, that is, a God who holds and moves us—individually and together, past and present and future, in sickness and health—as God's common good and purpose in Word and Spirit (for example, 5.A.1).

2. *Foreign Contexts*

We have seen these sets of activities in previous chapters. But Christians are encouraged to seek the face of God not only in their Scriptures and rituals and churches. As Israel created its Scriptures and liturgies and nation, it also struggled with (what we call) the various religions of Canaan, Egypt, Assyria,

Persia, and Rome. Early Christian practices and teachings took shape in interaction with Judaism as well as various Greek and Roman religions. Medieval theology dealt with the rise of Islam and more esoteric religions. And modern theologies deal not only with these disputes but also with Buddhism, Hinduism, and other religions discovered or created over the last couple of centuries. More to the point in Western cultures, we ought to think of the way individuals and groups of varying degrees of religiosity integrate themselves with and segregate themselves from each other by the ways they do and do not read the Bible, pray alone and together, attend church and synagogue, believe in a god more or less "personal."[3]

Much of the interaction has not been a pretty story. In the name of Yahweh's incomparability, Israel sometimes covenanted to slay "anyone who would not seek Yahweh" (2 Chr 15:13).[4] Tales of Christian anti-Semitism play a shameful role in Christian history; we might also think of how stories of the Crusades, Christian supported colonialism and racism, tyranny and torture can scarcely be told enough. Here God seems to become (or becomes) problematic. Why the God of *these* Scriptures rather than the Tanak or Qur'an or the Upanishads? Why not the Tripitaka? Why the God of *these* rituals rather than Judaism's Passover, Islam's Ramadan? Why the God of the Church rather than the Synagogue or Ummah? Why not the Sangha? Why, in sum, the God of *this* religion rather than some other theistic or non-theistic religion?

But we ought also to recall that much of the interaction between such religions has brought out some of the best of the human spirit. Israel is called to be a light to the nations. Cyrus rescues Israel. A Roman soldier recognizes Christ. A person wonders if he or she ought to become Christian or Jew, Buddhist or Hindu. A community ponders developing a missionary strategy which aims to deal fairly and lovingly with others. Others might simply wonder what the similarities and differences are between Christianity and other religions. The tales of the positive ways religions have treated each other and others in history is often lost. In any case, how can we seek God in a world of many religions?

This question will be answered differently depending on whether we use the word religion to circumscribe the best or the worst, the most natural or supernatural, the most important or trivial of human concerns. We ought not to be excessively preoccupied with such debates, not least because the contexts for seeking God are broader than any religious contexts. That is, we also engage God not only in the contexts of Scripture and worship, our churches and religions but also in a broader context yet: the world. The physical world attests the glory of God—so says not only that world but also our Bible and liturgy. And so does our human world, its inner and outer space. I earlier suggested that as particular people in particular physical and social relations, we often find ourselves moving from one geographical setting to another, from one role to another, from one interpersonal relation to another, from one community to another, from past to present to future in our actions and affections (1.A.1). The God we find at work in these settings is the God of the Scriptures and liturgies, of church and religions—but now given full cosmic scope. Seeking the face of God in this movement will be no less difficult than seeking a quark, a community, a friendship, broader or deeper joys. But that God is at work in what is going on in the world is the claim of Bible and ritual, the Church and its missionary policy. We are not in a world different from the one we have been in at the Lord's Supper and elsewhere. We do not need *separate* resources—thoughts or affections or actions—to move in this world.

But here, by reputation, the problem is most severe. There are friends and strangers and enemies who stand and move in comparable ways but who find the spheres of Bible and worship, church and religions, some part of the world or the world itself alien, foolish, even perverse and absurd. This is the world of what we might call "godlessness."[5] The issue is not just, "Why *these* Scriptures, *these* rituals, *this* community, or *this* God?" but, "Why *any* Scriptures, *any* rituals, *any* religion, *any* God?" Here, indeed, it is not only God but also we (and even I) who become problematic. Some—particularly those in Judeo-Christian or at least theistic cultures where a vast majority loosely relates belief in God, use of the Bible, and church attendance with upward mobility—will surely regard questions raised by godlessness as impractical, for challenges to religiosity are not their questions. But even if we cannot raise such questions for ourselves, they are raised for us by the world in which we live.

3. *The Identity of the Cosmos*

The first part of this chapter briefly describes some sample contexts—quite ordinary contexts—in which people do and do not seek and find God. God is the God of this world (this cosmos); therefore, we seek the face of God in each and all of these contexts. These contexts remind us that on the one hand, we need to avoid thinking that the move into religious and secular contexts is inherently dangerous, as if here we move into lands which are intrinsically alien to God—lands in which God's face turns away from us. On the other hand, we need to avoid thinking that only when we move into religious and secular contexts, does genuine theological inquiry begin, as if here we move into lands where God finally goes public. In other words, our quest for the face of God must be cosmological, where our world (cosmos) is Jesus Christ glorified and followed and thought about, Scriptures studied and contemplated, liturgies celebrated and reformed, churches engaged in missions of saving love, the existence of Judaism and less comparable religions, sundry individual and communal and physical energies—frequently fragmented and spoiled and sinful. Our quest for the face of God must be a quest that holds together the God of this world. Seeking the face of God in a different world may (or may not) overlap with this world, but it will not have the particular features of the face of the God of *this* world.

And yet this cosmological context also suggests a problem. When we are at home in various domestic contexts, it might *seem* relatively easy to seek the face of God: God is the God of these narratives and prayers, the common good who holds together our diverse communal goods. At the same time, it might *seem* difficult if not impossible to seek the face of God when we move into various foreign contexts. How can we identify God before strangers and friends and enemies in the worlds of diverse religions and unbeliefs? How, given the diverse and conflicting energies of *this* world, can it possibly yield a quest for *this* God? It is no accident that problems seeking the face of God emerge most clearly as we move from the domestic policies (chapters 2–4) to the foreign policies (chapters 5 and 6) of this community. The cosmological context for God-issues is parabolic of a God who is *other than* (foreign to) us. And yet God is a God of *our* world (the domestic world in which we are at home). How so? In sum, who is this God of our domestic and foreign contexts, of our lives as Christians in a world of many religions and many forms of godlessness?

B. *God Is with Us*

1. *The Implicitness of the Doctrine of God*

One purpose of a doctrine of God is to answer this question. That is, the point of a doctrine of God is, for the Christian community, to articulate a set of teachings that identify God. But we need to be even more careful when we make the transition from practices to teaching in the case of the doctrine of God than we were when we made the same transition in previous chapters. Most of our discourse about God does not aim to teach about (or identify or refer to) God, and identifications of (or teachings about) God do not supply the cornerstone of our dealings with God. More often we aim to call upon and pray to God, re-tell stories about God's dealings with Israel and the Church, enjoy the consolations of God's presence, or suffer dark nights of God's hiddenness. A God whom we could only identify, refer to, or teach about would not be a God of all our lives. The problem of identifying God, far from taking the place of (or providing the take-off place for) our dealings with God, arises because of problems that arise within other discourses about God (for example, the problem of identifying God in a world of many religions and forms of godlessness).

The relative infrequency with which we need to identify God is surely part of the explanation for the remarkable fact that the doctrine of God has played a "largely implicit role . . . in much of the history of Christian dogma."[6] Certainly the Council of Nicaea (on God as Father, Son, and Spirit) and Vatican I (on natural theology) propose such teachings. But usually communal teachings on God must be read within teachings about other matters: Christ and icons, Bible and sacraments, creation and sin and salvation, faith and reason.

For example, Vatican II has documents on the modern world and atheism and religions, the Church and the churches, Scripture and tradition and revelation—but no single document on God. At least, if we attend only to the surface of these texts, God does not seem to be a major topic. And yet if we attend to the role that Vatican II's teachings about God play in relation to Vatican II's other teachings, we find a common pattern that is focused on God: the God we seek is God with us (*Dominus nobiscum*). To make this implicit doctrine of God explicit, we need some evidence of the pattern.

2. *Vatican II on God*[7]

For example, in various documents, Vatican II teaches that God is active, doing something or other—filling the physical, social, historical, and personal world with signs of God's presence and purpose (CMW no. 11); enlightening all religions with "Truth" (NCR no. 2); fostering the ecumenical movement (DOE no. 1); moving and ordering the varied gifts of the Christian community (DCC nos. 1–4, 9, 18, 40); giving special gifts to religious sub-groups, bishops, and laity (DCC nos. 43, 22, 33); enacting the sacred action of the liturgy (CSL nos. 7, 9) and the whole liturgical movement (CSL no. 43); inspiring the Scriptures which tell the history of salvation from Genesis through the Exile (DCR no. 11); and perfecting humanity in the particular figure Jesus Christ (CMW no. 45).

Who is God? The God of Genesis and Exodus, of the Kingdom and Exile, of Christ and the Spirit is the God active in word and deed in each and all of these times and places: such is the teaching of Vatican II. Clearly these documents make claims not only about us and our world but also and primarily about God: *Dominus* nobiscum. God is with us, not behind or beyond these activities but as agent of these acts. The documents presume the prior actuality of God in each of these occasions of human activity. The question, "Who is God in relation to our world?" has a priority over the questions, "Who are we in relation to God?" and, "How do we deal with conflicting quests for God?" It is this God who is Lord of our domestic and foreign contexts.

Further, in each case it is claimed that the human activity described is constituted by humans' responding to this God's activity—by cultivating the earth (CMW no. 39); talking and otherwise working with members of other religions (NCR no. 2); taking an active part in common projects and prayers and reforms of the ecumenical movement (DOE nos. 1, 4); directing the Church's pilgrimage toward "the time of the restoration of all things" (DCC no. 48); seeking out and supporting those called to poverty and chastity and obedience, to pastoral offices, to building up this world toward the kingdom (DCC nos. 43, 34–36, 31; ALP nos. 1, 9); actively participating in the Church's worship (CSL nos. 9, 14); seeking out what God is doing with the Scriptures (DCR no. 12); and, in all this, finding their own activity "perfected" in Jesus Christ (CMW no. 45). Clearly, as these documents articulate teachings about God, they also articulate teachings about us—our world, our church, our liturgy. Who are we? We are those with whom God is. Dominus *nobis*cum. The God confessed is a God with us. This "with *us*" means that we are those with whom God is. The question, "Who are we in relation to God?" is subordinate but essential to answering the question, "Who is God?"

Finally, in each of these cases, the authoring community sketches its own courses of action *as* it sketches God's courses of action. Here there is no competition between divine and human agency; instead, divine and human freedom increase in direct and not inverse proportion.[8] Vatican II is thus a communal policy centered on the conviction that God and people are active at each and every time and place—in all the modern world (intellectually, politically, culturally); in non-Christian religions, the ecumenical movement, all segments of the Catholic Church, the liturgy, the Bible; and most particularly in Jesus Christ who is the light of all the nations. The key question to ask of every document of Vatican II is, "When and where does this document envision God's active calling of individuals and groups to refashion God's creation as well as to oppose and suffer evil as imitators and disciples? To understand and apply these documents is to understand and apply this pattern of divine and human (and therefore double) agency at work throughout the documents—and to understand and apply all other passages in the light of this pattern.[9] Dominus nobis*cum*. If *God* is always with us and God is always with *us*, God is always *with* us in the sense that we can find no point in our lives when we do not find God first.

A detailed analysis of individual documents would, I believe, make the same point.[10] But what is striking throughout the documents is Vatican II's affirmation of the eternal richness of God's activity in both our domestic and foreign contexts, in both our more particular and more universal contexts. Vatican II's claim is that the God of creation and Israel, Christ and the Spirit, Church and churches, religions and world is the same God. Thus, one reading of the documents of Vatican II (taken "as a whole") implies a set of teachings about God, each of which is both context and application of the rule: Dominus nobiscum.

3. *Patterns in the Face of God*

So far, so good. Vatican II teaches that God is with us in comprehensively particular ways. But there are also problems with how Vatican II teaches about God. Each example of divine and human activity above—from the Scriptures through the modern world—is a context of divine and human activity, a context for seeking the face of God. That is, the Scriptures, worship, the Church, other Christian communities, Judaism, non-Christian religions, and the joys and griefs of the modern world each count as a context, a sphere, or *locus* (place) of divine and human activity. These contexts are irreducible to each other. For example, seeking the face of the God who is with us in the Church cannot be reduced to seeking the face of God in our worship. Again, seeking the face of the God who is with us in the joys and griefs of modernity cannot be elucidated in terms more basic than itself (for example, it cannot be elucidated in terms of the elucidation of seeking the face of God in the truths of various religions).[11] The contexts of divine and human activity are irreducible to each other. But we need to ask, "What are *the relationships between* these contexts of divine and human activity? How do all these spheres amount to a God who (we pray) will bless us and keep us, a God whose face will shine upon us and be gracious to us (Num 6:24-26)?" This is the question about which Vatican II is not clear.

We need to be careful not to make this criticism too simplistic. Vatican II clearly does not permit us to say that any of these contexts are the *exclusive* theater of divine and human activity; there are *many* such contexts and therefore many spheres of divine and human activity. Further, Vatican II does not permit us to isolate these *loci* from each other. That is, Vatican II does not permit us to live as if God only periodically intervenes and we ought occasionally to respond in our Scriptures, our worship, our common life as a Church, the non-Christian religions, the joys and griefs of our personal and social lives. Vatican II's "God with us" is comprehensive and therefore requires patterns of relationships between these contexts of divine and human activity. But what are the patterns of relationships between these contexts?

Consider the problem another way. It may be true that "in the major questions of the knowability of divine saving action and its realization. . . . the Council has remained outside all technical theological positions"—whether the theologies of Cullmann or Bultmann, Ebeling or Barth, or even the classical "schools" of Catholic theology like "'Thomism,' 'Scotism,' 'Molinism,' etc."[12] Certainly part of what would be involved in remaining "outside all technical theological positions" would be avoiding the claim that God shows his face *only* in events of saving history; existential self-understanding; word-events; Jesus Christ; acts of existing, revolutionary *praxis*; or more ordinary politics. But if Vatican II avoids such claims, this has not always been to Vatican II's advantage. That is, many things can be said about the collapse of biblical theology during and after Vatican II, the rise of charismatic appeals to the activity of the Spirit and liberationist appeals to God's revolutionary praxis on behalf of the oppressed, the ecumenical consensus developing on a range of issues, the proliferation (as well as deconstruction) of metaphysical schemes for handling divine and human activity. But the conflicts involved in these popular and academic movements are primarily (if not solely) conflicts over the God whom we call upon by name. In these cases, to disagree on when and where God is *active* can lead to disagreements over who God *is*—or, better, because we disagree on who God is, we disagree over whether and when and where God acts. Post-Vatican II conflicts have not been solely or even primarily over world or Church or the relationship between the two but over God. They have been conflicts over the face of God. Little wonder the decade of Vatican II ended just as the culture and other Christians cried ambiguously (once again) that God was dead, faceless. Like Dorothy and her friends in *The Wizard of Oz*, we found ourselves praising God "because of the wonderful things he does," only to find that the fearsome or kind wizard could help but not deliver us home.

In sum, the diversity and conflict of our cosmological contexts for seeking the face of God are governed by the rule that God is with us as we (you and I and others) engage in human activity throughout the cosmos, dialogue and work with members of other religions, pray with other Christians, make the Catholic Church into a communion of saints, celebrate the liturgy, and find ourselves in the mirror of the Bible (DCR no. 7). Seeking the face of God must be cosmological. But it must also seek the face *of God*. Yet the documents provide no way systematically to relate divine and human activity in Christ and the Spirit, Scripture and liturgy, Church and religions and world. Vatican II provides several contexts of divine and human activity, but no one of these is clearly the one by which to order their practices and settle conflicts. The documents call for "God is with us" to be their central teaching, ruling all other teachings; but they do not tell us which of the myriad examples of how God is with us ought to guide the others.

This, of course, should not be surprising. The beauty and dullness, usefulness and irrelevance, truth and mistakes of different sections of the documents of Vatican II are a reflection of the pilgrim community who wrote and received them. But the key task of the theological quest for the face of God is to solve this problem.

C. *Arguments Before the Gods, Religions, and Unbeliefs*

1. *Four Options*

To seek the face of God is a cosmological quest in the sense that we engage in such a quest from within a set of practices ranging from Scripture and liturgy through the common goods of the Church to our mission in the religious and non-religious world (5.A). Furthermore, the subject matter of our quest is the God who is with us (5.B). But given the difficulties in relating the many ways God is with us, how can we seek the face of God in a world of many gods, religions, and unbeliefs? This question is related to a number of other difficult questions. Why do some seek and not find, while others find without seeking? Why does God sometimes hide when sought—as well as stand ready to be found when not sought? (Here I am thinking of the paradoxical ways Scripture depicts our quest for God, exemplified in such passages as Cant 3:1; 5:6; Hos 5:15; Isa 65:1; Rom 10:20.) How is a God who relates to us in such inscrutable patterns a fit subject and object of inquiry?

There is no consensus among Christians on the answer to such questions. Thousands of books have been written on the diverse problems raised by our life in a world of many gods, many religions, many forms of godlessness. It would be one of the heights of foolishness to claim to even address (much less resolve) the controversies involved. The justification for the following remarks is that my proposal is relatively modest: seeking the face of God has a different shape in relation to different audiences; many arguments among theologians result from taking one of these audiences as the only or the primary audience.

Let us begin by ruling out two ways of handling issues of audiences, that is, ways which restrict us to *either* domestic *or* foreign contexts for seeking the face of God. Restricting ourselves to domestic contexts is typical of particularists who are not catholic (or Catholics who are not catholic) (1.A). Let us call them "fideists." A fideist might argue that we seek the face of God only in the context of select faith-practices; seeking the face of God will be practical and intelligible only to those who heed a call to repent, join in these practices, and assent to these teachings.

The key benefit of this kind of fideism is its insistence that the theological rule (God is with us) is not a rule we need or can suspend. As we live and move in a religious and secular world, we abide in the same world as the God of Scripture and worship and Church; we do not move into a different world and God does not have a different face—and therefore we do not need radically different resources to seek the face of God in this world fairly and truthfully. The key problem with fideism is that it offers us no instruction on how we are to follow God's movement in this religious and secular world. We must simply call such worlds to repent. In effect, fideism restricts the quest for God to the scriptural, liturgical, and ecclesial; our domestic contexts provide our only resources and audience for seeking the face of God. But what about other contexts in which we live and move?

On the other hand, restricting ourselves to foreign contexts is typical of catholics who are not particular (catholics who are not Catholic) (1.A). Let us call them "modernists," for they sometimes suggest that seeking the face of God must be a quest intelligible to and applicable for any "modern" person. Such a modernist might argue not from specific faith-practices but from the setting of activities in which we all supposedly engage, arguing that these practices require God (or the symbol "God"). The key benefit of this position is its insistence that we always be willing to give a reason for the hope that is in us; mainstream Christian communities have by and large tried to train their members in articulating the intelligibility and applicability of their quests not only for each other but also for others. The key problem with this position is how contexts which are distinctive of (or internal to) no particular community can provide contexts for seeking the face of a God who is with particular peoples in particular ways. (Many modernists say that such a God must be replaced by another religious object [1.A.4]; they are part of the non-theological but religious audience discussed below.) In effect, this kind of catholicism restricts the quest for God to foreign contexts; the only important resources for identifying God are the resources provided by some universally religious, human, or cosmic activity.

I am not offering decisive arguments against fideism and modernism, pure Catholicism and pure catholicism. But if modernists are correct, the previous three chapters are wrong; and if fideists are correct, the final two chapters are wrong. It is not simply that their teachings are wrong but the practical contexts are somehow depraved. Christians who agree with Vatican II's "God is with us," even if they are occasionally tempted to fideism or modernism, will be satisfied with nothing less than a quest for God which embraces contexts both domestic and foreign.

But even if we agree on ruling out fideism and modernism, there remain two other major options for relating domestic and foreign contexts. We might permit ourselves to seek the face of God not *only* in contexts distinctive of the domestic life of the community but *also* in contexts foreign to ourselves and common to other communities. Or we might permit ourselves to seek the face of God not only in contexts distinctive of the domestic life of the community but *also* in contexts foreign to ourselves and common to other communities—as long as such foreign contexts are *also* of a piece with the domestic policies of our community.[13]

In what follows, I propose an experimental contest between these third and fourth options to see which one can best show us how to seek the face of God in contexts domestic and foreign. Which option can best guide Christians before audiences of theists, other religions, and various forms of godlessness? This emphasis on the relativity of our arguments on God to different audiences will eventually tilt the theological balance in the direction of the fourth option: we ought to permit ourselves to seek the face of God not only in contexts distinctive of the domestic life of the community but *also* in contexts foreign to ourselves and common to other communities—as long as such foreign contexts are of a piece with the domestic policies of our community. But recall that the aim is not to say everything that might be said to these audiences but enough to support the thesis of the chapter (that is, seeking the face of God is seeking the God of unrestricted importance for each and every occasion of our lives).

2. Three Audiences

a. THEISMS

Presume we are addressing an audience of theists, that is, people who believe in God. This audience would include our fellow Christians—as well as others who are theistic by their self-avowals enacted in lives of response to and mutual engagement with God's perfect agency. I do not wish to veto more functional construals of theism (for example, "Our god is whatever provides the central focus for our lives."); but the notion that God is an agent to whom we respond seems almost built into our ordinary uses of "God"; we do justice neither to non-theistic or theistic faiths by stretching the concept of God to embrace both. We do well to consider non-theistic religious audiences separately (as I shall do in the next section). In any case, the focus for an audience of theists is not on any *particular* context of divine and human agency; theists have different scriptures, different rituals, different communities. The focus is on one common ground among *all* the contexts: the engagement of our finite and God's infinite agency; the central problem is how such an engagement can be lived and thought

Take the example of Cardinal Newman's sermon on "The Infinitude of the Divine Attributes."[14]

> . . . [T]he attributes of God, though intelligible to us on their surface,—for from our own sense of mercy and holiness and patience and consistency, we have general notions of the All-Merciful and All-holy and All-patient, and of all that is proper to his Essence,—yet, for the very reason that they are infinite, transcend our comprehension, when they are dwelt upon, when they are followed out, and can only be received by faith. They are dimly shadowed out, in this very respect, by the great agents which He has created in the material world.

There are three main thoughts here: our own sense of mercy and holiness and patience and consistency in the agencies of our world, the infinitude of such perfections when attributed to God, and a relationship between the two on which we can dwell and which we can follow but which transcends our comprehension. This is "our own" sense of mercy and patience—as Newman puts it, "[T]he grace and loveliness which beam from the very face of the visible creation are cognisable by all, rich and poor, learned and ignorant."

This is a broad context for seeking the face of God. But seeking the face of God is not seeking this or any other context. Seeking the face of God includes seeking an infinitude of divine attributes. As we stand in and move through the spheres of divine and human activity, we seek a God of infinite perfection, engaging creatures grateful for God's mercies, humbled by God's holiness, consoled by God's patience, and in an infinitude of other ways sharing in the divine life bestowed on us.

It seems consistent with Newman's proposal to argue that "[t]he perfections we ascribe to God belong to a much wider class of predicates (I will call them 'character traits') which are used: a) to evaluate the *intentional actions* of agents, and b) to evaluate *agents* on the basis of their actions."[15] We call some of our friends, say, patient and merciful. We do this because they perform certain patient and merciful actions. But we do not merely value individual episodes of patience and mercy, for any such episode "must fit into a wider pattern of action which represents an ongoing continuity in the way the agent conducts his life." Such is how we render character traits not simply general but particular to this friend. We might say that, in this way, we give character traits a "face." For example, if we are to grasp the force of the predicate "patient" when attributed to a parent, a philosopher, or a military commander, "we must look at the way the *general* characteristics of patient action appear concretely in these *particular* undertakings" (that is, being a parent, a philosopher, a military commander). The movement between the general and the particular "constitutes an ongoing inquiry in which norms develop and are revised." Ultimately we are pressed to "tell an agent's story" in order to display the particular ways he or she holds together in multi-layered ways her or his character traits.[16]

Similarly, we think about God's acts as God acting wisely and patiently—not simply in individual episodes but continuously. The narratives of our Scriptures are complex renditions of this One's identity as the One we call upon by name in our worship, praising and thanking and beseeching God for the diverse goods bestowed on us in our individual and communal lives. Thus, we teach about God's character traits as we teach about our descriptions and assessments of each other.

It takes extraordinary skill to make the affirmations and negations involved in teaching the infinitude of this One's perfections. I will shortly return to a central problem in thus speaking analogously of God. But we must address the question, "What *sort* of way of seeking the face of God is this?" Begin with the third type of argument above (5.C.1). In teaching about God this way are we appealing to resources *external* to or foreign to our faith because they are common to other theistic faiths? Now surely Christian theism shares with other theisms the attribution to God of various perfections. In fact, the more *general* the attribute, the more our web of descriptions might overlap with the generalities of other theisms. These are what Newman calls "general notions" which "dimly shadow" God's perfections. But we have also seen that *general* character traits do not do justice to the *particular* ways they are enacted. Newman's sermon took the kenosis of Jesus Christ ("as if by a specimen") as the starting point for his reflections on the eternally rich being of God,[17] and he thought of this Jesus Christ in the context of ways Christians worship and imitate and follow Christ. A full identification of God would involve offering a narrative "that ties events"—particular and general—"together in a meaningful pattern and relates this pattern to the purposive activity of God."[18] The events that need to be tied together are biblical narratives and our life of worship, the common goods of church life as well as our experiences of mercy and patience and holiness. The fuller the description, the more particular—and the more particular the less generally theistic. The central aim of seeking the infinitude of God's perfections is to answer questions like, "Who is God?" and, "Who are we?" not, "What shall we do about those who think differently?" The central aim, in this view, is *internal* to particular ways of engaging God (who, we find, has always engaged us first). Newman's exercise is an instance of the fourth rather than the third option for seeking the face of God.

So particular are the perfections of this God that we may be tempted to confess that any overlap with other theisms is only apparent, overwhelmed by the particular ways the abstract label theism is displayed in the philosophies and scriptures and rituals of diverse ways of living. Calling Christianity a theism, this argument goes, distorts more than illuminates. However, the temptation to downplay theistic common ground is to be resisted, no matter whether or how we label it. This sort of knowledge of God would not have to be over valued: we could simply say that in this case what is proposed by theists also happens to be an authentic doctrine of the Christian community; a part of one "complex whole" can be a part of another "complex whole"—no matter how small a part.[19]

In short, seeking the face of God theistically is more like the fourth than the third option above: we can appeal directly to resources common to other communities—as long as such resources are *also* resources of our own community. Only in this way do we think of the God who is with *us* not simply in those attributes some others also ascribe to God but also and primarily in the particular form such attributes take in the particular ways God relates to us.

The main problem with teaching God theistically is not how we abide in and follow the perplexing ways the infinitude of divine perfections are showered on our meager theisms in the diverse ways we worship and build communities in our world. The main problem is that we "can 'conceive of divine perfection' *qua* applying predicates of perfection to God without disrupting their defining semantic relations. But we cannot 'conceive of the divine perfection' qua offering detailed description of how these perfections are exemplified by God."[20] God (as Newman puts it) transcends our comprehension. We dwell upon and follow out this infinitude, but it "can only be received by faith." In still other words, "God's love, though rooted in a mode and scope of agency which radically transcends us, becomes available to our understanding when it grasps us in an action which we recognize as God's own."[21] But what is it, then, we are doing when we "conceive of divine perfection" in this second sense? And what about non-theistic ascriptions of perfection? Here we must—as theologians concerned with theism only too rarely do—turn to another audience in relation to whom we seek the face of God.

b. RELIGIONS

One way to think through questions about perfection is by presuming to address a religious audience—in the following way. The God who is with us is, under one description, "the ultimate . . . mystery of our being" (NCR no. 1). In claiming that God is the ultimate mystery, Vatican II is interacting with a peculiarly modern use of the notion of religion. In this modern tradition, a religion is taken to be a set of practices (ritual and moral, individual and communal) and teachings (beliefs, action guides, and valuations) centered on something of ultimate importance.[22] To confess that God is the ultimate mystery is to claim that God is of unrestricted importance. To teach that God is of unrestricted importance is to identify God as the One of unrestricted primacy and uniqueness.

However, in the world in which we live, God is not the only candidate for such primacy and uniqueness. Vatican II goes on to discuss other candidates in Hinduism, Buddhism, Islam, and other religious "ways" of living (NCR no. 2). There are, we might say, many ways to be religious (for example, Christian and Jewish, Muslim and Hindu, Buddhist and Confucian, Humanist and Marxist, perhaps even Communist and Americanist). Many of these religions have analogous practices and teachings: myths or sacred narratives, symbols and rituals, ethical and other doctrines, social and institutional expressions, experiences and affections. But these patterns of activity have a different shape according to how they center on something or other (stars, gods, humanity, nature, various ideals, being, God) as of supreme importance, the object and subject of our ultimate concern and loyalty. This audience, in short, is not always theistic. They do not always think that they live and move in spheres where creaturely agency is engaged by divine agency. A religiously pluralistic world is constituted by different spheres—samples of human activity engaging that which diverse people take to be of ultimate importance through diverse myths and symbols, diverse ritual and moral actions, diverse religious communities and affections, diverse policies toward our world. A central chore of students of religions is to understand the identities and oppositions, the similarities and

differences, and other patterns of relationships between the
practices and teachings of these religions.

Part of seeking the face of God in this sphere is offering what
we might call a logically individuating description of something of unrestricted primacy.[23] Take, for example, Karl
Barth's interpretation of Anselm's one argument (*unum
argumentum*). God, the argument goes, is that than which a
greater cannot be conceived; but it is greater to exist than be
conceived; therefore, God exists. Anselm offers this proof,
Barth points out, in the context of prayer. He stands in "God's
presence, on which the whole grace of Christian knowledge
primarily depends, the encounter with him which can never be
brought about by all our searching for God however thorough
it may be, although it is only to the man who seeks God with a
pure heart that this encounter comes."[24] God cannot not be.
The actuality and the possibility of the knowledge of God as
well as the transition between the two are given by God and
God alone (*CD* 2/1, ch. 5). "The Reality of God," then, is that
of the One who loves in freedom in the Trinitarian richness of
the perfections of divine loving and of divine freedom (*CD*
2/1, ch. 6). This God is the One who is in what he does, who
lovingly seeks and creates fellowship with us with the freedom
to be both transcendent and immanent.[25] The theologian thus
shapes our language to attest God's self-attestation, never permitting any descriptions to dominate the One described, never
separating description and reality. All apologetics are "supplementary, incidental, and implicit" (*CD* 2/1:8).

Here is a model of seeking the face of God, at least in this
sense: God is of unrestricted primacy. No matter what category one chooses—abstractions like reality, images like light
and darkness, or more ordinary concepts like person—God is
of unrestricted importance in that category. Indeed, the whole
of the *Church Dogmatics* might be read as the ongoing selection of categories (given by revelation and Scripture, Church
and culture) within which the case can be made that the God
who is with us is of unrestricted primacy. The theologian thus
sets herself or himself the task of redescribing in myriad ways
this One than whom a greater cannot be conceived, using
Scripture and Church proclamation and "secular parables"

(that is, lights of creation which become "extraordinary witnesses" to Jesus Christ's self-attestation).

This is not a fideistic argument of the first type we saw above; reasons are offered and arguments are made—indeed, one argument (*unum argumentum*). Neither is it an argument of the third type, permitting us to appeal to reasons shared with other communities (for example, "something or other is of ultimate importance") no matter how that common ground relates to our own practices and teachings—although there certainly are such versions of this ontological argument. It is an argument of the fourth type, for the resources used are resources *internal to* the prayerful practices and creedal teachings of the Christian community. Barth, we have seen, permits resources to be used which partly overlap with those of other religious and secular communities, but only if such secular parables are *also* resources internal to the Christian community (4.C.3). The strategy is the fourth rather than the third type—a faith seeking faith (*CD* 1/1:14).

There are, of course, two objections to the Anselmian strategy for seeking the face of God. First, it is not necessarily better to exist than to be conceived; clearly there are a great many things we can conceive which do not exist. But, Barth (evasively) responds, that is precisely why this argument is so apt theologically. Reasons for God are reasons for a *particular* God—a God who reveals the name by which we call upon him, a God whom we hear in the Scriptures, find proclaimed in the Church and attested by Israel and the world. This is a God who is other than we are and who therefore calls for an other sort of reason-giving. "Totally other"? Obviously not, Barth came to say: the paradigm of the face of God is Jesus Christ, the One who is *other than* we are in the unique ways this One moves *on our behalf*, even unto death.

A second counter-argument claims that God (if God exists) is not of unrestricted importance. Instead, this argument goes, something else is the ultimate mystery of our being: the gods or certain people, nature or humanity, justice or love or something else. Barth resists the temptation to respond in any but "supplementary, incidental, and implicit" ways to such challenges. All religions *as* sets of practices and teachings are forms of "unbelief"—including and particularly Christianity as a religion (*CD* 1/2:297–325). Theological witness, he will say, is to the God and Father of Jesus Christ, not our own or any other religion. Still, we may find truths in other religions—secular parables of our practices and teachings on creation and reconciliation and salvation.

The first objection is, I believe, more powerful than the second; Barth's counter-argument to the second is more powerful than his counter-argument to the first. But the main point does not hang on technical objections to Anselm's ontological argument.[26] It is important to recall the reason for bringing up Barth's argument in the first place: to illustrate thinking of "divine perfection." Anselm's argument is, we might say, typical of the "thickness" of the religious sphere of activity Christianly conceived. We can imagine what it would be *like* for a Buddhist to make a *similar* (not identical) case about nibbana: nibbana would become that than which a greater cannot be conceived; this teaching could be unpacked by redescribing it in myriad ways, using Buddhist scriptures and other practices of the Buddhist community. Adjudicating the argument between Christian and Buddhist construals of that which is of unrestricted value would involve adjudicating sundry practices and teachings in relation to the God of loving freedom and the enlightened emptiness of nibbana.

Thus, on the one hand, there is at least this common ground between Christian and Buddhist claims: each ascribes ultimate importance to something or other. This is common ground we do well not to ignore. And yet thinking of God as that than which a greater cannot be conceived or the subject and object of ultimate importance is not the same as thinking of nibbana. Thinking God is thinking an infinitude of divine perfections to which our character traits are analogous, while thinking nibbana is thinking freedom from conditioned existence (including our character traits). Christian and Buddhist cultural linguistic systems are partly overlapping and partly opposed in ways that need to be spelled out in detail by assessing not only God and nibbana but also the practices and teachings, scriptures and rituals, communities and philosophies each permits and requires—and doing this by taking up particular practices and teachings.[27]

This, in fact, is the central practical objection to Anselm's argument—not that it is an argument, not that it is an argument of the third type, but that it is a *single* argument (an *unum argumentum*) in a world that calls for diverse arguments for diverse audiences. Just as identifying God theistically left us the project of thinking through the infinitude of divine perfections in relation to our character traits, so the religious sphere leaves us the task of seeking diverse patterns of relationships between religions. How shall we proceed?

Thus far I have been discussing what is involved in the activity of identifying God as the One of unrestricted importance. But it is important to remember that most of our discourse about God does not aim to "identify" (or "refer to") God and that identification of or teachings about God do not supply the cornerstone of our dealings with God (5.B). Recall from the previous chapter that the issues among religions are also soterial. Mapping patterns of relationships between religions is, then, ultimately a matter of taking stands on the Christian, general, and relativist soterialisms discussed in the previous chapter. The Christian case on God in relation to other religions will not only be arguments on God but also on the way this God is with us in word and sacrament and Church, raising all humanity to share in God's life. To be a Buddhist is to use different scriptures, celebrate different rituals, build up different communities with different domestic and foreign policies than a Christian does. Little doubt there are parts of these religious "complex wholes" which are or can be or ought to be part of the Christian complex whole (5.C.2.a). However, other parts of these complex wholes are mutually exclusive.

In the face of such oppositions, it is important not to confuse answers to the questions, "Who is God?" and, "Who are we in relationship to God?" with the question, "What do we say and do about those who answer these questions differently than we do?" God is the God who is with us. We are those with whom God is. God is (and therefore we ought to be) out to raise all humanity to share in God's life (4.A.1). How God is doing this with the *specific* practices and teachings of these religions is one of the great unresolved theological questions—one for which we are required to find an answer.[28]

In any case, it is time to address another audience. By their own self-avowals, many are not Christian, theistic, or even religious in any sense discussed thus far. (How) can we seek the face of God in relationship to this audience?

c. GODLESSNESS

I earlier proposed that one of the contexts that makes identifying God problematic is godlessness. The godless deny God. Like theisms and the religions, godlessness comes in interesting as well as trivial and dangerous forms. But what distinguishes the godless from our previous audiences is that, unlike theists and the religious, they embody denials. For example, if some call themselves atheists, we know what they are *not*—not what they *are*. A denial of the God who is with us is compatible with an endless series of affirmations—or so it seems to those for whom what we are not is the midpoint of a tale that begins and ends in the affirmations of Genesis and Revelation, of reconciliation and anointing. Theravada Buddhists, religious naturalists, and humanists, as well as relativists and nihilists sometimes call themselves atheists. Perhaps they are, on some level, theists or religious but without knowing this;[29] if so, we might argue on God with them in the way we argue with theists or the religious. But what if, no matter how deep they dig into themselves or how high they climb beyond themselves, they are not theists or religious?

Consider the way John Courtney Murray distinguishes between the godless person of the "modern" and "postmodern" age. The godless person of modernity, says Murray, is the godless person of the academy *or* the marketplace—that is, one who embodies *either* "the will to understand the world, *or* to make a living in it, without God."[30] On the other hand, the godless person of post-modernity is *either* the godless person of political revolution *or* the theater—that is, one who embodies the will to transform the world *or* to exist absurdly, without God. What is crucial for our purposes is Murray's insight that there are many forms of godlessness, none of which can be reduced to the others.

In still other words, godlessness has no *internal* coherence. The godless Darwin does not speak for the godless Marx, at least on the issue of godlessness; Marx does not speak for the godless Nietzsche on this issue; the post-modern godlessness of Beckett does not speak for modern liberal or conservative godlessness.[31] Thus, part of the force of Murray's distinction between modern and post-modern godlessness is that there is no *single* problem of godlessness, no *single* audience, and therefore no *single* way we can address all these audiences. Some forms of godlessness will martyr some of us; other forms will value our contribution to their conversation. The world of this godlessness is neither good nor evil but a highly ambivalent world—a world of both joys and griefs. In relationship to this audience, there will be no single way to seek the face of the God who is with us. Before this audience we stand powerless, if not always totally silent.[32]

Why is the lack of internal coherence in godlessness so important for theological inquiry (here, for seeking the face of God in a world of many religions and forms of unbelief)? John Courtney Murray provides an essential clue when he reminds us of "the Godless man in the Bible." This godless person in the Bible includes the godless philosopher as well as godless people outside Israel and the Church (ancient and modern and post-modern). But (Murray rightly claims) the "biblical fool is the prototype of the perennial godlessness *of the people of God*"—"the archtype of *the unbelief of believers*."[33] In sum, the biblical paradigm of godlessness is our own. As Vatican II puts it, believers often "conceal rather than reveal the authentic face of God" (CMW no. 19). *We* conceal the very face of the God we are called to seek. What distinguishes our godlessness from the godlessness of others is that it is the godlessness of those who are not—or not only—godless before the academy or marketplace, political revolution or the theater but godless *before God*. This godlessness is much deeper and more serious than intellectual, economic, political, or aesthetic godlessness. In still other words, the deepest challenge to seeking the face of God in a world of many religions and unbeliefs is that those doing the seeking of this face deny that God by the lives they lead and the sorts of persons they are. And no doctrine of God can cure the godlessness of its doctors.

However, precisely because the central (but not the only) problem of godlessness is internal to our community and our individual characters, godlessness can scarcely be our first or last word. We can be godless, but God cannot be "human-less."[34] Even our own godlessness is only the mid-point of a tale from creation through sin toward salvation—a journey in which our central proof of the God who is with us will be the love of the faithful for God and neighbor (CMW no. 21). While God may (as Scripture sometimes says) hide until the godless seek, more often our hope is that God will find even those who do not seek precisely because our godlessness can be only this mid-point. How so? Consider the opportunities presented to Christians by two different forms of godlessness.

First, some godless are interested exclusively in our world. They are intrigued by what Christians call the joys of creation. They may think, for example, that they can "explain" us by various physical and social, psychological and historical "causes."[35] Second, other unbelievers challenge us with lives maimed and mutilated, deprived of longevity or the capacities of mind and heart to enjoy life; with the deaths of speechless infants and the suicides of adults. This godlessness does not focus on the joys of good creation but the griefs of our world.

We seek the face of God in very different ways before these two forms of godlessness. Concerning those who fall victim to the beauty of God's world, we need to remember that they may "only go astray in their search for God and their eagerness to find him; living among his works, they strive to comprehend them and fall victim to appearances, seeing so much beauty" (Wis 13:6-7). This type of godlessness can teach us much about the beauty of God's world. For example, we can agree with these godless that our activity before God has a physical and social matrix. It is as embodied creatures that we read and hear the Scriptures, baptize with water and oil, eat and drink the Lord's Supper, respond to calls to marriage and virginity, feed the poor and heal the sick. Surely if this material world is part of the setting of God's activity, we too ought to study that world. This interaction with and study of our world is not the fideistic journey which implies that there are no connections between the claims we make about the cosmos and the claims we make about God; it is also not the modernist argument that our teachings about God can be derived from our teachings about the cosmos. It is also not what I earlier called the third type of argument (for example, that the claims we make about the world raise "limit questions" which require or permit us to see God at work) (2.C.2). Finally and most crucially, it is not a strategy of the fourth type which proposes that our arguments about the world are sometimes identical with arguments about God. It is, instead, an effort to map patterns of relationships between our teachings about God and our teachings about the world.[36] It has ceased to be simply seeking the face of God and has become a quest to understand our world. Seeking ways to understand our world is an important quest, but (as we shall see in the next chapter) it is a sort of inquiry different from seeking the face of God.

Considering those who focus on the tragedies of our world, Christians often ought to remain speechless before such tragedies. Christians can seek the face of God before this audience by retelling the story of their betrayal of Jesus, recalling how not even their sin destroyed God's creation and how this One's death and resurrection is salvation. We can give reasons why we baptize dying infants, forgive our sinners, anoint our suicides, console our sufferers. But the one thing we cannot do is give reasons for such tragedies, for there is nothing there for which we might give a reason but our sin—and sin is the paradigm of irrationality (whether we locate it in the diabolically fatal powers of the cosmos, the inner dynamics of the will, or elsewhere). We can, in short, seek the face of God in relation to this audience by locating tragedies in a world which is other (although not totally other) than the world of the godless. But note that we find ourselves once again talking about the world, not God. The issue is once again the comprehensive character of our convictions about God—but now the occasions are absurd or tragic. Our inquiry is once again not into any of our four types—it is a different sort of inquiry that calls for a different chapter.

I am not suggesting that such responses will satisfy the godless. We would need to know more about their specific objections to our Scriptures, our liturgies, our Church as well as their alternative before we could more fully respond to their objections. But seeking the face of God before these forms of godlessness challenges us to show how seeking the face of God relates to particular occasions of human activity in their and our world.

3. *A Missionary Community*

As it turns out, then, seeking the face of God in a world of many forms of religion and godlessness is a complex enterprise in which we have different roles. For example, the different contexts in which we are called to identify God explain why Vatican II's modes of reference to God are so diverse. We seek the face of God when we call upon this God by name in liturgical and personal prayer; when we retell the story of this One as creator of the world and savior of Israel, as the God of Jesus Christ and the communion of saints; when we engage in "human activity throughout the cosmos" (CMW pt. 1, ch. 3); when we test the adequacy of any of our images and judgments about God. The Bible, the liturgical and more broadly communal life of the Church and the churches, the creative and redemptive activities of all individuals and groups, and all the other examples of human activity sketched above are a web of private and public events, particular and more universal occasions of human activity.

The God of Vatican II is a God who, far from calling us to choose between such practices, calls us to shape such activities in particular ways. Such occasions of human activity throughout the cosmos are formed into a pattern as a Vatican II community takes up its commission to weave the activities of all humanity as well as its own into the body of the Christ who is its presiding promise that divine and human activity are distinct and yet one. Thus, Vatican II's claim is that the God of the Bible *is* the God present and at work in this community's liturgical celebrations, in its efforts to become a sacramental communion of saints, in its relations with other Christians—as well as in the practices and teachings of other religions and all humanity, particularly those who are in any way poor or afflicted. Finally, a community shaped by Vatican II's communal policy relates this pattern to the activity of God by that ongoing reform of its activities which heeds the call of the Spirit to shape themselves into the new humanity and thus to live on pilgrimage toward the new heaven and new earth which this God will graciously bring to perfection (CMW no. 39).

If we had to select one document within Vatican II that makes this point, the best constitutional policy for identifying God—

the document which (on these if not other issues) sets the norm for the others—would be Vatican II's Decree on the Church's Missionary Activity. To require that we seek the face of God in a world of many gods, many religions, many forms of godlessness is to require that we become a missionary community, under the missionary activity of the God whose face we seek. We engage in this activity in various stages, often intermingled (CMA no. 6). Thus, the practical context of our argument begins with the example of our lives and the witness of our words, extends through the preaching of the gospel and assembling of the people of God, and moves to the forming of the Christian community in particular churches in particular lands (CMA nos. 11–18). At this beginning and middle and end (2.A.2), we train ourselves and our children, our monks and our lay people to give reasons for the hope that is in them, finding common ground here and opposition there, working from the former as well as overcoming the latter. In the case of both common ground and opposition, "whatever good is found to be sown in the hearts and minds of men, or in the particular customs and cultures of peoples, far from being lost is purified, raised to higher level and reaches its perfection, for the glory of God, the shame of the demon, and the happiness of men. Thus, missionary activity tends towards eschatological fullness." (CMA no. 9). All of this is in imitation of the "wonderful exchange" [*admirabile commercium*] of the Incarnation.[37]

Thus, there is no single way of seeking the face of the God who is with us before audiences which partly overlap and partly compete with our quest. Training our children and families, our parishes and ministers, our neighbors and ourselves in seeking the face of God is a highly relative and particular affair. The key context of divine and human action is not *only* creatures engaged with ultimate importance *or* with God in general but human beings engaged in a variety of practices, domestic and foreign, centered on Jesus Christ—the Jesus whose identity is constituted in relation to us (*pro nobis*), binding his identity to particular contexts internally and externally. Seeking the face of God in such contexts includes identifying God as the One who, in the infinitude of perfections, is of unrestricted importance. Just as identifying God is a matter of our contexts individually and as a whole, so also it is a matter of unpacking God's attributes individually and as a whole, describing how God is with us on all occasions. Thus, our quest for the face of God has a Catholic particularity.

But seeking the face of God is not simply learning to identify God in diverse contexts. It is most importantly living a life that enables us to tie events together in a pattern which can "broaden and complete our field of reference by describing the ultimate context in which we live our lives."[38] Because it broadens our field of reference, we can see the point of the third strategy above (5.C.1) which does not fear appealing to resources we share with other theistic, religious, and human communities; but because it completes our field of reference, we can see why our strategy must be of the fourth type: no quest for the face of God will be complete unless it holds together the God of our lives (human and religious and theistic) with the God of the biblical narratives whom we call upon by name in our public and private devotions as the common good of all humanity. Thus, our community ought to permit its members to seek the face of God using resources common to other communities—as long as such resources are or ought to become *also* authentic practices and teachings of our own community. This, by the way, does not rule out discovering resources which are not those of our community; but such resources will not be *essential* to Christian *communal* identity, even though they might be essential to the work of individuals and small groups within the community.

In still other words, every effort to identify God includes as at least one of its premises an argument from faith. This is equivalent to claiming that seeking the face of God must *include* a call to repent and believe for the kingdom of God is at hand. But we do not have a way of identifying and otherwise seeking the face of God that is forceful in any situation and for every occasion past, present, and future. Seeking the face of God is prospective as well as retrospective—and therefore an essentially unfinished task.

Finally, seeking the face of God is a cumulative enterprise. There is, for example, no single argument for all audiences, but only "the cumulation of probabilities" as we live and think our way in the world.[39] But it might be deceptive to call the argument cumulative if this suggests that the better argument grows progressively or that arguing on God were a matter of piling up reason upon reason. There are progressive features to our arguing as we repent of mistakes we have made in following the infinitude of divine attributes, in living and thinking the God of unrestricted importance for our lives, in discerning God at work in the joys and griefs of our world. But arguing on our effort to identify the God whose face we seek never exhausts the infinite wealth of its abidingly interesting object. The argument may be cumulative, but its subject matter is better characterized as mystery, in the sense suggested by Gerard Manley Hopkins:

> [Y]ou know there are some solutions to, say, chess problems so beautifully ingenious, some resolutions of suspensions so lovely in music that even the feeling of interest is keenest when they are known and over, and for some time survives the discovery. . . . Christ is in every sense God and in every sense man, and the interest is in the locked and inseparable combination, or rather it is in the person in whom the combination has its place. Therefore, we speak of the events of Christ's life as the mystery of the Nativity, the mystery of the Crucifixion and so on of a host; the mystery being always the same, that the child in the manger is God, the culprit on the gallows God, and so on. Otherwise birth and death are no mysteries, nor is it any great mystery that a just man should be crucified, but that God should fascinates—with the interest of awe, of pity, of shame, of every harrowing feeling."[40]

Seeking the face of God implies developing a repertoire of practices and teachings interesting enough to sustain an eternal quest. The mystery of double agency—of God's particular agency and our particular agencies—is that it prompts a permanent inquiry into how it is that the Spirit is shaping humanity into the body of the Christ after whom one segment of humanity is named. How the Spirit is doing that in comprehensive ways in the particular joys and griefs of our world is the subject of a final chapter.

6

Seeking the New Heaven and the New Earth

Jesus Christ "holds all things in unity" (*ta panta en auto synesteken*) (Col 1:17; cf. Wis 1:7; Heb 1:3). This confession is particular in that it is a claim about Jesus Christ and all the particulars of our cosmos—including us and you and me. But the confession is also catholic, universal, comprehensive, even cosmic. It speaks of Jesus Christ holding together not one thing or some things but all things—not only our liturgy (ch. 2) and our Bible (ch. 3) and Church (ch. 4) and our quest for the face of God (ch. 5) but ourselves and our world (ch. 6). It has to do with "all things"—not only (as we shall see) joys and griefs external to us but also those internal to us (for example, your and my characters). If the confession is cosmic, then so must the mandate to seek the humanity of God also be comprehensive.

But there are two key challenges to the ecological universalism of Colossians. First, our inquiries are limited (finite). Certainly this is true of us as individuals. Our individual quests are limited by time and space; by opportunities granted and gained, taken and lost; by our intelligence and will and affections; and by other particularities of our characters. There are also severe limits to the quests we engage in together. How can we hold together inquiries into our genetic structure, the diverse friends and institutions with whom we commune, and the galaxies?

Second, inquiry can be perverse and trivial. For example, inquisitive people (like curiosity) can kill more than cats. There are Grand Inquisitors as well as saintly ones. Not all inquisitions are valuable. Still other inquiring minds (as some popular tabloids remind us) want to know the most trivial of things in the silliest (if not perverse) ways. In sum, seeking the humanity of God is, we ought to say, cosmic in its limits, in its depravities, and in its scope.

This chapter will propose a way to deal with this fact (or these facts). I shall propose that, *in and with other contexts and topics of theological inquiry, seeking the humanity of God is also our and your and my*—all three are crucial—*inquiry into the new heaven and new earth God is preparing in Word and Spirit.* Such is the fifth and final sub-thesis supporting the main thesis of the book (1.B). Backing up this sub-thesis will require (A) our showing that this cosmic context yields a set of problems distinct from those in previous chapters and therefore requires strategies for inquiry quite distinct from those thus far proposed. I shall propose that this context escalates the perils and possibilities of theological inquiry because the "narrative unity" of our quest is constantly undercut by our efforts to hold together *our* joys and griefs and the joys and griefs of *others*. But (B) we can seek and find the narrative unity of our quest as we become particular characters, holding together our own and others joys and griefs in a unified narrative. The saints are limited exemplars of our quest for patterns of relationships between our heaven and earth and the new heaven and new earth—patterns of relationships we have (by and large) not yet found. However, (C) seeking and finding such patterns of relationships depends centrally on a Trinitarian vision of God, who is creator of us and our world, who has spoken to us in Jesus Christ, and who is forming us into a people of love. By chapter's end it will be clear that the mandate to seek the new heaven and new earth is the presiding way of signaling the (permanently?) unfinished character of theological inquiry into the humanity of God.

A. *The Quest for a Unity for Our Lives*

1. *Identifying with the Joys and Griefs of the World*

First, consider a problem raised in chapter 1 (1.A.1), implicit in subsequent chapters, but able to be clearly formulated only in this final chapter. Catholic Christians, we have seen, engage the scriptural texts, celebrate word and sacrament, build up the communion of saints, and seek the face of God in contexts domestic and foreign. But while we more or less consistently succeed or fail in these tasks, we never do *only* these things. We also have parents and children, families and friends, jobs and professions, neighborhoods and citizenships and economies, needs and powers, affections and beliefs shared with near and distant neighbors. In short, Catholics and other Christians engage in such specifically Christian activities only as they move within a broader world—a world of other texts and rituals and communities and religions; a world of the technologies for outer space and therapies for inner space, of natural history and art, of executive and legislative and judicial powers; a world of vast riches and massive poverty. In sum, we live in a world of numerous joys and griefs. It is within (or, let us say, *internal to*) this world that we must negotiate our diverse and conflicting interactions with the particular and concrete events of our lives.

From this point of view, any consideration of the Scriptures or liturgies or churches or religions "in themselves" (for example, the previous chapters) is relatively abstract; that is, it is abstracted from the fact that our inquiries into the Scriptures and rituals and community and religions are undertaken from the midst of the physical, social, historical, and personal energies that constitute the world. For most of us (that is, for those not called to or stuck in some varieties of the monastic life), the previous practices and teachings must be sought and found in the context of this world as a whole. By and large, to be a Christian includes thus identifying with the joys and griefs of the world: we (among others) *are* these joys and griefs. To say that inquiry is cosmic is to say it embraces this world. This fact demands its own chapter.

But equally important is the fact that no one ever stands and moves only in *the* midst of things or in the world as a whole. If most of us are lay people in some respects, we are all monks in some other respects. That is, the world is not only "the world" but "*our* world"—a world, then, in which our joys and griefs are *limited*. For example, the Christian community is called to enact its faith "from within [internal to] the struggles and hopes of the poor"; and yet, for most of us, "the will to live in the world of the poor can only follow an asymptotic curve: a constantly closer approach that can, however, never reach the point of real identification with the life of the poor."[1] The world is our (your and my) world, not always their (her and his) world. No one has affections and thoughts uninfluenced by some particular communities, some particular rituals, some particular texts. Insofar as we engage in some particular practices, we remain monks from someone's point of view.

Granted, our monasteries are never absolutely isolated. We walk on the same ground as most others. This is why essays on the practices and teachings involved in any aspect of the Christian life are incomplete without essaying the patterns of relationships between that feature and its rivals and resources. This is why previous chapters proposed that a particular practice or activity required finding patterns of relationships between that practice and some *other* practices and teachings. If we were not in the world in the first chapters, we will not get there by announcing the topic in this last chapter. Thus, previous chapters have dealt with the world (or, at least, our world). From this point of view, *this* chapter is an abstraction *from* the others (rather than, as is also true, the others being an abstraction from this one). The world is not a single thing, and so we rarely deal with it except in piecemeal fashion: and so have previous chapters. We *are* some—but not all—joys and griefs. Some joys and griefs are internal and some external to us. How can we relate these two species of joys and griefs?

Note that the problem here is *not* seeking the patterns of relationships between Catholic and Christian teachings (1.A.2) or between Christian teachings and religious or other truth-claims (1.A.3). The problem is the very different problem of dealing with the fact that some joys and griefs are internal and some external to our world (1.A.1). One of the ways our inquiries become depraved is by our confusing or separating such internal and external joys and griefs. Some of us, in the name of the cosmic scope of our inquiries, deny our limits. For example, we may refuse to admit that there are inquiries external to our own. We may also refuse to see that our inquiries are ours, internal to us. Still others, in the name of the limits of our inquiries, deny their cosmic scope. What, then, is the relationship between the two? How do we seek in a world of so many joys and griefs?

2. *A Narrative of our Joys and Griefs*

It is only in the face of such questions that we can see the point of as well as a problem with the thesis of Vatican II's Pastoral Constitution on the Church in the Modern World:

> The joy and hope, the grief and anguish of the people of our time, especially of those who are poor and afflicted in any way, are the joy and hope, the grief and anguish of the disciples of Christ as well, and nothing that is genuinely human fails to find an echo in their hearts (CMW no. 1).

An implication of the previous section (6.A.1) is that if we identify *with* no joys and griefs, we will not be able to *identify* such joys and griefs; in other words, if no joys and griefs are internal to us (for example, if we have no experiences of joys or griefs), we will not be able to teach anything about the relationships between internal and external joys and griefs. The thesis of Vatican II's Pastoral Constitution presumes that we have some joys and griefs, that we know from experience and practice some of the hope and anguish of the afflicted, and that we are the sort of people who resonate with the laughter as well as the tears of authentic humanity.

But the Pastoral Constitution's thesis is also problematic. The confession that "nothing that is genuinely human fails to find an echo in their hearts" is itself an echo of a line from a comedy by a classical Latin playwright, Terence. Ironically, in its original context, the line is used by a busybody who is offering an excuse for prying into other people's business. Confronted with his prying, the busybody exclaims, "I am human: I think nothing human is alien to me." But the line has long been used by Christians as an expression of the mandate to love our neighbor.[2] The relationships between Terence and Vatican II are less important for us than a more general question suggested by Vatican II's intentional or unintentional echoing of the classical world. Can the thesis of the Pastoral Constitution be made good without defying our limits? How can any *particular* community echo the hope and anguish of *all* humanity?

Vatican II's strategy for answering such questions has become familiar. We ought to engage in the activities of "reading the signs of the times and of interpreting them in the light of the Gospel" (CMW nos. 4–10). These tasks, we learn, amount to aiming "to discern in the events, needs, and the longings which [we] share with other people of our time, what may be genuine signs of the presence or of the purpose of God" (CMW no. 11). These signs are sought and found (Vatican II proposes) in a humanity at once powerful and weak, boundless yet limited (CMW nos. 9–11) in the dignity of individual human persons (CMW pt. 1, ch. 1), the community of humankind (CMW pt. 1, ch. 2), and (climactically) human activity throughout the cosmos (CMW pt. 1, ch. 3).

The climactic description of human activity in part 1, chapter 3 of the Pastoral Constitution (entitled Human Activity [*navitate*] Throughout the Cosmos) is especially important. Here humanity activity is depicted in a narrative with four acts.[3] First, "human activity corresponds to the plan of God" so that "the achievements of the human race are a sign of God's greatness and the fulfillment of His own mysterious design" (CMW no. 34). Such is a centerpiece of the *joys* of our individual and communal lives. Yet in act two we learn that this same human activity can "put an end to the human race itself"; therefore, human activity, "purified and perfected" by Christ and the Spirit, needs to overcome the disorder of sin (CMW no. 37). Such self-deconstructive capabilities are typical of our *grief* and anguish.

Third, thus purified and perfected, human activity builds up a community of love on the pattern of Jesus Christ, who, as crucified and risen, summarizes human history (CMW no.

38). Here we identify with the joys of creation and the griefs we cause and suffer as the way of enacting the hope of salvation *in diverse ways,* for "the gifts of the Spirit are manifold." Finally, because "*God* is preparing a new dwelling and a new earth in which righteousness dwells," we are spurred "to develop this earth" and nurture "the fruits of our nature and enterprise." We will find these joys and griefs, "illuminated and transformed," when Christ hands an "eternal and universal kingdom" to the Father (CMW no. 39). Thus, whenever this community finds individuals and groups engaged in this sort of activity, creative and redemptive, it will find God working and accommodate its activity accordingly (see CMW no. 44).

In sum, the central teaching about our world is nothing fancier than the claim that we are God's good creatures, agents and victims of evil, set on a journey toward salvation by God in Word and Spirit. Human activity has the shape of this narrative (or these narratives) of creation and sin, salvation now and in the future. Here, then, in general terms is our solidarity with the joys and griefs of humanity, set in an unfinished narrative which embraces the "already" and the "not yet."

3. *The Problem of Narrative Unity*

How does this narrative help us relate internal and external joys and griefs? In general terms, this narrative provides the context which enables us to address the occasions of joy and grief we share with human kind *by locating such internal and external joys and griefs within these particular narratives of creation and sin and salvation.* But what does it mean to locate internal and external joys and griefs within these particular narratives? Here is another controversial question for theological inquiry. For example, the Pastoral Constitution proposes that the relationship between the Church (one set of internal joys and griefs) and world (one set of external joys and griefs) is "mutual" and "reciprocal" (CMW pt. 1 ch. 4).[4] But what does this mean? What sort of mutuality and reciprocity is at stake here? Is reciprocity a compromise between those who focus on what the Church has to give to the world (conservatives?) and those who focus on what the world has to give to the Church (liberals?)? Does Vatican II teach (or announce) that Catholics are good modern men and women, equipped to move with ease in and between the realms of politics and culture and economics? Are we left perched on a boundary between our identities as Christians and worldlings, left to be mediators in a world of conflict?

We hope not. Consider the following four implications of the four acts of Vatican II's narrative. First, locating internal and external joys within *narratives* of creation implies that our dignity as individuals and our life as a community are constituted in a physical *and historical* world. And this, as Genesis implies, is good. The description of our joys and griefs as internal and external might suggest that our identities are constituted exclusively as creatures in physical and social *space*. But the first act of Vatican II's narrative of human activity reminds us that our activity is temporal as well. This temporality is part of what it means to be God's good creature.

This implies that theological inquiry is undertaken by individuals within a physical, social, and historical world. Our endeavors to relate internal and external joys and griefs are undertaken within this world. Thus, the patience that it takes to relate internal and external joys and griefs is not simply called for by the fact that the goods of communal life are always accompanied by evils; this patience is also called for because human activity is an historical life, bound to the trajectories and rhythms of time. This time is, of course, finite—limited by, for example, when we are born, when we live, when we die.

These are claims about all of us—Jew and Greek, male and female, slave and free. They are "metaphysical claims"— "claims about absolutely general features of the world," some wish to say.[5] They are claims which pervade every context in which we live and move. This does not mean that all of us agree with all parts of this story and these claims. In fact, we live in a world where only *some* of us share this story and these claims.

In fact, this suggestion that we, as individuals in a physical and social and historical world, are divided from each other within this world requires explicating the second act of the story: we are agents and victims, doers and sufferers of evil.

We are agents or doers of evil in that we cause others as well as ourselves to suffer; we are victims of evil in that we suffer the evils done by others. If we are individuals in a physical and social and historical world, such evils will be diverse—internal as well as external to us. They jeopardize both our individuality and our physical, social, and historical circumstances.

What, then, is the point of locating such evils in a narrative? At their best, Christian convictions about sin and suffering have been bounded by two presumptions. On the one hand, evils are not God's creatures. They are not any thing—at least if by "thing" we mean one of God's creatures. On the other hand, if evils are not God's creatures, neither are they illusory. The grief and anguish of our time are not "really" joy and hope. Evils are real. Perhaps the closest Christians have come to characterizing evil accurately is to confess that it is absurd, without rhyme or rhythm or reason.[6] In any case, evils are a second act of the story, irreducible to the first act; evils are the radical interruption of any attempt to tell a unified story of our lives.

This second act of the narrative is our solidarity with the griefs and anguish of the people of our time. Once again, these are claims about all of us, although not all of us agree with them. What we think is evil depends on what we think there is.[7] But not everyone agrees that we are individuals in a physical and social and historical world; not surprisingly, then, we will disagree on evil and sin and suffering.

The third act of the story is a tale not of the past or present of evil and sin and suffering. The third act is a story of our movement toward the future, centered on a community of love which identifies with the joys of creation and the griefs we cause and suffer as the way of enacting our hope of salvation. Because we do this as creatures, we do this as individuals and communities in a physical and social and historical world. Because we are also agents and victims of evil, we do this as a sinful community of sinners. Once again, this third act of the story is not the story of a "well-balanced" individual or community. The narrative does not have this sort of equilibrium.

Thus, even this community of salvation is not the end of the story. We remain creatures and sinners in a sinful Church and so on the way toward salvation. Our salvation history is lived in hope—a quest for a *new* heaven and a *new* earth when we will find our joys and griefs (Vatican II says) "illuminated and transformed." There will be these *same* joys and griefs but now *transformed*, a *new* heaven and earth, a resurrection of the flesh. Thus, locating our joys and griefs in the fourth act of this narrative means that the problem of relating internal and external joys and griefs is ultimately a problem of relating our internal and external joys and griefs *now* and in the *new* heaven and earth.

In sum, identifying (as Vatican II requires) with the joys and griefs of the people of our time is locating internal and external joys and griefs in a unifying and unified narrative. In this sense philosophers as diverse and opposed as Alasdair MacIntyre and Charles Taylor are right that the "unity of human life is the unity of a narrative quest"—"a quest or a journey in which various forms of evil are encountered and overcome".[8] And yet it is no easy chore holding together these narratives—or these acts of a single narrative. In fact, much of the history of Christianity has been the story of an argument over whether we ought to "stress" the joys of creation (some Catholics), the griefs of our sin and suffering (some Protestants), or the tearful hopes of a creation eagerly awaiting the apocalypse (some Eastern Orthodox). But Christians nowadays ought to agree that creation and sin and salvation are not rivals among which we ought to choose; instead, they form a set of narratives whose unity we seek.

Nonetheless, the very description of the four acts of the narrative suggests that this narrative unity is (at best) very fragile. At each stage of the story we saw conflicts emerge—conflicts over the joys of creation, the griefs of this creation, the diverse ways Christians enact solidarity with those joys and griefs, which of the joys and griefs of this earth will endure and which will be transformed. But if this narrative generates so much conflict, how can it support a community called to identify with the joys and griefs of the people of our time? How can it provide a context for a mutual or reciprocal relationship between Church and world, between internal and external joys and griefs?

B. *The Characters of Our Humanity*

1. *The Character of a Saint*

Part of the resolution of the problem of the narrative unity of our life is that this unity is concretely embodied in particular individuals in particular physical, social, and historical circumstances. Traditionally, such individual exemplars of the Christian life have been called "saints," "holy" persons. But who are the saints?

"Seeking God" (spiritual masters tell us) is a characteristic of these saints—seeking God in *all* things.[9] But the long tradition of producing saints in and for diverse cultures shows us how diverse our individual exemplars of seeking God are. For example, Catholics celebrate saints who were martyrs and pastors, doctors of the Church and virgins, members of religious orders and widows. In each of these cases, what is at stake is not primarily teachings or doctrines *about* (or criteria of) sainthood but *examples* of saints. Further, what is at stake in such examples is not primarily the diverse "practices" in which they engage: their heeding the Scriptures, celebrating sacraments, contributing to the common goods of the Church, living a life centered on God's loving majesty, heeding the right teachings. What is at stake is the people who engage in these practices and propose these teachings; what is at stake is not primarily "seeking" but particular people seeking the humanity of God. What is at stake, let us say, is their "identity" or "character," that is, that which makes them (and us) irreducibly unique individuals.[10]

Issues of character are the most personal (or, others might say, existential or spiritual) moment of Catholic particularity. Relative to the Christian narrative of creation and sin and salvation, one way to describe our character is to say that "that which makes us irreducibly unique individuals" is simultaneously *internal* to us (for example, our individual needs and powers) and *external* to us (for example, given to us by our physical, social, and historical circumstances). If this is so, we can say that our character is constituted by how we relate these internal and external joys and griefs over the course of time. In still other words, our character is constituted by how you and I hold together your and my particularity and the variety of contexts in which we live and move.

But even putting the issue in terms of character may be too abstract. The unity of Vatican II's narrative of "human activity throughout the cosmos" is concretely enacted as the narrative of creation and sin, salvation now and in the future becomes *my and your* narrative, that is, as it becomes the narrative of your and my life. For example (to rehearse the four acts of Vatican II's narrative relative to our character), Christians do not simply confess creation of "heaven and earth, of all things visible and invisible" (Constantinopolitan Creed). The "I believe" of the Christian creeds implies that you and I are specific characters in a particular space and time with specific needs and powers, beliefs and affections (gratitude and wonder before such a world).[11] Further, it is you and I who are each poor and afflicted in various ways—hungry and thirsty, naked and sick, widows and orphans, strangers and captives to sin and death. Much of our refusal to take seriously Vatican II's focus on "those who are poor and afflicted in any way" is a refusal to recognize who *we* are—agents and victims of the diverse forms of poverty and affliction in our world. Our creaturely character is constantly jeopardized by the evils we do and suffer.

Our vocation to holiness, then, is a call to be a particular person as we seek ways to relate joys and griefs internal and external to ourselves over the course of time. The ways we do this are (as Vatican II says in the third act of the story) "diverse." This raises a large problem for seeking the humanity of God. That is, Catholics have examples of saintly martyrs and saintly pastors, saintly doctors and saintly widows. But we are often clearer about what Christian character amounts to for martyrs and pastors and members of religious orders than we are for other vocations. The central problem in suggesting how seeking the humanity of God bears on our characters is that "there is as yet hardly a single person venerated as a saintly parent or a saintly merchant or a saintly politician or a saintly professor (except, of course, of theology)."[12] The examples might be expanded: we seek not only saintly parents but sons or daughters of parents, not only merchants but consumers of merchandise, not only politicians but citizens, not only saintly professors but saintly students. The point is that seeking and finding saintly examples of such characters is often no easy chore.

The adjective (saintly) is important. Soren Kierkegaard once said that Christianity "has erected a barrier with a view to preventing these things from coalescing completely into one: Christianity and a living, Christianity and a career, Christianity and a fiancee, etc."[13] Part of Kierkegaard's worry (obsession, perhaps) was that Christian discipleship can become identified with worldly professions, forgetting what he calls its peculiar "inwardness" (that is, its internal joys and griefs). Those called to poverty remind us that becoming a Christian is not identical to making "a living"; those called to virginity and celibacy remind us that becoming a Christian is not identical to seeking or finding a "fiancee." We need to remember that the saintly parent or merchant may not be identical to what our culture calls the successful parent or merchant.

However, Kierkegaard's concession that the barrier is never complete is crucial.[14] The adjective (saintly) and the noun (parent, merchant, etc.) are not opposed, as if we could be saints in our inwardness (whether alone or together) no matter what the shape of our public lives as sons and daughters, spouses or parents, merchants or consumers, citizens or politicians, teachers or students.

It is precisely because our narrative quest is incomplete in such ways that we need the fourth act of the story, calling us to seek the new heaven and new earth not only in the cosmos but also in our characters in this cosmos. Admittedly, some characters in our community will attest to the continuities and some to the discontinuities between our heaven and earth and the new heaven and earth. Some will marry and some will be virgins. Some will give money to the poor and others will become poor. Some will go to some wars and others will refuse.[15] But such distinctions between our diverse characters are subordinate to distinctions *within* each of us, for the fourth act of the narrative shows that our characters are constituted also as we look forward to our resurrection and eternal life.

2. *Before and with Each Other*

My point here is not to describe fully (much less dramatize) the diverse patterns of relationships different characters seek and find as they and we become the saints we and they are called to be. We discern saints from whom to learn (and become saints ourselves) in particular circumstances that generate a continual reformation of our quest for the characters we are called to become. What I have proposed is that the problem of the narrative unity of our quest is a problem of the narrative unity of our characters. But how does this proposal help us explicate Vatican II's insistence that the relationship between internal and external joys and griefs is mutual or reciprocal?

We are irreducibly unique characters in particular physical and social and historical contexts, agents and victims of evil, and on the way to salvation. This is who we are, let us say, "before and with each other." In saying that this is who we are *before* each other, I mean that others are genuinely different from us, separated from us by geography and citizenship, age and historical era; I also mean that I am genuinely different from others, separated from them by my needs and powers, affections and thoughts, geography and citizenship, age and historical era. They have their own joys and griefs, internal to them, as I have mine. In saying that this is who we are *with* each other, I mean that we stand related to each other in our movement from nature through grace to glory.

My character, then, is not only my internal joys and griefs but also my external joys and griefs. If my character is my irreducible individuality and this individuality is constituted by internal and external joys and griefs, then my reciprocal relationship to others is *internal* to who I am and am called to be. More concretely, love—always patient and kind, never jealous or boastful, rude or selfish, delighting in the truth and enduring until we know as fully as we are known (1 Cor 13:4-12)—is the central disposition and act of the Christian saint.

Much of theological inquiry in the world is figuring out how to dramatize and describe this movement before and with each other in our always diverse and often competing families and friends, our jobs and professions, our politics and philosophies, our religions and theologies. For now, I will restrict myself to one problem created by this movement. The fact that our quest is before and with each other in these ways means that, as we engage in thus seeking the humanity of God, a Christian can sometimes share more about the world with the world than with her or his fellow Christians. Think of the way Christians side with some members of the world against others (including their fellow Christians) in affairs of the mind and heart, body and soul, politics and philosophies, businesses and nation-states. The mutual or reciprocal relationship between Church and world is not the reciprocity of those Catholics or Christians who seek to preserve their own identities at the expense of the joys and griefs of others.

But note that in such cases, we share more with the world *about the world*, not about the practices which seem to this world so other-worldly: heeding the Bible, worshipping, being built up by and building up the communion of saints, loving those who afflict and persecute us, becoming not simply citizens or philosophers but saints. Our solidarity with the world is always piecemeal, for the joys and griefs we share with the world are not our *only* joys and griefs; there are also the joys and griefs of our worship and Scriptures, our communal life and mission, the needs and powers of our characters. Therefore, we will always be strange to that world *in the midst of* our solidarity. The mutual relationship between Church and world is not the reciprocity of those utopias where each heart is perfectly transparent to other hearts; it is the reciprocity of hearts (to use the metaphor from Vatican II [6.A.2]) which resonate with or echo (rather than replace or mute) authentic humanity. The "character of the saints" will thus be recognizable but strange to the world, for our quest is for a new heaven and earth.

3. *Objecting to Character*

There are three major objections to the proposal that part of the resolution of the problem of narrative unity is that such unity is enacted in our characters, for example, in the ways each of us holds together our joys and griefs throughout the temporal course of our lives before and with each other. One

objection is that this resolution has too *little* to do with our
(modern) world; a second objection is that it has too *much* to
do with our (modern) world. We will learn important lessons
responding very briefly to these two objections. A third objection is more directly theological and will require a longer
response.

The argument thus far (the first objection goes) has been cir-
cular. I have suggested that Vatican II summarizes a *narrative*
for holding together joys and griefs internal and external to us
(6.A); I have also proposed that, within this narrative, our
character is constituted by the way you and I and others relate
such internal and external joys and griefs before and with each
other in lives we hope will be transfigured into a new heaven
and new earth (6.B.1, 2). But (this argument continues) it is
easy to break the circle in which the narrative seems to presume the account of character and vice-versa. For example, it
is wrong to think that attention to our (particular) characters
provides us with a field of interest that embraces all of us (that
is, is catholic). Buddhists are skeptical of this preoccupation
with our characters, souls, or selves. For others, Nietzsche's
proclamation of the death of God has become much less interesting than his proclamation of the death of our selves. More
concretely, any given reader might ask, "What is the relationship between *my* character and Vatican II's narrative?" This
question suggests that the account thus far emphasizes more
the way Christian saints are before than with others. Its reciprocity is the reciprocity of those who have already set the
terms of the conversation.

There is no single answer to this objection, for any answer
will depend on knowing about the character of the questioner.
For example, if the questioner is seeking a *single* way to relate
the joys and griefs of our characters to the joys and griefs of
this narrative, such a quest is futile. There is no single path into
the catechumenate, no single way to read Scripture or build up
the communion of saints, no single way to live and move in our
world, no single set of rules to guide all our inquiries into God,
no single way to seek the humanity of God which undercuts the
particularities of our characters.

On the other hand, if the questioner is (like Nietzsche) suggesting "in a cheerful and affable way" that our irreducible in-

dividuality is constituted by our will to "be alone" rather than live "before and with others," we will have to call her or him to repentance—or pray that God will do what we so often cannot.[16] In sum, if seeking the humanity of God includes relating the internal and external joys and griefs particular to our characters, then there can be no single way of relating our character to the narrative of those joys and griefs.

The second objection is that our claim that the sources of our character are internal as well as external is only a peculiarly modern way (and therefore only *one* way) of talking about our character.[17] This second objection argues that modernity is by and large corrupt. In taking as its cue "solidarity with the joys and griefs of the people of our time," the discussion of character emphasizes the way we are with other people but not the ways we need to stand before them, refusing to let modernity set the agenda for Christians.

But I have not claimed that our quests for a way to relate the internal and external joys and griefs of our characters are *the* (much less the *only*) problems generated by the comprehensiveness of the mandate to seek the humanity of God. There is (Christians ought to claim) no *single* thing called the cosmos or the world or reality but only a number of things (physical events, plants, animals, societies, human beings, and so forth) variously related—sometimes causally; sometimes generically; sometimes through loose acquaintances; sometimes by unified purposes; and sometimes through "partial stories that run parallel to one another, beginning and ending at odd times."[18] Some Christians have thought we could write out a systematic scheme of such things and relations (including our sundry needs and powers), much in the way that the first chapter of Genesis presents an orderly view of the seven days of creation. Other Christians have been skeptical of such order, much in the way that the second chapter of Genesis presents a more lavish and less orderly depiction of God's creation.[19] We do not need to decide here how to hold these two "partial stories" together. But we do need to discipline the way we talk about the cosmic context of theological inquiry by *not* claiming that any *single* problem sets the agenda. The problem of relating internal and external joys and griefs of our character is not *the* (or the *most important*) way to describe ourselves. It is not a key that will unlock all or even most doors. It is simply one problem that will help us understand seeking the humanity of God in a cosmic context.

It is important to recall that Vatican II's Pastoral Constitution on the Church in the Modern World does not aspire to offer a thoroughly comprehensive map of our lives in this world. It is more particular than that, especially when it claims to deal with the "more urgent problems deeply affecting the human race at the present day" (CMW, Pt. 2, preface). The urgency at stake here is the urgency with which the gospel narratives move—within themselves as well as between the orderly creation account of Genesis 1 and the eschatological re-creation of the Book of Revelation. Urgency is highly circumstantial. What is urgent, pressing, and impelling for one individual or group, one place or time is tedious, trivial, and boring for another. The urgency of the story-teller or poet is not always that of the preacher or eucharistic assembly. The urgency of a particular local Christian community is not always that of wider church bureaucracies. The urgency of the Church is not always that of the world. The urgency of a small part of the world is not always that of a particular individual being tortured or maimed. The urgency of one dying in solitude is not the urgency of those caring for a corpse or its relics. A complete dramatization and description of seeking the humanity of God would have to deal with these and many other occasions for theological inquiry, holding apart our diverse characters and practices and teachings as well as seeking patterns of relationships between them.

But as we engage in this quest, we need to remember that our teachings, like the teachings of most religious and other communities more generally, are limited by the definiteness of our aims, our competence, our historical circumstances.[20] We ought to be theologically agnostic about much of what goes on in our world; indeed, if we think of the diverse physical energies that constitute the world in which we live, we might even say we must be theologically agnostic about *most* of what goes on, at least until we know more. We ought not to aim to teach everything about ourselves, our physical and political world, and especially our God. We need skills in discerning which of our teachings are necessary and accidental, unconditional and conditional, permanent and transitory, irreversible and reversible.[21] Here above all we need "unity in what is necessary, freedom in what is doubtful, and charity in everything" (CMW no. 92).

Thus, in response to the objection that the discussion of character concedes too much to modernity, I say that it does concede something, but not too much. Problems of character are simply one of the urgent problems facing our efforts to seek the humanity of God in a cosmic context.

In sum, in response to objections that the above proposals about character are not modern enough or are too modern, I am suggesting that we undertake the mandate to inquire comprehensively as neither apologists for nor polemicists against our world. For all of their differences, both apologists and polemicists agree that modernity is a *single* thing, within which (or outside of which) we must stand and move. Their agreement on this issue overshadows their disagreement over whether we ought to fight a defensive (apologetical) or offensive (polemical) war. However, in suggesting that the problem of relating internal and external joys and griefs is simply one urgent problem among many, I side neither with liberal apologists of modernity nor with conservative (or postmodern) critics. Instead, I side with communities which confess a world at once powerful and weak, capable of the noblest deeds and the foulest (CMW nos. 4–10)—a world that needs a narrative which embraces its particularities, its power, and its powerlessness.

These are not complete responses to objections that character seems to lean alternately toward ways we are with and before each other. But does not this incompleteness indicate that discussions of our characters are even more deeply wrongheaded? The most important objection to any notion that character can provide a source of narrative unity comes from those Christians who are wary that preoccupation with our characters (or souls or selves) will lead us to forget that it is in losing ourselves that we find ourselves.[22] This objection is more specifically theological than the first two. That is, it suggests that the claim that seeking the humanity of God includes seeking our characters risks underplaying the real object of our quest, that is, God. The following section will make the opposite case, that is, that only once we enact our quest in cosmic fashion can we seek and find the humanity of God.

C. *The Humanity of the Triune God*

1. *Inquiry before and with God*

Important as other urgent problems might be, they pale before the central claim of Christian anthropology that we are characters in particular contexts, agents and victims or evil, and on the way to salvation *before and with God.* The crucial task for *theological* inquiry is not *only* relating the internal and external joys and griefs of our individual and collective lives in history. The crucial issue is also not *only* the way our characters are constituted in a physical, social, and historical world as agents and victims of evil loving our enemies and enduring suffering in hope. The crucial issue is that our human activity in the cosmos, individually and together, is lived and thought "before and with God."

By "before God" I mean before the face of the God who is genuinely other than us as creator and savior of our world; by "with God" I mean that the God who is of unrestricted importance is the God who is with us, calling us to be co-workers with God, to cultivate the earth with God (1 Cor 3:9; CMW no. 57). Thus, theological inquiry is not simply interested in our characters in a physical and social and historical world but in those characters before and with God. We are not simply interested in the diverse ways we are agents and victims of evil but in the way sin and suffering disorder and render absurd our lives before and with God. We are not simply interested in the diverse gifts and tasks and characters we have in our journey toward salvation but in salvation before and with God. And this means that when we speak of our quest for the new heaven and earth, we are not only seeking our characters as creatures and sinners on the way to salvation. We are seeking (as Vatican II summarizes the fourth act) how *God* "is preparing the new earth in which righteousness dwells" (CMW no. 39). Our narrative quest for a new heaven and a new earth is centrally a quest before and with this God.

But how can this be? How can it be that our lives (as a narrative quest before and with each other) are also a narrative quest before and with God? How can this be, when our lives are the lives of Jews and pagans, heretical and orthodox Christians— all of us with our diverse and conflicting practices and teachings, our diverse characters in a small corner of a dark cosmos?

The general answer to these questions is quite simple. Our lives before and with each other can be lives before and with God only if the mutual or reciprocal relationship between *our* internal and external joys and griefs is not only external to (distinct from) God but also internal to God. Our mutuality or reciprocity must be bound to a mutuality or reciprocity that is *internal to* the character of God. If this is so, the reciprocity between Church and world is, then, not a life balanced between Church and world, between our life as disciples and our careers, our friends, our citizenships, our affections. This reciprocity is instead a testimony to the reciprocity between God and our world promised in Word and Spirit.

This will require some unpacking, for the claim that this reciprocity is ultimately a reciprocity *internal* to the character of God is the claim that Christians have articulated in the doctrine of the Trinity.[23] We have seen the triune God at work in each of the preceding chapters. Recall the God we learn to call upon in prayer in the catechumenate (2.A.3), the interactions between Father and Son and Spirit in the gospel narratives (3.A.2), the confession that Christ is our hope (4.B), and the suggestion that we are a missionary community in relationship to the mission of the triune God (5.C.3). But it is crucial that the drama and logic of the triune God can be fully displayed only in this last chapter, that is, in the context of our particular inquiry throughout the entire cosmos. To understand why this is so crucial, consider how a doctrine of the Trinity arises out of the links between this and previous chapters.

The God who is with us (we saw) is of unrestricted importance and holiness and glory. We stand and move in our world with this God *before* us. But the God who is with us is not simply of unrestricted importance, the beginning and end of all things. One claim implied in the gospel narratives is that God is *with* us in the particular character Jesus Christ, cradled and coffined on our behalf (2.A). The God of our cosmos is also the God of this Israelite, Jesus. The *particular* character Jesus Christ is of unrestricted importance—*homoousios* or consubstantial with the Father (to use the ancient lexicon). In this sense, this Jesus Christ is, in power and powerlessness, "the humanity of God".

But we also have seen that the Gospels narrate a particular character in particular circumstances who, over the course of time, enacts salvation *on our behalf*. In fact, we saw earlier that these gospel narratives set the context for Vatican II's identification of the joys and griefs of Christians and other people: precisely because nothing is alien to Jesus Christ, in the measure that we are disciples of this Christ nothing that is human will fail to find an echo in our hearts (3.B.3). But how is this so? As a particular individual, Jesus Christ is different from us, external to us or *extra nos*. Jesus Christ is the humanity of God with us—but is a way of being *with* us that remains *before* us. How, then, can this One be for us if Jesus remains before us? How can we hold together and apart those respects in this Jesus Christ that are external and internal to us, in Himself for us and for us in Himself, before and with us? In still other words, how can we glorify, follow, and think this One not only as a particular individual but also as a particular individual of catholic significance? (ch. 3, n. 19)

We cannot, at least if this "we" is all of us—Jew and Greek, male and female, slave and free, creatures and sinners seeking salvation. I cannot, at least if my character is constituted not only by the joys of creation but also by griefs inherited or constructed in my quest for salvation. We or I *alone* cannot do this. I do not mean that we cannot *attempt* to do this and even *seem to* succeed. We can try to live alone, whether our loneliness be the isolation of our characters or communities or historical era from others. But because our characters are constituted before and with others, the effort to stand and move alone is ultimately the absurdity Christians call sin.

How, then, is the God of the Israelite Jesus Christ (who is also the God of the cosmos, of all being, we used to say) our God and my God and your God? God must do a *new* thing, pouring the Holy Spirit into our hearts as a foretaste of the new heaven and earth. The Holy Spirit must be poured forth into our hearts, transforming us from within and so enabling us to pattern our lives on Jesus Christ. The transformation is from within in several senses. The Spirit shapes our individual characters into saints. But with and against pietisms that make born-again individuals the foundation of the faith, the Spirit also shapes from within our social life into a Church and eventually a new Jerusalem. Further, with and against social gospels that make one local or universal community the goal of our faith, the Spirit shapes from within our heavens and earth into a new heaven and earth.

But what is most important at this point is that God does not do this *alone* (no more than we or you or I seek the new heaven and earth *alone*). God is before and with *us*. Personally and socially, historically and eschatologically, God is *before* us (and so *holy*) but also *with* us (and so Holy Spirit). God's "before and with us" is not simply who God is in relationship to us but who God is. God *enacts* a reciprocal form of solidarity with us because God *is* this reciprocity. In other words, God is creating and redeeming the practices and teachings and patterns of relationships of our quests. The patterns God is creating and redeeming are ultimately the patterns God *is* in Word and Spirit, graciously creating and saving, calling us into the reciprocity which constitutes God's own life. In still other words, not only is Jesus Christ in *his* way the humanity of God but so are we in *our* way, in the power of the Spirit. Thus, God's way of being before and with us in Word and Spirit is the origin and ground and goal of our own need and power to be before and with each other. Such is how God creates a new heaven and new earth faithful to our heaven and earth as transformed by Jesus Christ.

2. *The Joys and Griefs of Inquiry within Tradition*

I am not, of course, suggesting that this is a necessary or sufficient treatment of the Trinity. It is not a sufficient treatment because it leaves a score of problems about the relationships between God's "before and with us" and humanity's "before and with each other." In other words, it leaves a score of problems about the relationship between what has been called the "immanent" and "economic" Trinity—the way the triune God forms and transforms our practices and teachings, our characters and communities.[24] But it is not even a necessary treatment. Certainly Trinitarian Christians would agree with some of the claims I have made in speaking of the humanity of the triune God; insofar as these Christian agree, we might speak of such claims as some of the necessary features of inquiry into the triune God. On the other hand, neither I nor any Trinitarian Christian would claim that we can articulate the doctrine of the Trinity only as the interaction between the ways we are before and with each other and the ways God is before and with us. But there is another way to reinforce the main point I am trying to make here, namely, that the context for the doctrine of the Trinity is the cosmic scope of our need to hold together the internal and external joys and griefs of our lives. That way is to sketch a version of the origins of the doctrine of the Trinity in the Christian tradition. Jaroslav Pelikan has proposed that the

> . . . climax of the doctrinal development of the early church was the dogma of the Trinity. In this dogma the church vindicated the monotheism that had been at issue in its conflicts with Judaism, and it came to terms with the concept of the Logos, over which it had disputed with paganism. The bond between creation and redemption, which the church had defended against Marcion and other Gnostics, was given creedal status in the confession concerning the relation of the Father to the Son; and the doctrine of the Holy Spirit, whose vagueness had been accentuated by the conflict with Montanism, was incorporated into this confession. The doctrine believed, taught, and confessed by the church catholic of the second and third centuries also led to the Trinity, for in this dogma Christianity drew the line that separated it from pagan supernaturalism and it reaffirmed its character as a religion of salvation.[25]

Going one step further than Pelikan's narrative, we might argue that the climax of this development was Augustine's "discovery of personality,"[26] when Augustine proposed that the doctrine of the Trinity was complete when it held together not only this world of Jew and Greek and Christian but also his and any individual's world as a vestige of the Trinity.

In this reading, the doctrine of the Trinity was one doctrine within this "religion of salvation"—a doctrine that *set apart* (orthodox) Christian from (heretical) Christian and *set apart* early Christianity from Judaism and paganism. This story involves much sin and suffering. Our confession that the God of Jesus Christ is the God of Israel was often undercut by our anti-Semitism. Our agreement with Israel that the God of Israel was the God of all creation often vacillated between separating ourselves from that world and accommodating ourselves to it philosophically and politically. We sometimes burned our heretics and destroyed their books. Such separations also contributed to battles among Christians East and West, Trinitarian and Unitarian. And the personality Augustine discovered could be, in later historical contexts, a force for the radical separation between the individual and the community with which democratic as well as totalitarian regimes continue to struggle.

But it is more important to note that the doctrine of the Trinity was the product of a debate which not only held us apart but also *held together* heterodox and orthodox Christians, *held together* Jew and Greek. In this version of the story, the doctrine of the Trinity was a way of identifying God (that is, teaching who God is) that held together an entire world—a world of Jew and Greek, mainstream and marginal Christians. Further, Augustine (to use my lexicon) showed (or tried to show) how the triune God holds together not simply the (external) joys and griefs of Jew and Greek and Christian but also the (internal) joys and griefs of his own and our own irreducible individuality. Our characters are vestiges of the Trinity (he suggested) in that the internal and external joys and griefs of our character are held together in a journey before and with the triune God.

Thus, my point is not that we simply need to retrieve the doctrine of the Trinity. Our Jews and Greeks, our heretics and orthodox are not identical with those of the first centuries of Christianity. We are external as well as internal to the joys and griefs of the first centuries of Christian life and thought; we stand before and with them in our heaven and earth (as they stand before and with us in their new heaven and earth). Seeking the new heaven and new earth within our heaven and earth is an enterprise which looks forward as well as backward—but ultimately forward. The point is that we learn from this tradition that the doctrine of the Trinity hangs together with a vision of the cosmos, including the role of our characters in that cosmos—and not only our characters but those of Christians past and future. The point is that we need to do for our time what Christians past did for theirs, preserving the joys and transforming the griefs—with our passions and actions focused not on the joys and griefs of this tradition but on how God is preparing the new heaven and earth in this tradition.

Thus, these claims about the complex interrelations between the triune God and our worldly characters, between Jesus Christ as the humanity of God and our own lives as the humanity of God remain another unresolved issue rendering theology a genuine inquiry. The triune God stands surety for a full range of unresolved problems for theological inquiry. In sum, the most challenging particularist theologies focus on the ways Jesus Christ is the shape of things to come. The most challenging catholic theologies focus on the unfinished ways the Spirit is moving to shape humanity into the new humanity. The most challenging Catholic particularist theologies are those which seek to relate the practices and teachings of the Christian community to those of our common humanity in ways that engage what God is doing for all humanity in Word and Spirit. That, the reader will recall, is the main thesis of this book.

3. *Will We Seek Forever?*

Some might be tempted at this point to find a resolution of Trinitarian and other unresolved problems by seeking other contexts and other claims. Perhaps in other contexts God will rearrange the words of Scripture (or spaces between the letters) so that we can clearly read God and ourselves in that text—or perhaps the Scriptures will be abolished (3.C.1). Perhaps there liturgical activity ends in a final Sabbath rest—or perhaps sacramental activity begins in unanticipated ways (2, introduction). Perhaps in these other contexts the Scriptures and sacraments and Church and religiosity and world will pass away in favor of an other world. Then again, perhaps we will become those scriptures of which Paul spoke, will celebrate a baptismal meal of eternal praise, know a new Jerusalem, a new heaven and earth.

Or perhaps then there will be no more teachings or doctrines, belief or truth-claims, action-guides or commands. The last thing many of us would look forward to is being permanently a student, one taught teachings by a teacher. But some say that we ought to explain what we can and leave other things in the hands of God so that "God should forever teach, and man should forever learn the things taught him by God."[27] Perhaps we will find these practices and teachings woven with other practices and teachings analogically, dialectically, or in ways no one has yet dreamed.

Perhaps patterns of relationship will be at the margins of other glories. But it may also be that hope for resurrection is of a piece with broader hopes for our physical and social world. Finally, perhaps here inquiry will, as Western Christians have by and large contended, end: ". . . faith has already found but hope still seeks him. But love has both found him through faith and seeks to have him by sight, where He will then be found so as to satisfy us, and no longer to need our search."[28] Or perhaps inquiry is more catholic, as some Eastern Christians hold when they say that "it is not one thing to seek and another to find, for the gain from the seeking is the seeking itself."[29] More likely, whether our seeking ends or not is less important than the One we seek. In other words, the key recommendation is "seek the One who is forever" rather than "seek God's face forevermore."[30] But in the hands of a new Origin or Hegel, Augustine or Aquinas, Theresa of Avila or Dorothy Day perhaps we will see that all of these possibilities are somehow true and right.

In some ways, all we can do with the notion of seeking the humanity of God is what we can do with any theological topic: experiment with it, mine and unpack it, check and probe how it turns out when essayed in different contexts, try to press it into service as far as is possible without permitting it to monopolize thought and action, inscribe other topics into it and it into other topics. If the effort is successful, we can begin to understand why some topics can be *one* fit description of the *whole* of the Christian life. But something more is at stake also. As we probe a particular topic, we locate it in particular contexts, articulate rules which govern those contexts, and relate it to other contexts and rules. If this effort is successful, we can begin to understand why a topic can be the *only* fit description of *part* of the Christian life. The more comprehensive the contexts and teachings and relationships of a particular topic, the more crucial that topic is for theology. But it is never the *only* description of the *whole* of life—or one description of just *any* form of that life.

The case I have aimed to make is that seeking the humanity of God is an activity constituted by relating the practices and teachings of the Christian community to those of our common humanity in ways that engage what God is doing for all in Word and Spirit. What is ultimately at stake in unresolved issues is how we will find the "good fruits of our enterprise freed of stain, burnished, and transformed" in the new heaven and earth (CMW no. 39). Exactly which of these practices and teachings are residue and which will be transfigured into the new heaven and earth, we do not know. Exactly how God weaves together our Catholicity and catholicity, the internal and external joys and griefs of our characters and circumstances depends on the relationship between inquiry now (earth) and then (heaven)—or inquiry now (in heaven and earth) and then (in the new heaven and earth). We journey in wonder and hope, but also in fear that we are not seeking the humanity of God.

Rather than pursue other worlds, my own preference for addressing unresolved issues would be to deepen our understanding of the practices, teachings, and patterns of relationships handled in this book—as well as to broaden the investigation to include still other practices (for example, our singing and preaching, para-liturgical devotions, church offices and canon laws, other institutions and character traits, other divine attributes and energies of the inner-Trinitarian being, our more trivial as well as doctrinally essential teachings). But I do not hesitate to pursue the context of God and Church and world triumphant because such a context is other-worldly or mythological. Neither would I wish to stop at the claim that we think and engage other worlds by analogy to this one. Perhaps what is at stake here is a calling to do one kind of theology rather than another—"lay theology," we Catholics still awkwardly put it. Lay theology is not a theology done about or by lay people but theology which focuses on our common vocation in and with our diverse callings—a vocation to seek the humanity of God in diverse contexts focused on Jesus Christ and the work of the Spirit in our world.

Perhaps, then, we can do no better than end with a parable about other worlds. There is a Christian tradition which has it that the apostles will join in our last judgment, the inquiry to end and begin all inquiries. And so we imagine Christ turning to us and asking, "What is your judgment?" What shall we say and do? Well, what *do* we say and do? We hold our enemies and strangers outside even our earthly kingdoms. Will we consent to the judgment of the Judge? Will we, say, let our lives stand surety for the lives of others? For some of us, if *we* are faithful, the Judge will hold *all* of us (including *them*) saved. For most of us, if *they* are faithful, the Judge will hold us saved. For all of us, since Jesus is faithful, we hope we shall all be saved. These "we" and "all" and "they" are parts of each of us, the humanity of God we seek in Jesus Christ and the Spirit.

Endnotes

Chapter 1

[1]Blaise Pascal, *The Provincial Letters,* trans. A. J. Krailsheimer (New York: Penguin Books, 1967) Third Letter, 60.

[2]Jaroslav Pelikan, *Reformation of Church and Dogma (1300–1700), The Christian Tradition: A History of the Development of Doctrine,* vol. 4 (Chicago and London: University of Chicago Press, 1984) ch. 5. My use of the phrase only partly overlaps with Pelikan's. "Catholic particularity," we shall see, is not a *single* thing. In what follows, "Catholic" (with a capital "C") roughly identifies those who consent to those early Christian creeds confessing "the holy, catholic Church"; "Catholic" is thus more specific than "Christian" but more general than "Roman (or Anglo- or other) Catholic." The adjective "catholic" (with a small "c") refers to a more general "universal."

The distinctions are rough. We shall see that, as with any theological distinctions, they can only be honed within particular contexts, in relation to particular topics and the aims we have in using such distinctions.

[3]Pascal, *The Provincial Letters,* 41–42 (on the Dominicans); 75, 182 (on the Jesuits); 290–294 (on popes); 43, 261 (on his friends).

[4]The best recent essays on individual theologians and groups of theologians are David F. Ford, ed., *The Modern Theologians: An Introduction to Christian Theology in the Twentieth Century,* 2 vols. (Oxford: Basil Blackwell, 1989).

[5]See Nicholas Lash, *Easter in Ordinary: Reflections on Human Experience and the Knowledge of God* (Charlottesville: University Press of Virginia, 1988).

[6]Charles Taylor, *The Sources of the Self: The Making of the Modern Identity* (Cambridge: Harvard University Press, 1989) 13 and pt. 3, has argued "the affirmation of ordinary life" is a peculiarly modern affirmation, often simply meaning "the life of production and the family." But the "ordinary"

Christian life does not always include what the world calls job and family (as contemplative orders remind us); further, even when the Christian life does include job and family, it also includes much more. When I define practices as I have above (that is, as "ordinary, common sensical, and idiomatic activities"), I realize that there is no universal agreement on what "ordinary activities" are.

[7]George A. Lindbeck, *The Nature of Doctrine: Religion and Theology in a Postliberal Age* (Philadelphia: Westminster Press, 1984) 74. However, my own proposals are less influenced by Lindbeck's view of the nature of doctrine (see 2.C.2 below) than by the sorts of teachings he proposes as ingredients in the "emerging consensus" of a "Christian internationale"; see George A. Lindbeck, "Ecumenism and the Future of Belief," *Una Sancta* 25 (1968) 3-17. On the benefits and burdens of any quest for an "essence of Christianity," see S. W. Sykes, *The Identity of Christianity. Theologians and the Essence of Christianity from Schleiermacher to Barth* (Philadelphia: Fortress Press, 1984).

[8]Shall we say, then, that the problem of relating "theology" and "theologians" is (thus far) a particular species of a more general problem of relating object and subject, "objectivity" and "subjectivity"? If so, the advice offered here will be of little help, since it advocates addressing such questions in relationship to particular subjects and objects (contexts and subject matters) rather than subjectivity and objectivity in general.

[9]For the general logic of diverse "patterns of relationships" between "authentic (here authentic Catholic and Christian) doctrines" and "truth-claims" or "rights-claims," see William A. Christian, Sr., *Doctrines of Religious Communities: A Philosophical Study* (New Haven and London: Yale University Press, 1987); and "Domains of Truth," *American Philosophical Quarterly* 12 (no. 1, January 1975) 61-68. For the triumvirate of natural theological, correlational, and ad hoc strategies, see David Kelsey, "Method, Theological," *The Westminster Dictionary of Theology,* eds. Alan Richardson and John Bowden (Philadelphia: Westminster Press, 1983) 363-368; and James J. Buckley, "Barth, Schleiermacher, and Theological Decisions," *Barth and Schleiermacher: Beyond the Impasse* (Philadelphia: Fortress Press, 1988) 178-186. Although I have been influenced by William Christian's distinctions between various sorts of doctrines (for example, his distinctions between truth-claims or beliefs and rights-claims or action-guides, between governing doctrines and primary doctrines), I will not make systematic use of them here.

[10]"Prescription Against Heretics," *Ante-Nicene Christian Library,* eds. Rev. Alexander Roberts and James Donaldson, vol. 15, *The Writings of Tertullian,* vol. 2, trans. Peter Holmes (Edinburgh: T. & T. Clark, 1870) ch. 7, 9-10, and ch. 12, 16.

[11]Karl Barth, "The Humanity of God," *The Humanity of God,* trans. John Newton Thomas (Atlanta: John Knox Press, 1960) 37-65. Read in the way I will suggest (particularly in chs. 3 and 4), this Reformed theologian is a "catholic particularist," although more "particularist" than "Catholic."

[12]See, for example, Gordan Kaufman's claim that "the image/concept of God serves as a focus or center for devotion and orientation"—a focus which must be represented "on a continuum running from highly mythical and sym-

bolical images—God as a personal being who loves and cares—to the more abstract notion of the cosmic ground-of all humanity." *The Theological Imagination: Constructing the Concept of God* (Philadelphia: Westminster Press, 1981) 32, 51.

[13]See Aristotle, *Metaphysics,* trans. Richard Hope (Ann Arbor: University of Michigan Press, 1960), Book Epsilon, 1025b–1026a. However, for Aristotle's ultimate sympathy with the gods, see W. J. Verdenius, "Traditional and Personal Elements in Aristotle's Religion," *Phronesis* 5 (1960) 56–70.

[14]See Yves M.-J. Congar, O.P., *A History of Theology,* trans. and ed. Hunter Guthrie, S.J. (Garden City, N.Y.: Doubleday & Co., 1968) 25–49; Frank Whaling, "The Development of the Word 'Theology,'" *Scottish Journal of Theology* 34 (no. 4, August 1981) 289–312.

[15]See Lindbeck's notion of "samples" of "competent speakers" in *The Nature of Doctrine,* 79, 82, 90, 99, 113, and Francis Schussler Fiorenza's notion of the "paradigmatic ideals" of Christian "praxis" in *Foundational Theology: Jesus and the Church* (New York: Crossroad, 1984) 304, 306.

[16]My sympathies with the "Radical Reformation" will periodically emerge. But I am convinced that dialogue with this wing of the Reformations cannot be productive until Catholics of various sorts have decided how they will nurture those among themselves who have the charisms Roman Catholics have located in religious orders; see ch. 4.

[17]Karl Barth, *CD* 4/3,1: 881. If the theologians discussed here were placed in different contexts in relationship to different topics, their arguments might become debates between theologians rather than about theology. If so, I would have to practice more of the theology of polemic and ridicule Pascal outlines in *The Provincial Letters,* Letter 11. However, it would be a polemic *ruled* in various ways, particularly by a love which "inspires a hearty desire for the salvation of those whom we attack" (p. 172). Verbal war would be a just war, fought not with the Bomb but with conventional weapons.

[18]See Albert R. Jonsen and Stephen Toulmin, *The Abuse of Casuistry: A History of Moral Reasoning* (Berkeley: University of California, 1988) especially the critique of Pascal in pt. 5. However, unlike Jonsen and Toulmin, I think that casuistically generated consensus is always relative to particular contexts and topics; to universalize casuistry is to guarantee (as Pascal suggested) an "accommodationist" theology. See chs. 5 and 6 below on "occasion-comprehensiveness."

Chapter 2

[1]See Karl Barth's ingenious exegesis of Leviticus in *CD* 2/2:358, 363.

[2]*The Documents of Vatican II,* CSL nos. 7, 9, 14 (= *Acta Apostolica Sedis* 56 [15 February 1964] 100, 101, 104). For further patterns of relationship between Jesus Christ and various features of the liturgy, see CSL nos. 2, 5, 83,

102. Vatican II's deceptively simple claim that liturgy is "activity" merits much closer scrutiny than I will be able to give it here (particularly in relation to traditional theories of sacramental causality or modern theories of symbol). The key texts of Vatican II for this chapter are its recommendations for reform of the baptismal rite in CSL nos. 64–70 and especially CMA no. 14.

³Aidan Kavanaugh, *On Liturgical Theology* (New York: Pueblo Publishing Co., 1984) 111. Western theologians frequently charge Eastern theologians with having an *exclusively* (in contrast to *distinctively*) liturgical theology; for a counter-argument, see Vigen Guroian, *Incarnate Love: Essays in Orthodox Ethics* (South Bend, Ind.: University of Notre Dame Press, 1987), pt. 2 (Liturgical Ethics). I realize that the poverty of my efforts compared to those of liturgical theologians may end up supporting their claims rather than my own.

⁴The "as" in this sentence is crucial, lest we fall into the mistake of identifying our own baptism and that of John the Baptist. As we will see in the next chapter, Jesus's baptism is important theologically only as an act in a cumulative narrative.

⁵*The Rites of the Catholic Church,* [as Revised by Decree of the Second Vatican Ecumenical Council and Published by Authority of Pope Paul VI. English Translation prepared by The International Commission on English in the Liturgy (New York: Pueblo Publishing Co., 1976)] 20–106. Subsequent references (for example, RCI no. 100) are to paragraphs on these pages. References in footnotes are references to the paragraphs of the official commentary; references in the body of the text are to the prayers of the rite itself. For functionally equivalent rites which are not as textually massive, see Max Thurian and Geoffrey Wainwright, eds., *Baptism and Eucharist: Ecumenical Convergence in Celebration* (Geneva: World Council of Churches and Grand Rapids, Mich.: William B. Eerdmans Publishing Co., 1983) 3–96.

⁶Aidan Kavanaugh, *The Shape of Baptism: The Rite of Christian Initiation* (New York: Pueblo Publishing Co., 1974) xiii, 115. Kavanaugh's description is crucial for my thesis. Like Kavanaugh, I will label this set of practices in a variety of ways (for example, rite of Christian initiation, baptism, catechumenate, Christian initiatory polity or policy) and be wary that any single description will fragment the assemblage of practices at stake.

⁷RCI nos. 6–7; cf. nos. 19, 98, 155.

⁸Kavanaugh, *The Shape of Baptism,* 135; cf. 49, 64, 135, 143, 158, 161, 178. Sacramental symbols, then, are not primarily symbols in general but acquire their force in the context of specific rituals precisely because they condense the action in apt ways.

⁹See Hans Frei, *The Identity of Jesus Christ: The Hermeneutical Bases of Dogmatic Theology* (Philadelphia: Fortress Press, 1975) p. xii; *RCI* nos. 12, 9, 6a, 14, 69.

¹⁰RCI nos. 6b, 7b, 17–19, 23, 98–99.

¹¹RCI nos. 3, 41, 133.

[12]*RCI* nos. 66, 153, 25; cf. nos. 7, 22, 25.

[13]*RCI* nos. 27, 235, 7d, 37; cf. no. 6c.

[14]See R. L. Grimes, *Beginnings in Ritual Studies* (Lanham, Md.: University of America Press, 1982), preface; see also Erik H. Erikson, "Ontogeny of Ritualization," *Philosophical Transactions of the Royal Society of London,* series B, no. 772 (1966) 251:337–50.

[15]"Protocatechesis," par. 3, *The Works of Saint Cyril of Jerusalem,* trans. Leo P. McCauley, S.J. and Anthony A. Stephenson (Washington, D.C.: The Catholic University of America Press, 1963) 1:71.

[16]*RCI* nos. 5, 67.

[17]See Wayne Proudfoot, *Religious Experience* (Berkeley: University of California Press, 1985) 112. On the relationship between "experience" and "doctrine," see also John A. Berntsen, "Christian Affections and the Catechumenate," *Worship* 52 (no. 3, May 1978) 194–210.

[18]See, for example, Kavanaugh, *The Shape of Baptism,* ch. 6, for an analysis of why water-baptism, anointing, and the laying on of hands have become the focus of specifically Christian disputes about baptism.

[19]If we (with Ronald Thiemann) take the doctrine of revelation as part of an account of God's identifiability (namely, God is a God of prevenient grace in matters of knowledge as elsewhere), then we might say that God reveals by creating and redeeming a world in which seeking we shall find—a world which includes, amidst many other activities, the activity of inquiring. See Ronald F. Thiemann, *Revelation and Theology: The Gospel as Narrated Promise* (South Bend, Ind.: University of Notre Dame Press, 1985). But "revelation" is not always used in this way.

[20]For this common patristic use of the catechumenal rule in relation to Scripture, see Beryl Smalley, *The Study of the Bible in the Middle Ages* (South Bend, Ind.: University of Notre Dame Press, 1964) 124.

[21]Joseph Fitzmyer, S.J., *The Gospel According to Luke X-XIV,* The Anchor Bible, vol. 28a (Garden City, N.Y.: Doubleday & Co., 1985) 915. For further biblical exploration of the theme, see Marvin H. Pope, *Song of Songs,* A New Translation with Introduction and Commentary, The Anchor Bible, vol. 7c (Garden City, N.Y.: Doubleday & Co., 1977) especially 416–417, 526–527; R. Alan Culpepper, "Appendix I: The Technical Meaning of *zeteo* and *darash,*" *The Johannine School: An Evaluation of the Johannine-School Hypothesis Based on an Investigation of the Nature of Ancient Schools* (Missoula: Scholars Press, 1975) 291–299.

[22]On Manichees, see Peter Brown, *Augustine of Hippo: A Biography* (Berkeley and Los Angeles: University of California Press, 1969) 111; on pragmatists, see John Dewey: "Prayer is the 'seek and ye shall find,' the inquiry of science. . . . The scientist seeks and finds something,—results," quoted in R. W. Sleeper, *The Necessity of Pragmatism: John Dewey's Conception of Philosophy* (New Haven and London: Yale University Press, 1986) 29.

[23]John Wesley, *The Works of John Wesley. Sermons* (Nashville: Abingdon Press, 1984) 1:659. It is noteworthy that Matt 7:7 is included in a gospel read-

ing at Roman Catholic liturgies celebrated "For Any Need" in the *Lectionary for Mass* (New York: Catholic Book Publishing, 1970) 1052.

[24]See Mircea Eliade, et al., "Initiation," *Encyclopedia of Religion,* ed. Mircea Eliade (New York: Macmillan Publishing Co., 1985) 7:224–38; Barbara G. Myerhoff, et al., "Rites of Passage," *Encyclopedia of Religion* 12:381–402.

[25]On the burdens and benefits of my appeals to "common sense," see Clifford Geertz, "Common Sense as a Cultural System," *Local Knowledge: Further Essays in Interpretive Anthropology* (New York: Basic Books, Inc., 1983) 73–93; S.A. Graves, "Common Sense," *Encyclopedia of Philosophy,* ed. Paul Edwards (New York: Macmillan Publishing Co., 1967) 2:155–160; Bernard J. F. Lonergan, S.J., *Insight: A Study of Human Understanding* (rev. ed.; London: Longmans, Green and Co., 1958) chs. 6 and 7; Stephen Toulmin, et al., *Introduction to Reasoning,* chs. 10, 12, 18. Chapters 5 and 6 below take up this issue as the problem of developing a "comprehensive" notion of inquiry.

[26]*RCI* no. 8.

[27]See Julian N. Hartt, *Theological Method and Imagination* (New York: The Seabury Press, 1977) 19.

[28]See Augustine, "On the Catechizing of the Uninstructed," trans. S.D.F. Salmond, *A Select Library of the Nicene and Post-Nicene Fathers of the Christian Church,* ed. Philip Schaff (Grand Rapids, Mich.: William B. Eerdmans Publishing Co., 1978), vol. 3. Augustine's combination of narrative and doctrine with a close attention to rhetorical questions of audience is exemplary, particularly his recommendation that the narrative should be taught "in such a manner as to give, for each of the affairs and events which we narrate, causes and reasons by which we may refer them severally to that end of love from which neither the eye of the man who is occupied in doing anything, nor that of the man who is engaged in speaking, ought to be turned away" (ch. 1.1, p. 283; ch. 6.10, p. 289).

[29]Or perhaps I ought to say that these are the issues which can be most clearly related to the catechumenate, for there is no consensus that these are the crucial issues. For an introduction to the story of the modern rise and postmodern deconstruction of "truth," see Robert C. Solomon, *Introducing Philosophy: A Text with Readings,* (3rd ed.; New York: Harcourt Brace Jovanovich, Inc., 1985) ch. 6. But Solomon's tale conveniently skips over intricate medieval discussions of the issue, brilliantly summarized in Josef Pieper, *Living the Truth* (San Francisco: Ignatius Press, 1989).

[30]See Richard Swinburne, *Faith and Reason* (Oxford: Clarendon Press, 1981). Swinburne's treatment of natural theology is unusual in giving careful treatment to a "period of investigation" akin to the catechumenate, but he unfortunately exempts foundational truths from such an investigation; see *Faith and Reason,* 9, 12, 15, 161 and 66–71, 72, 53, 66, 82, 88. On the link between this kind of natural theology and foundationalism, see Alvin Plantinga, "The Reformed Objection to Natural Theology," *Philosophical Knowledge,* Proceedings of the American Catholic Philosophical Association, vol. 54, John B. Brough, Daniel O. Dahlstrom, and Henry Veatch, eds. (Washington, D.C.: American Catholic Philosophical Association, 1980) 49–62.

[31]For the various options, once truth as correspondence is abandoned, see Solomon, *Introducing Philosophy* ch. 6. Just as there are different sorts of natural theologians, so there are different sorts of correlationalists; for other examples, see David Ford, ed., *The Modern Theologians*, vol. 1, pts. 2 and 3. On the notion of correlation at the "limits" using diverse "models of truth," see David Tracy, *Blessed Rage for Order: The New Pluralism in Theology* (New York: The Seabury Press, 1975) chs. 5 and 6; as well as David Tracy, *The Analogical Imagination: Christian Theology and the Culture of Pluralism* (New York: Crossroad, 1981) 62–63, 160–67.

[32]See Jürgen Moltmann, *The Theology of Hope: On the Ground and the Implications of a Christian Eschatology*, trans. James W. Leitch (New York: Harper and Row, 1967) 85, 118. As Bruce Marshall has shown, Lindbeck's own preference is for a definition of truth as correspondence; see Bruce D. Marshall, "Aquinas as Postliberal Theologian," *The Thomist* 53 (no. 3, July 1989) 353–402. However, because Lindbeck's *The Nature of Doctrine* does not fill in the relationship between intrasystematic and ontological truth, I think it also permits (without requiring) Moltmann's position.

[33]See Lindbeck, *The Nature of Doctrine*, 63–69 (on "truth"); 128–129 (on ad hoc apologetics); and 132–134 (on the catechumenate). For other claims about being "ad hoc," see Hans Frei, *The Identity of Jesus Christ*, xii; David Kelsey, *The Uses of Scripture in Recent Theology*, 165–166; Ronald Thiemann, *Revelation and Theology*, 75. Once again, not all "ad hoc-ists" are in agreement, particularly on issues of truth; for sympathetic criticisms, see William Werpehowski, "Ad Hoc Apologetics," *Journal of Religion* 66 (no. 3, July 1986) 282–301; William Placher, *Unapologetic Theology: A Christian Voice in a Pluralistic Conversation* (Louisville: Westminster/John Knox Press, 1989), ch. 8 and pp. 167–168. For further discussion of Lindbeck, see also James J. Buckley, "The Language of Dogma and Theological Discourse," *The Catholic Theological Society of America Proceedings*, ed. George Kilcourse, (1987) 42:140–143.

[34]See also Hans Urs von Balthasar's effort to subordinate knowledge and faith to *doxa* in his *The Glory of the Lord: Theological Aesthetics*, vol. 1, *Seeing the Form*, trans. Erasmo Leiva-Merikakis, eds. Joseph Fessio, S.J., and John Riches (San Francisco: Ignatius Press, 1982) 140, 151, 174. Yet it remains unclear how Balthasar holds together what he calls "the subjective evidence" (*The Glory*, pt. 2) and "the objective evidence" (*The Glory*, pt. 3) for the primacy of *doxa*. I am suggesting that "the process by which the thing itself [the form of the crucified Christ] impresses its form on us on its own initiative" is not simply the "event" of baptism (*The Glory*, 578) but the whole continuum of practices which constitute the catechumenate.

[35]See William A. Christian, Sr., *Doctrines of Religious Communities: A Philosophical Study* (New Haven and London: Yale University Press, 1987) ch. 4, for a clear formulation of the logical principles at stake.

[36]See Yves J.-M. Congar, O.P., "The Notion of 'Major' or 'Principal' Sacraments," *The Sacraments in General: A New Perspective*, eds. Edward Schillebeeckx, O.P., and Boniface Willems, O.P. (New York, N.Y., and Glen Rock, N.J.: Paulist Press, 1968) 21–32.

Chapter 3

[1]See Walter Lowe, "Christ and Salvation," Peter Hodgson and Robert H. King, eds., *Christian Theology: An Introduction to Its Traditions and Tasks* (2nd ed.; Philadelphia: Fortress Press, 1985) 241–245.

[2]"The Rule of St. Clare," *Francis and Clare: The Complete Works,* trans. and introduction by Regis J. Armstrong, O.F.M. Cap., and Ignatius C. Brady, O.F.M. (New York: Paulist Press, 1982) ch. 10, 222. "And those who do not know how to read should not be eager to learn. Rather, let them devote themselves to what they must desire to have above all else: the Spirit of the Lord and His holy manner of working. . . ."

[3]See, for example, Robert A. Bennett and O. C. Edwards, *The Bible for Today's Church, The Church's Teaching Series,* prepared at the request of the Executive Council of the General Convention of the Episcopal Church (New York: Seabury Press, 1979) vol. 1, ch. 1.

[4]See the analysis and articles collected in Stanley Hauerwas and Gregory Jones, eds., *Why Narrative?* (Grand Rapids, Mich.: William B. Eerdman Publishing Co., 1989).

[5]See, for example, DCR nos. 4 and 18.

[6]The influence of Hans Frei's *The Identity of Jesus Christ: The Hermeneutical Bases of Dogmatic Theology* (Philadelphia: Fortress Press, 1975) on the next few paragraphs will be obvious. For a sympathetic critique of Frei, see William C. Placher, "Paul Ricoeur and Postliberal Theology: A Conflict of Interpretations," *Modern Theology* 4 (no. 1, October 1987) 35–52. For Barth as Frei's master explicator of biblical narratives, see David Ford, *Barth and God's Story* (Frankfurt: Peter Lang, 1981); William Werpehowski, "Narrative and Ethics in Barth," *Theology Today* 43 (no. 3, October 1986) 334–353.

[7]On this concept of particularity, see Bruce Marshall, *Christology in Conflict: The Identity of a Saviour in Rahner and Barth* (Oxford: Basil Blackwell, 1987) especially 42–47.

[8]See Ronald F. Thiemann, *Revelation and Theology: The Gospel as Narrated Promise* (South Bend, Ind.: University of Notre Dame Press, 1985) 87–91, 130–140; Dale Patrick, *The Rendering of God in the Old Testament* (Philadelphia: Fortress Press, 1981). We might even say that if Jesus is the focus of the gospel narratives, *God's* kingdom is the focus of the stories Jesus tells.

[9]For an argument that the constellation of fellow human beings most essential to the gospel narratives includes John the Baptist and Mary, the Twelve (including Peter and John), and Paul, see Hans Urs von Balthasar, *The Office of Peter and the Structure of the Church,* trans. Andree Emery (San Francisco: Ignatius Press, 1986) 136–145.

[10]Augustine, *The Confessions,* trans. John K. Ryan (New York: Image Books, 1960) XI, 2, 4 (279).

[11]See especially Christopher Morse, *The Logic of Promise in Moltmann's Theology* (Philadelphia: Fortress Press, 1979) ch. 4.

[12]See the argument of Peter Carnley, *The Structure of Resurrection Belief* (Oxford: Clarendon Press, 1987) for whom "[t]he Easter stories . . . are told and retold for the purpose of alerting the hearer to a possibility of present experience" (p. 367), a liturgically focused experience of Christ.

[13]From a wealth of literature on Jesus the Teacher, see Jack Dean Kingsbury, *Jesus Christ in Matthew, Mark, and Luke* (Philadelphia: Fortress Press, 1981) 45f., 48f., 80f., 115f.; Hans Frei, *The Identity of Jesus Christ*, 141–142; A. E. Harvey, *Jesus and the Constraints of History* (Philadelphia: Westminster Press, 1982) 41–65; Benedict Thomas Viviano, O.P., *Study as Worship: Aboth and the New Testament, Studies in Judaism in Late Antiquity*, ed. Jacob Neusner, vol. 26 (Leiden: E. J. Brill, 1978); Jaroslav Pelikan, *Jesus Through the Centuries: His Place in the History of Culture* (New Haven and London: Yale University Press, 1985).

[14]The structure of Part 1 is so remarkable that Joseph Ratzinger goes so far as to say that "here for the first time in an official document of the magisterium a new type of completely Christocentric theology appears" ("Part One, Chapter One," *Commentary on the Documents of Vatican II*, ed. Herbert Vorgrimler [New York: Herder and Herder, 1969] 5:159). I will return to the non-Christological paragraphs of the Constitution in chapter 6.

[15]Each of the major documents of Vatican II begins with (rather than, as in the Pastoral Constitution on the Church in the Modern World, climaxes in) a Christological rule. See particularly CSL nos. 5–7; DCC nos. 1–5, 9–12, 19–20; DOE no. 2; DCR nos. 2–4; CMA nos. 2–4. Subsequent chapters will have such sections in mind.

[16]We could also say that the main function of Christological teachings is to hold together what the main body of Christian communities came to call the (1) "person" and "natures," (2) "work," (3) "states," and (4) *pro nobis* identity of Jesus Christ. Thus, with Karl Barth (*CD* 4/1:122–38), this teaching implies, on the one hand, an agreement with the custom of articulating doctrines of Christ's "person" and "natures," Christ's "work" (frequently centered around the "offices" of priest and king and prophet), and Christ's "states" (for example, Christ's humiliation and exaltation) in what Barth calls "so-called 'Christology'". On the other hand, "so-called" is important. The insistence that this One is who he is "on our behalf" generates a suspicion of "Christology" as a *locus* separate from soteriology and ecclesiology and anthropology; hence, Barth's terribly faint praise for "Christology" (or "Christocentrism"). We are not glorifying, following, or thinking about this One if we think we can teach who this One is in separation from what this One does over the course of time on our behalf.

[17]See "A Message to the People of God" [="The Church, in the Word of God, Celebrates the Mystery of Christ for the Salvation of the World"], *Origins, NC Documentary Service* 15 (no. 27, 19 December 1985), I.3 [= p. 445a]. Chapter 4 will address the most crucial question raised by the bishops: how is "the crucified Christ" a "perfecting" of human activity (II.A.2 [= p. 446b] and II.D.2 [= p. 449b])?

[18]Hans W. Frei, *The Eclipse of Biblical Narrative: A Study in Eighteenth and Nineteenth Century Hermeneutics* (New Haven and London: Yale University Press, 1974) 54, 142, 217ff.; as well as "The 'Literal Reading' of Biblical Narra-

tive in the Christian Tradition: Does It Stretch or Will It Break?" *The Bible and the Narrative Tradition,* ed. Frank McConnell (London: Oxford University Press, 1986).

[19]Rowan Williams, *Resurrection: Interpreting the Easter Gospel* (New York: The Pilgrim Press, 1984 and London: Darton, Longman, & Todd, 1982) 84; see also Gene Outka, "Following at a Distance: Ethics and the Identity of Jesus," *Scriptural Authority and Narrative Interpretation,* ed. Garrett Green (Philadelphia: Fortress Press, 1987) 144–160 (especially the distinction between [1] differences between Jesus Christ and us and [2] "points of correspondence" between Jesus Christ and us).

[20]See Edward Farley and Peter Hodgson, "Scripture and Tradition," *Christian Theology: An Introduction to Its Traditions and Tasks,* eds. Peter C. Hodgson and Robert H. King (rev. and enlarged; Philadelphia: Fortress Press, 1985) ch. 2. For a "pragmatist position" that is much clearer than Farley and Hodgson on the problem of the diverse "interpretive interests" we might have, see Stephen Fowl, "The Ethics of Interpretation or What's Left over After the Elimination of Meaning," *The Bible in Three Dimensions: Essays in Celebration of Forty Years of Biblical Studies in the University of Sheffield,* eds. David J. A. Clines, Stephen E. Fowl, and Stanley E. Porter (Sheffield: JSOT Press, 1990) 379–398. Fowl seems to permit (without requiring) an interpretive interest in what I am calling the theological subject matter of the text in a way Farley and Hodgson do not.

[21]For example, I think that when we ask about the "literal sense" of Scripture we are sometimes asking about the subject matter (Is the subject matter God? Events? Ideals? If all of these, how are they ranked and related?), sometimes about the context (Is the context the author? the author's intention? the author's community? the way the contemporary community uses the text? If these or others, how are they ranked and related?), and sometimes about the text of Scripture itself. Or we might say that asking about the *sensus literalis* is closely related to asking for the "truth" of the text, and then much will depend on the issue of the definition and test of truth raised in the previous chapter. But, again, I also think it is easier to understand the problems of relating subject matter, text, and context before trying to understand problems of "taking the text literally."

[22]See Beryl Smalley, *The Study of the Bible in the Middles Ages* (South Bend, Ind.: University of Notre Dame Press, 1964) 1, 12, 95; Hans Urs von Balthasar, *The Glory of the Lord: A Theological Aesthetics,* vol 1: *Seeing the Form,* trans. Erasmo Leiva-Merikakis, eds. Joseph Fessio, S.J., and John Riches (San Francisco: Ignatius Press, 1982) 527–56.

[23]Ibid., 529. My emphasis.

[24]Terry Eagleton, *Walter Benjamin or Towards a Revolutionary Criticism* (London: Verso Editions and NLB, 1981) 115–117. But the text is even now radiant rather than obscure; see Ronald F. Thiemann, "Radiance and Obscurity in Biblical Narrative," *Scriptural Authority and Narrative Interpretation,* 21–41.

[25]Hans Frei, *The Eclipse of Biblical Narrative,* 100. Note, then, that

questions about the subject matter of the texts arise only in specific contexts.

[26]"Performing the Scriptures," *Theology on the Way to Emmaus* (London: SCM Press, 1986) 42. On this view, Scripture's literal sense "is the sense whose discernment has become second nature to the members of the community" which performs the text; see Charles Wood, *The Formation of Christian Understanding: An Essay in Theological Hermeneutics* (Philadelphia: Westminster Press, 1981, 43).

[27]I do not find this mistake in Nicholas Lash, although I wonder if the method of correlation Lash elsewhere advocates (for example, *Easter in Ordinary: Reflections on Human Experience and the Knowledge of God* [Charlottesville: University Press of Virginia, 1988] 90) does not inevitably lead to it. For an argument that David Tracy's method of correlation leads to this problem (that is, in Tracy's terms, truth as "disclosure" grants systematic priority to the "event" over the "person" of Christ), see my review in *The Thomist* 46 (no. 4, October 1982) 626–631.

[28]Frei, *The Eclipse of Biblical Narrative,* 3; George A. Lindbeck, *The Nature of Doctrine: Religion and Theology in a Postliberal Age* (Philadelphia: Westminster Press, 1984) 117; Thiemann, *Revelation and Theology,* 146. Thiemann also claims that "how the text does in fact tie its language to the world of a believer in any particular communicative situation cannot be explained within theology's descriptive competence" (p. 150). Much depends on what is meant, particularly by "explain." But it would be more correct to say that there are *too many* ways to describe and explain this (rather than that this is beyond theology's descriptive competence) for any theology to pretend it has done so.

[29]David Kelsey, *The Uses of Scripture in Recent Theology* (Philadelphia: Fortress Press, 1975) 7.

[30]David Kelsey, "Biblical Narrative and Theological Anthropology," *Scriptural Authority and Narrative Interpretation,* 122.

[31]For a brilliant summary of the collapse of Christological dogma, see David Friedrich Strauss, *The Life of Jesus Critically Examined,* ed. Peter C. Hodgson, trans. George Eliot (Philadelphia: Fortress Press, 1972) 757–784.

[32]Albert Schweitzer, *The Quest of the Historical Jesus: A Critical Study of Its Progress from Reimarus to Wrede,* trans. W. Montgomery (New York: MacMillan Publishing Co., 1968) 6–7.

[33]See Gordon E. Michalson, Jr., *Lessing's "Ugly Ditch": A Study of Theology and History* (University Park and London: The Pennsylvania State University Press, 1985).

[34]For further remarks on Scripture (including a view of what happens when people from diverse religions argue over the same Scriptures), see James J. Buckley, "The Hermeneutical Deadlock between Revelationalists, Textualists, and Functionalists," *Modern Theology* 6 (no. 4, July 1990) 325–339. For counsel on issues internal to the Christian community, see L. Gregory Jones and Stephen Fowl, *Reading in Communion: Scripture and Ethics in Christian Life* (London: S.P.C.K., 1991).

Chapter 4

[1] "Soterial" (as defined in the *Oxford English Dictionary*) means "relating to salvation"; we shall see that there is no general consensus on what "salvation" is or whether it is important. As a rule, we ought to be wary of inventing new words, reviving archaic uses, or using technical language when non-technical language will do the job. But the risk of making these mistakes is justified when our current vocabulary cannot do justice to problems that need solving. By this chapter's end, I hope to show that such is the case with regard to salvation. Thus, "soterial action" is "*action* relating to salvation"; "soteriology" is a set of *claims about* what constitutes such soterial action; and what I will later call "soterialism" is the effort to show *patterns of relationships between* diverse and competing soterial actions and soteriologies. What I more concretely mean by "soterial," "soteriology," and "soterialism" will emerge as this chapter explores soterial action.

[2] I have learned a great deal about diverse kinds of ordinary, idiomatic, and common sensical soteriological wisdom from Paul Ricoeur, *The Symbolism of Evil*, trans. Emerson Buchanan (Boston: Beacon Press, 1967) and statistical research (which takes its cue from Ricoeur) in William C. McCready and Andrew M. Greeley, *The Ultimate Values of the American Population*, Sage Library of Social Research, vol. 23 (Beverley Hills: Sage Publications, 1976). But both the philosopher and the sociologists share a confidence in a method of correlation which, for reasons articulated in section C below, I do not share.

[3] Referred to as DCC by chapter (c.) and paragraph number (no.).

[4] The best book on this score remains George A. Lindbeck, *The Future of Roman Catholic Theology* (London: SPCK, 1970).

[5] See Avery Dulles, S.J., *Models of the Church* (Garden City, N.Y.: Doubleday, 1974); Synod of Bishops, "The Final Report," p. 446b (2.B.3). Both Dulles and the bishops are correct in showing how important it is to take the key documents of Vatican II as (pastoral) descriptions of practices as well as (dogmatic) articulations of teachings. I prefer the bishops' talk of "descriptions" of the Church to Dulles's talk of "models" (although offering descriptions usually involves "models"); but these are descriptions of purposes and goods (rather than simply "descriptions").

[6] See James M. Gustafson, *Treasure in Earthen Vessels: The Church as a Human Community*, Midway Reprint (Chicago: University of Chicago Press, 1976). I take Vatican II to describe a church whose primary common goods are the ones mentioned above; a theologically full description would have to include other common goods discussed by Gustafson (for example, our "language," "interpretation," "memory," and "understanding") and others, but these would be adiaphorous to the primary (that is, doctrinally essential) common goods.

[7] See Karl Rahner, *TI* 6:270–94 (The Sinful Church in the Decrees of Vatican II) for this phrase.

[8] JBF, referred to by paragraph number. For international dialogues, see *Growth in Agreement: Reports and Agreed Statements of Ecumenical Conversa-*

tions on a World Level, eds. Harding Meyer and Lukas Vischer (New York: Paulist Press and Geneva: WCC, 1984).

[9]I borrow the expression "Comparative Dogmatics" from a course I took many years ago from George Lindbeck at Yale University. It suggests an ongoing debt, without (I hope) burdening Lindbeck with the specifics of my analysis.

[10]On the crucial teaching that traditions can complement each other in ways that allow each tradition to confess that the other "has come nearer to a full appreciation of some aspects of a mystery of revelation than the other, or has expressed them better," see DOE no. 17. The axiom that *alien* churches can teach each other *new* things prefigures the way subsequent chapters will suggest that alien religious and secular communities may teach the Christian community truths Christians had not previously known.

[11]Thus, they implicitly agree that, in the case of their teaching on justification, there is an identity between the "Christianness" and the "truth" of their proposal (see 3.C.2.b).

[12]See especially the questions raised by Carl J. Peter, "Justification by Faith and the Need of Another Critical Principle," *JBF,* 304–315.

[13]Hans Frei, "Theological Reflections on the Accounts of Jesus' Death and Resurrection," *The Christian Scholar* 49 (1966), 291.

[14]See Gene Outka, "Following at a Distance: Ethics and the Identity of Jesus," *Scriptural Authority and Narrative Interpretation,* ed. Garrett Green (Philadelphia: Fortress Press, 1987) 144–160 (especially 152–153, 157–158). In what follows I aim to show how we do not have to choose, on certain crucial scores, between what Outka calls "following after" and "imitating" Jesus Christ.

[15]See Michael Root, "The Narrative Structure of Soteriology," *Modern Theology* 2 (1986) 145–158; "Dying He Lives: Biblical Image, Biblical Narrative, and the Redemptive Jesus," *Semeia* 30 (1984) 155–169. The Lutheran Root is primarily if not solely interested in the way the crucified Christ generates discontinuities and even paradoxes in soteriological discourse, whereas the Catholic Buckley is interested primarily if not solely in continuities and even close analogies between ourselves and the soterial patterns made possible by Christ.

[16]Vladimir Lossky, "Redemption and Deification," *In the Image and Likeness of God,* eds. John H. Erickson and Thomas E. Bird (Crestwood, N.Y.: St. Vladimir's Seminary Press, 1974) 109.

[17]"He will not be content that the story occurred and he fulfilled it for his person, but he mingleth it with us and maketh thereof a brotherhood, that he might be a common good and heirship for us all; he setteth it not in a *praedicamento absoluto,* but *relationis,* to say that he hath done so not for his own person or sake, but as our brother and for our sole good; and will not be otherwise regarded and known of us, save as he who with all this is ours and we in turn his and so we belong together mostly intimately, so that we cannot be more closely tied, like those alike have one father and are set in the like common and undivided inheritance and can assume, glory and take comfort in all his power, glory, and goodness as in our own." (Martin Luther, quoted by Karl Barth, *CD* 1/2:215, from *Pred.ueb. Mc.* 16:1f; *E.A.* 11,208). See also St.

Thomas Aquinas, *The Three Greatest Prayers: Commentaries on the Our Father, the Hail Mary, and the Apostles Creed,* trans. Laurence Shapcote, O.P. (London: Burns Oates & Washbourne Ltd., 1937) 80.

[18]See John Meyendorff, *Byzantine Theology: Historical Trends and Doctrinal Themes* (2nd ed.; New York: Fordham University Press, 1979) ch. 4. Note that the problem I raise for Lossky is a problem *internal to* the Eastern tradition; see Rowan Williams, "Eastern Orthodox Theology," *The Modern Theologians,* vol. 2, ch. 8, for differences among Eastern Orthodox on this issue. Clearly not all Eastern Orthodox are subject to the following critique of Lossky.

[19]Vladimir Lossky, *The Mystical Theology of the Eastern Church* (Crestwood, N.Y.: St. Vladimir's Seminary Press, 1976) 17, 19, 200.

[20]Lossky, "Redemption and Deification," 106–107. For a critique of turning the classic trinitarian categories of person and nature into an anthropology, see James J. Buckley, "Re-Trieving Trinitarian Teachings: A Review Discussion," *The Thomist* 48 (no. 2, April 1984) 274–296. As I see it, soterial *action* is a more central issue than issues of "person" or "nature," "individual" or "community."

[21]When I think of the monastic life at its best, I think of the descriptions of Jean Leclerq, O.S.B., *The Love of Learning and the Desire for God: A Study of Monastic Culture,* trans. Catharine Misrahi (New York: Fordham University Press, 1961), particularly the focus on the monastic life as a "quest for God" (pp. 24 and *passim*); see also Friedrich Wulf, "Decree on the Appropriate Renewal of the Religious Life," *Commentary on the Documents of Vatican II,* trans. William Glen-Doepel, et al. (New York: Herder and Herder, 1968) 2:347 (n. 11).

[22]We might also call them "catholic soterialisms" (in contrast to what we might have called "Catholic soterialisms" of the previous section). A good recent discussion (although not advocacy) of a range of general soterialisms—from Greece and Rome through Hinduism and Buddhism to the Enlightenment and Marxism—is provided by Edward Schillebeeckx (see below). For samples of clear advocacy of a theological version of general soterialism, see Gordan Kaufmann, "Evil and Salvation: An Anthropological Approach," *The Theological Imagination: Constructing the Concept of God* (Philadelphia: Westminster Press, 1981) 157–171; Henry Nelson Wieman, *Man's Ultimate Commitment* (Carbondale, Ill.: Southern Illinois University Press, 1958) 11, 13, 293–294. For samples of soteriological theories of religions (theistic and non-theistic), see Frederick J. Streng, *Understanding Religious Life* (2nd ed.; Enrico, Cal.: Dickenson Publishing Co., Inc., 1976) particularly p. 7; Paul Wiebe, *The Architecture of Religion* (San Antonio: Trinity University Press, 1984) 19, 24, 112. I will unpack the distinction between "religious" and "non-religious" in chapter 5.

[23]Edward Schillebeeckx, O.P., *Interim Report on the Books Jesus & Christ,* trans. John Bowden (New York: Crossroad, 1981) chs. 1 and 2; *Christ: The Experience of Jesus as Lord,* trans. John Bowden (New York: The Seabury Press, 1980) pt. 1. Page numbers in the following paragraph are to this edition of *Christ.*

[24]See Schillebeeckx's "Dominican Spirituality," *God Among Us: The Gospel Proclaimed,* trans. John Bowden (New York: Crossroad, 1983) 232-248.

[25]Schillebeeckx, *Interim Report,* p. 133.

[26]Schillebeeckx, *Christ,* 672 (Schillebeeckx's emphasis). The context is a discussion of Manichaeism. Such anti-soterialists (as we might call these Manichees) are the most difficult group to place because their claims are so anomalous in relation to all three groups. For example, from the point of view of soterial relativists, anti-soterialists ought to be located alongside general soterialists because their claims are as general or universal as those of any soterialist (for example, "There is no evil" or "There is evil but there is nothing we can do about it"); but, from the point of view of general soterialists, anti-soterialists belong beside soterial relativists because they deny one of the conditions for getting the general soterialist's key claim off the ground. The terrorism of revolutionary dualism is heresy from all these points of view; see Jon Gunnemann, *The Moral Meaning of Revolution* (New Haven and London: Yale University Press, 1979) ch. 3. See also my remarks on the logic of unbelief in 5.C.2.c below.

[27]Richard B. Brandt, "Ethical Relativism," *Encyclopedia of Philosophy,* ed. Paul Edwards (New York: The Macmillan Company, 1967) 3:74-78. See also Jack W. Meiland and Michael Krausz, eds., *Relativism: Cognitive and Moral* (South Bend, Ind. and London: University of Notre Dame Press, 1982); Martin Hollis and Steven Lukes, eds., *Rationality and Relativism* (Cambridge: The MIT Press, 1982). I have taken for granted the truth of arguments that not all religions seek "salvation." For the relativity of "salvation" and related notions in various religions, see Willard G. Oxtoby, "Reflections on the Idea of Salvation," *Man and His Salvation: Studies in Memory of S. G. F. Brandon,* eds. E. J. Sharpe and J. R. Hinnels (Manchester: Manchester University Press, 1973) 17-37; Douglas Davies, "The Notion of Salvation in the Comparative Study of Religions," *Religion* 8 (1978), 85-100; John Bowker, *Problems of Suffering in Religions of the World* (Cambridge: Cambridge University Press, 1970); Peter Berger, *The Sacred Canopy: Elements of a Sociological Theory of Religion* (Garden City, N.Y.: Doubleday & Co., Inc., 1967) ch. 3 (The Problem of Theodicy). For theological treatments attuned to this relativity, see Joseph DiNoia, O.P., "The Universality of Salvation and the Diversity of Religious Aims," *Worldmission* 32 (no. 4, Winter 1981-82) 4-15; David H. Kelsey, "Struggling Collegially to Think About Evil: An Interpretive Essay," *Occasional Papers: Institute for Ecumenical and Cultural Research* (no. 6, September 1981) 1-6; Terrence W. Tilley, "The Use and Abuse of Theodicy," *Horizons* 11 (no. 2, Fall 1984) 304-319.

[28]William James, *The Varieties of Religious Experience: A Study in Human Nature* (New York: Collier Books, 1961) 400, 407; see also William James *Pragmatism* (Cambridge: Harvard University Press, 1975) lecture 8. For a soteriological reading of James, see Henry Samuel Levinson, *The Religious Investigations of William James* (Chapel Hill: The University of North Carolina Press, 1981). For a powerful critique of James, see Nicholas Lash, *Easter in Ordinary: Reflections on Human Experience and the Knowledge of God* (Charlottesville: University Press of Virginia, 1988) chs. 2-8 (where James is read in less relativistic ways than I have suggested).

[29]Note, then, that if cross and resurrection form a sequential unity, the Lutheran "simultaneity" model is subordinated to the Catholic "transformation" model, at least with regard to Christ. The cross, as Jon Gunnemann puts it, is not "the paradigm" of what I call soterial action—or it is the paradigm *only* in relationship to life and resurrection and promised return; Gunnemann, *The Moral Meaning of Revolution,* especially ch. 5. My quarrel below will not be with the storied relations Barth describes between Jesus' death and resurrection but with the ways this crucified and risen One stands with and for us.

[30]See also Jürgen Moltmann, *The Crucified God: The Cross of Christ as the Foundation and Criticism of Christian Theology,* trans. R. A. Wilson and John Bowden (New York: Harper and Row, 1974) particularly the ways Moltmann here (like Barth everywhere) focuses on the (particular) "personal name, Jesus" (p. 85) while striving to find (catholic) "points of correspondence" or "patterns" for dialogue between this Jesus Christ and psychological and political liberation strategies (pp. 291–294).

[31]Note, then, that Barth is both critic and example of soterial relativism (as is Lossky of orthodox soterialism and Schillebeeckx of general soterialism). He is critic when relativists apply their position to Jesus Christ; he is example when he finds their stand on other issues to be "secular parables" of the kingdom. When he ought to be critic and when example depends on particular cases. See, for example, Stanley Hauerwas, *Suffering Presence: Theological Reflections on Medicine, the Mentally Handicapped, and the Church* (South Bend, Ind.: University of Notre Dame Press, 1986), where Hauerwas combines a deep respect for what medicine has to teach us about salvation with reasons for thinking "medicine needs the church." Barth and Hauerwas may not agree on this particular case, but their ad hoc strategy is similar.

[32]No more than in the case of Lossky or Schillebeeckx do these criticisms amount to a thoroughgoing critique of Barth. I will, for example, not touch on Barth's paradoxical claims about "nothingness"; see David Ray Griffin, *God, Power, and Evil: A Process Theodicy* (Philadelphia: Westminster Press, 1976), 164–166.

[33]Karl Rahner, "Virginitas in Partu. A Contribution to the Problem of the Development of Dogma and of Tradition," *TI* 4:160. Do "dialectical" descriptions make salvation an instance of a process in which reconciliation (synthesis) not only abolishes but preserves an evil (antithesis) which is built into the nature of creation (thesis)? In context, it is clear that Rahner here uses the notion of "dialectical" opposition much more informally.

[34]Compare the "Instruction on the Contemplative Life and on the Enclosure of Nuns," (*Documents of Vatican II,* 656–675), where Israel's exodus and episodes of solitude in the life of Christ are warrants for the claim that a "certain degree of withdrawal from the world and some measure of contemplation must necessarily be present in every form of Christian life. . . ." I have not taken up the issue of "church offices" for two reasons. First, "church offices" are essential practices of a community, but subordinate to other common goods; I think that the ways Roman Catholics have institutionalized "religious" and "lay" life are more distinctive (for better and worse) of "Catholic particularity" than are the offices of priesthood, episcopacy, and/or papacy. Second, even if a reader does not grant this first reason, we still lack what John

O'Malley calls an adequate "historiography" (or, as I would say, narrative) of office—from its ritual location in eucharistic liturgies of ordination to its shape in diverse political cultures; see John O'Malley, S.J., "Priesthood, Ministry, and Religious Life: Some Historical and Historiographical Considerations," *Theological Studies* 49 (no. 2, June 1988) 223–257.

Chapter 5

[1]On the interaction between the way the face of God (particularly the face of Christ) is "at once the mark of unique personality and the embodiment of receptivity to others," see Frances Young and David F. Ford, *Meaning and Truth in Corinthians* (Grand Rapids, Mich.: William B. Eerdmans Publishing Company, 1987) especially pp. 248–255.

[2]See 2.A.2 as well as Charles Wood, *The Formation of Christian Understanding: An Essay in Theological Hermeneutics* (Philadelphia: Westminster Press, 1981) especially pp. 39–41, 46–47, 67–68, 100–101 (on Bible as Word of God).

[3]Such are the issues pollsters find useful in the United States. See *Religion in America: 50 Years: 1935-1985, The Gallup Report,* report no. 236 (May 1985) and *The People, Press, and Politics,* A Times Mirror Study of the American Electorate Conducted by the Gallup Organization September 1987 (Times Mirror, 1987).

[4]This includes anyone "whether high or low degree, man or woman" (2 Chr 15:13). Here is a paradigm of the egalitarianism of the Grand Inquisitor and other inquiring minds. Most shocking is Yahweh's promise that unless they (thus?) seek, he will desert them; by the end of the story, he does not.

[5]I will later return to the discussion of "godlessness" in John Courtney Murray, S.J., *The Problem of God: Yesterday and Today* (New Haven and London: Yale University Press, 1964) ch. 3. "Godlessness" is preferable to "atheism," for (1) it focuses the issue on "God," (2) it does not permit us to avoid the issue of atheistic religions (for example, Buddhism), and (3) atheism is defined in diverse and opposed ways depending on how "theism" is used and defined; see Michael Buckley, *At the Origins of Modern Atheism* (New Haven and London: Yale University Press, 1987) especially pp. 337ff. Compare Vatican II's helpful understatement, "The word atheism is used to signify things that differ considerably from each other" (CMW no. 19).

[6]Jaroslav Pelikan, *Christian Doctrine and Modern Culture (Since 1700), The Christian Tradition: A History of the Development of Doctrine,* vol. 5 (Chicago and London: University of Chicago Press, 1989) 182–183. Another part of the explanation for the implicitness of the doctrine of God is that, until modernity, it was widely (if not universally) presumed that all of us knew how to identify God; the debate was over whether God exists or creates or saves us.

[7]All references to the documents of Vatican II are by paragraph numbers.

[8]On the "direct and not inverse proportion" of divine and human freedom, see Kathryn Tanner, *God and Creation in Christian Theology* (Oxford: Basil Blackwell, 1988) 85. Tanner rightly shows how theologians as diverse as Aquinas, Barth, and Rahner follow this rule. However, to be persuaded to share Tanner's worry that Roman Catholic theology's use of this rule does not do justice to divine sovereignty (p. 162), I would have to be persuaded not only that some theologians jeopardize divine sovereignty but also that our essential practices (for example, liturgical and ecclesial) and teachings (for example, Vatican II) permit such jeopardizing.

[9]On "double agency," see Austin Farrer, *Faith and Speculation: An Essay in Philosophical Theology* (New York: New York University Press, 1967) v, although I think that Farrer's distinction between "the theology of nature" and "the theology of revelation" (p. 86) cannot do justice to non-theistic religions.

[10]For example, see the reading of Vatican II's teachings on revelation and Scripture and tradition by Joseph Ratzinger, Alois Grillmeier, and Beda Rigaux, "Dogmatic Constitution on Divine Revelation," *Commentary on the Documents of Vatican II,* ed. Herbert Vorgrimler, trans. William Glen-Doepel et al. (New York: Herder and Herder, 1969) vol. 3, especially pp. 179, 227–28, 248, 261.

[11]I borrow this formulation from David Burrell, who speaks not of spheres of divine and human activity but of "paradigmatic uses of *actus,*" where a paradigmatic use of "act" is such that "we cannot elucidate that paradigm use in terms more basic than *actus* itself." See David Burrell, C.S.C., *Aquinas: God and Action* (South Bend, Ind.: University of Notre Dame Press, 1979) 116–118, 131, 162–163, 173–175.

[12]Joseph Ratzinger, "Dogmatic Constitution on Divine Revelation, Chapter 1: Revelation Itself," *Commentary on the Documents of Vatican II,* vol. 3, pp. 160, 172, 173.

[13]I hope the nature of these third and fourth options will become clear as I show how they might address different audiences. Those interested in a careful formulation of these options as they generate arguments in many religious communities will want to consult William A. Christian, Sr., *Doctrines of Religious Communities: A Philosophical Study* (New Haven and London: Yale University Press, 1987) especially p. 100. Those interested in specific representatives of these four options might consider Kierkegaard or so-called Wittgensteinian fideists (fideism), John Hick or Gordan Kaufmann (modernist), John Macquarrie or David Tracy (third type), Donald MacKinnon or Hans Frei (fourth type). These four options are also comparable to a typology developed by Hans Frei and nicely summarized by David Ford in his introduction to *The Modern Theologians: An Introduction to Christian Theology in the Twentieth Century,* 2 vols. (Oxford: Basil Blackwell, 1989). Frei and Ford have five rather than four types because they divide my third type into two subgroups, one of which systematically correlates internal and external reasons (for example, Tracy) and one of which does not systematically correlate them (for example, Schleiermacher).

[14]John Henry Cardinal Newman, "Infinitude of the Divine Attributes," *Discourses Addressed to Mixed Congregations* (new impression; London: Longmans, Green, and Co., 1909) 305–322 (here, p. 318). All subsequent

quotes from Newman are from this sermon, pp. 314, 309. Note that I am beginning with the problem of "identifying," "referring to," or "teaching about" God. But it is crucial (to repeat a point I made at the beginning of the previous section [5.B]) that we cannot identify (or refer to or teach about) a God whom we can only identify (or refer to or teach about). Thus, "identifying God" is only part of "seeking the face of God." By section's end we shall see that arguments over how to identify God are of a piece with much larger questions about God's relationship to us and our relationship to God.

[15]Thomas E. Tracy, "The Moral Perfections of God," *The Thomist* 47 (no. 4, October 1983) 473–500 (here p. 485). How Tracy's proposal relates more exactly to Newman's would depend on how Newman (like Tracy) would take human beings to be the key examples of "the great agents which [God] has created in the material world."

[16]Ibid., 485, 488, 489, 490. My emphases.

[17]Newman, "Infinitude of the Divine Attributes," 309. Even here, however, we are not bereft of analogies, for (Newman romantically continues) the incarnation "is, if we may use human language, a prodigality of charity, or that heroic love of toil and hardship, which is poorly shadowed out in the romantic defenders of the innocent or the oppressed, whom we read of in history or in fable, who have gone about the earth, nobly exposing themselves to peril for any who asked their aid."

[18]Thomas E. Tracy, *God, Action, and Embodiment* (Grand Rapids, Mich.: William B. Eerdmans Publishing Company, 1984) 78. For some other metaphysical options on this issue, see Owen C. Thomas, ed., *God's Activity in the World: The Contemporary Problem* (Chico, Cal.: Scholars Press, 1983).

[19]Christian, *Doctrines of Religious Communities,* 120, 167. Shall we call this mode of identifying God "natural theology"? At one time I devoted several pages of this chapter to an excursus on natural theology. But the very fact that my discussion was an excursus implied that the question is not of fundamental importance for the chapter; I therefore decided it ought best to be handled elsewhere. Any effort to explain my position would involve unpacking the following two points: 1. Vatican I taught only that God "may be (*posse*) certainly known by the natural light of reason." Vatican I's formulation was not even definitively rejected by the reputed enemy of all natural theology, Karl Barth (*CD* 2/1:84). The reason for this is that Vatican I *can be* read as permitting only a "natural theology" *internal* to the faith. 2. Natural theology was practiced in parts of the world when there was (or was thought to be) considerable overlap among our notions of human as well as divine agency; where such common ground persists, we may take advantage of it—but this world will not necessarily provide any crucial, practical clue for God's dealings with other worlds.

[20]Tracy, "The Moral Perfections of God," 497. This is, Tracy points out, precisely the opposite of Thomas Aquinas, for whom the words we use for divine perfections are used literally of God, while the words are used inappropriately as far as our way of signifying these perfections. I obviously agree with Tracy's compassionate critique of Aquinas, but I realize the issues are terribly complex. However, the problem of thinking the perfections remains, whether we put the issue in Tracy's or Aquinas' terms.

[21]Tracy, "The Moral Perfections of God," 500.

²²This account is heavily influenced by George A. Lindbeck, *The Nature of Doctrine: Religion and Theology in a Postliberal Age* (Philadelphia: Westminster Press, 1984) ch. 2; by Ninian Smart's description of the practices of diverse religions in *The Religious Experience of Mankind* (3rd ed.; New York: Charles Scribner's Sons, 1984); and by William Christian's discussions of unrestricted primacy valuations in *Meaning and Truth in Religion* (Princeton: Princeton University Press, 1964, 1966) and *Oppositions of Religious Doctrines: A Study in the Logic of Dialogue Among Religions* (London: Macmillan and New York: Herder and Herder, 1972) ch. 5. Again, I am less interested in arguing for a particular theory of religion or religions than suggesting how an argument on the existence of God might relate to diverse and even opposed views of religions.

²³See Christian, *Meaning and Truth in Religion,* especially chs. 3 and 4 for how diverse predicates perform this function (for example, "x" is most powerful, most holy, of ultimate concern, etc.).

²⁴Karl Barth, *Anselm: Fides Quaerens Intellectum: Anselm's Proof of the Existence of God in the Context of His Theological Scheme,* trans. Ian W. Robertson (Richmond, Va.: John Knox Press, 1960) 38. See also Hans Frei, *The Identity of Jesus Christ: The Hermeneutical Bases of Dogmatic Theology* (Philadelphia: Fortress Press, 1975) ix, 155–156.

²⁵This enables Barth to disagree with theologies which separate inquiry into God's (i) being and (ii) activity. For example, Jean Calvin says that "[t]he most perfect way of seeking God, and the most suitable order is not for us to attempt with bold curiosity to penetrate to the investigation of his essence, which we ought more to adore than meticulously to search out but for us to contemplate him in his works whereby he renders himself near and familiar to us, and in some manner communicates himself." (*Institutes of the Christian Religion,* ed. John T. McNeill, trans. Ford Lewis Battles (Philadelphia: Westminster Press, 1960) bk. 1, ch. 5, sec. 9 (= vol. 1, p. 62). But, Barth would say, to investigate this One's works is to investigate his essence—although we do not do this out of bold and meticulous curiosity but as a phase of grateful adoration.

²⁶On the evasiveness of Barth's reading of Anselm and his argument, see John H. Hick and Arthur C. McGill, eds. *The Many-faced Argument: Recent Studies on the Ontological Argument for the Existence of God* (New York: The Macmillan Company, 1967) and James J. Buckley and William McF. Wilson, "A Dialogue with Barth and Farrer on Theological Method," *Heythrop Journal* 26 (1985) 274–293.

²⁷On God and Nibbana, see Christian, *Doctrines of Religious Communities,* 126–144.

²⁸Generally speaking, it is compatible with Vatican II to say that, with regard to different aspects of different religions, we may be pluralistic (for example, hold that these aspects of those religions are equal and valid paths to God), exclusivistic (for example, hold that the Christian way excludes some aspects of some other religious ways of living), or inclusivistic (for example, hold that other religions are constituted by practices and teachings identical to Christian practices and teachings); see Gavin D'Costa, "Theology of Religions," *The Modern Theologians,* 2:ch. 14 (from whom I have borrowed the labels "pluralism, exclusivism, and inclusivism" but defined them in slightly differ-

ent ways than D'Costa). Thus, on the issue of the salvation of non-believers, I agree with George Lindbeck that we ought to *permit* (without doctrinally *requiring*) answers ranging from claims that we are all anonymously Christian to scenarios of decisions we might make in dying or at the final judgment (*The Nature of Doctrine,* 55–63). But the real theological work lies between these extremes, as we sort out current identities, oppositions, and other patterns of relationships between religions one by one—as Augustine did for his time in canvassing the 288 supreme goods of the ancient world in *Concerning The City of God Against the Pagans,* trans. Henry Bettenson (Harmondsworth, England: Penguin Books, Ltd., 1972) bk. 19. As Vatican II suggests (NCR no. 4) the place to start and end for Christian theology is Judaism.

[29]The argument that we are all crypto-religious abides even when crypto-theism becomes implausible. Thus, Paul Wiebe, *The Architecture of Religion: A Theoretical Essay* (San Antonio: Trinity University Press, 1984) 26, argues that "the profound [in my idiom, that which is of unrestricted importance] is a formal and necessary human reality that is present within any possible way of dwelling on earth, whereas God is peculiar to the monotheistic ways of dwelling. . . ." I find the arguments of soterial relativists more plausible.

[30]John Courtney Murray, S.J., *The Problem of God: Yesterday and Today* (New Haven and London: Yale University Press, 1964) ch. 3, p. 87.

[31]See Martha Nussbaum's strategy for drawing the differences between herself and Samuel Beckett in "Narrative Emotions: Beckett's Genealogy of Love," *Ethics* 98 (no. 2, January 1988) 225–254; re-printed in Stanley Hauerwas and Gregory Jones, eds., *Why Narrative?* (Grand Rapids, Mich.: William B. Eerdmans Publishing Co., 1989) pp. 216–248. What is refreshing about Nussbaum is that, while she is certainly not a theist, she also knows she is not "religious" (in the way I use that term above); see her *The Fragility of Goodness: Luck and Ethics in Greek Tragedy and Philosophy* (Cambridge: Cambridge University Press, 1986). I do not deny that the godless frequently *do* speak for each other, acting as if they share a godlessness which overrides their disagreements on other issues. But they do not agree on which of them *best* speaks for the others.

[32]See Origen's comparison of the theological apologist to Jesus' response to his inquisition in *Contra Celsum,* trans. Henry Chadwick (Cambridge: Cambridge University Press, 1965) 3–4.

[33]Murray, *The Problem of God,* 79 (My emphases). Unfortunately, Murray does not discuss the possibility of the deep connections between the godlessness of believers and the godlessness of modern and postmodern men and women. See also 2.C.2 above.

[34]See *CD* 3/4:652. We do not have to share Barth's dialectics of the impossible possibility of godlessness; we might more simply say that our godlessness is the absurdity we call sin. Godlessness has no "logic" to it—or whatever logic it does have depends on its setting in nature and grace and glory.

[35]See, for example, the tradition summarized in J. Samuel Preus, *Explaining Religion: Criticism and Theory from Bodin to Freud* (New Haven and London: Yale University Press, 1987).

[36]For a philosophically acute treatment of this issue (under the rubric of the

"occasion-comprehensiveness" of our teachings), see Christian, *Doctrines of Religious Communities,* 188, 226. For the application to issues of causality, see also William A. Christian, "Religious Valuations of Scientific Truths," *American Philosophical Quarterly* 6 (no. 2, April 1969) 144-150.

[37]CMA no. 22. The Latin phrase is not translated in *Documents of Vatican II,* 839; see *Indices Verborum et Locutionum Decretorum Concilii Vaticani II.* 14. *Decretum de activitate missionali ecclesiae. Ad Gentes* (Bologna: Istituto per le Scienze Religiose, 1983) 21.

[38]Thomas F. Tracy, *God, Action, and Embodiment* (Grand Rapids, Mich.: William B. Eerdmans Publishing Company, 1984), 79.

[39]John Henry Newman, *An Essay in Aid of Grammar of Assent* (Garden City, N.Y.: Doubleday & Co., 1955) 230.

[40]See "[Letter] To Robert Bridges," *A Hopkins Reader,* ed. John Pick. (rev. ed.; Garden City, N.Y.: Image, 1966) 408–409. Joseph Bochenski, [*The Logic of Religion* (New York: New York University Press, 1965) 109] calls this sense of mystery "axiomatic mystery," pointing out that these kinds of mysteries are not peculiar to theology.

·Chapter 6

[1]Gustavo Gutierrez, "Theology from the Underside of History," *The Power of the Poor in History,* trans. Robert R. Barr (Maryknoll, N.Y.: Orbis Books, 1983) 194; *We Drink from our Own Wells: The Spiritual Journey of a People,* trans. Matthew J. O'Connell (Maryknoll, N.Y.: Orbis Books, 1984) 126. I presume that "from within" does not merely mean that we *think* about the poor, or even that we *see* as the poor see, having or acquiring or stealing their thoughts or perspective on things. "From within" refers not to our concepts or percepts of the poor but to a context from within which we *enact* discipleship.

[2]On the "tacit quotation" or "deliberate allusion" in the Pastoral Constitution, see Charles Moeller in Herbert Vorgrimler, ed., *Commentary on the Documents of Vatican II,* trans. W. J. O'Hara (New York: Herder and Herder, 1969) 5:87. On the context in Terence, see Sander Goldberg, *Understanding Terence* (Princeton: Princeton University Press, 1986) 14, 137; H. D. Jocelyn, "Homo sum: humani nil a me alienum puto," *Antichthon* 7 (1973) 14–46. A hidden issue here is how much the Pastoral Constitution is suggesting we deal with modernity on the model of the way Christians dealt with the classical world—and how much our situation is relatively unique.

[3]Alfons Auer calls an earlier version of this chapter "the most unmixed success in the whole history of the Pastoral Constitution," although a close study of the final version reveals a number of tensions; see "Part I, Chapter III," *Commentary on the Documents of Vatican II,* 5:182–202 (especially pp. 183, 187, 194–195, 200). In what follows I am experimenting with how this part of Vatican II can address the problem of relating internal and external joys and griefs. But the "fit" between Vatican II and this problem is not perfect. For ex-

ample, the Pastoral Constitution proceeds from treatment of "the Individual" (pt. 1, ch. 1) through "the Community" (pt. 1, ch. 2) to "Human Activity throughout the Cosmos" (pt. 1, ch. 3). A case could be made that we have here an infelicitous distinction between our individual and social "being" (pt. 1, chs. 1 and 2) and our "action" (pt. 1, ch. 3)—or "persons" (individual and communal) and the cosmos or "physical" world; hence, the abstractness of Vatican II's treatment of our diverse individuality and communities. I think it is more truthful to read the three chapters more "holistically," but arguing the case against competing readings will have to be reserved for another time and place.

[4]It would be possible at this point to typologize theologies on this issue as I have done in previous chapters on other issues. For example, on the model of 5.C, we might try to read Vatican II as teaching (in fideist fashion) that Christian joys and griefs can learn nothing really new from the joys and griefs of modernity; all our joys and griefs are "internal." We might try to read Vatican II as teaching that the *only* joys and griefs Christians have are those it shares with the people of our time—eliminating (in modernist fashion) Christian-specific joys and griefs. We might reject these two options in favor of Vatican II's "reciprocity," but read "reciprocity" as the systematic correlation of internal and external joys and griefs—or as an "ad hoc," unsystematic enterprise. As in previous chapters, I aim for something more than "ad hoc" and less than "systematic" correlation.

[5]See David Kelsey, "The Doctrine of Creation from Nothing," *Evolution and Creation,* ed. Ernan McMullin (South Bend, Ind.: University of Notre Dame Press, 1985) 179. I do not think much is at stake in whether we call such claims "metaphysical" or not—just as I do not think Christians have much stake in claiming that some of their truth-claims are "absolutely" general. We might be satisfied with showing that such truth-claims are analogous to what goes on in the Book of Proverbs, where Israel's sages pondered counting and otherwise sorting things out as they read the stories of the Torah and the visions of the prophets. God may have eschatological plans even for our abstractions.

[6]See, for one example, Bernard J. F. Lonergan, S.J., *Insight: A Study of Human Understanding* (rev. ed.; London: Longmans, Green, and Co., 1958), 667: "What is basic sin? It is the irrational. Why does it occur? If there were a reason, it would not be sin."

[7]Austin Farrer, *Love Almighty and Ills Unlimited* (London and Glasgow: Wm. Collins & Co., Ltd., 1962) especially ch. 2.

[8]Alasdair MacIntyre, *After Virtue: A Study in Moral Theory,* (2nd ed.; South Bend, Ind.: University of Notre Dame Press, 1984) 163, 203; Charles Taylor, *Sources of the Self: The Making of the Modern Identity* (Cambridge: Harvard University Press, 1989) 17, 48 (where Taylor quotes the passages from MacIntyre just cited). This agreement between MacIntyre and Taylor is important because they are opposed on many other crucial issues. Pressed to summarize their disagreement, I would say that MacIntyre emphasizes the griefs and Taylor emphasizes the joys of modernity. But one specific example is symptomatic of a crucial philosophical issue involved in seeking the humanity of God. Taylor contrasts two ways of conceiving our narrative quest on pp. 51–52: "One could [and MacIntyre does] put it this way: because we cannot but or-

ient ourselves to the good, and thus determine our place relative to it and hence determine the direction of our lives, we must inescapably understand our lives in narrative forms, as a 'quest.' But one could [and Taylor does] perhaps start from another point: because we have to determine our place in relation to the good, therefore we cannot be without an orientation to it, and hence must see our life in a story." The point of the rest of the chapter is not to deny the philosophical aspects of this debate their own time and space (and even a limited autonomy) but to suggest that, even if we resolve the philosophical problems, there are myriad theological problems left (as the reader will see by substituting "the humanity of God" for "the good" in the previous quote).

⁹See, for example, St. Ignatius of Loyola, *The Constitutions of the Society of Jesus,* trans. George E. Gass, S.J. (St. Louis: The Institute of Jesuit Sources, 1970), 165, par. 288; St. John of the Cross, *Spiritual Canticle,* trans. E. Allison Peers (3rd rev. ed.; Garden City, N.Y.: Image Books, 1961) 61ff., 260ff.; "Instruction on the Contemplative Life and on the Enclosure of Nuns," *Documents of Vatican II,* 656–675; Jonathan Edwards, *A Treatise on Religious Affections* (Grand Rapids, Mich.: Baker Book House, 1982) 300ff.; Gutierrez, *We Drink from Our Own Wells,* ch. 5.

¹⁰I am not here thinking of any specific proposal about the nature and importance of "character." Instead I am thinking of a complex and often inconsistent theological, literary, and philosophical tradition which extends from the Bible's diverse characters through patristic and medieval accounts of the virtues of character to Karl Rahner's "turn to the subject" or Hans Urs von Balthasar's treatment of "character" in the theater (*Theo-Drama: Theological Dramatic Theory,* vol. 1, *Prolegomena,* trans. Graham Harrison [San Francisco: Ignatius Press, 1988] especially pt. 3) as well as from Aristotle's ethics to the modern novel. But no one has done more to promote interest in (as well as suspicion of) issues of character in Christian theology in the English-speaking world over the last fifteen years than Stanley Hauerwas, particularly in *Character and the Christian Life: A Study in Theological Ethics,* (San Antonio: Trinity University Press, 1985).

¹¹See Kelsey, "The Doctrine of Creation," 180. I am, however, suspicious of describing this by saying that the doctrine of creation is an "existential" or "self-involving utterance" (pp. 178, 179), for this can suggest that there is some general agreement on how to be (or whether we ought to be) an existential "self." In other words, it can be the bearer of remnants of "the turn to the subject" Kelsey has so nicely criticized elsewhere; see his "Human Being," *Christian Theology: An Introduction to Its Traditions and Tasks,* eds. Peter C. Hodgson and Robert H. King (2nd ed.; Philadelphia: Fortress Press, 1985) ch. 6.

¹²James Tunstead Burtchaell, C.S.C., "Community Experience as Source of Christian Ethics," *The Giving and Taking of Life: Essays Ethical* (South Bend, Ind.: University of Notre Dame Press, 1989) 116. Roman Catholics ought even to qualify Burtchaell's exception, for our Lectionary lists as theologians (doctors) of the Church ordained males—all of whom, besides being teachers, are described as *primarily* something else: bishop, pastor, priest, deacon, abbot.

¹³See Kierkegaard's *Attack Upon "Christendom" 1854–1855,* trans. Walter

Lowrie (Princeton: Princeton University Press, 1944) 144. I would not deny that Kierkegaard's point might be correct (to generalize his proverb on "Protestantism, Christianly considered") "as a remedy [corrective] at a given time and place" rather than "as a principle for Christianity" (p. 34).

[14]A "complete" barrier would yield an individualism incompatible with the gospel. It must be said that Vatican II sometimes admits of a more individualistic (and, to this extent, more Kierkegaardian) version of character than I am presenting. For example, where I speak of "internal joys and griefs," Vatican II once speaks of our "interiority" (*interioritas*): "by her own interiority she rises above the universe of mere things: to this profound interiority she returns when she turns to the heart where the God who probes her heart awaits her, and where she herself discerns her proper destiny under the eyes of God" (*Interioritate enim sua* ["the power to know himself in the depths of his being," the English translation infelicitously says] *universitatem rerum excedit: ad hanc profundam interioritatem* ["his real self," the English translation says, more appropriately this time] *redit, quando convertitur ad cor, ubi Deus eum exspectat, qui corda scrutatur, et ubi ipse sub oculis Dei de propria sorte decernit* [CMW no. 14, my translation]).

In one sense, this text summarizes what, I will eventually propose, is near the heart of the matter: there is no "pure" interiority (for example, no "internal" without "external" joys and griefs), for we stand and move "under God"; this is what Kierkegaard called " the theological self, the self directly before God" (*The Sickness Unto Death*, trans. Howard V. Hong and Edna H. Hong [Princeton: Princeton University Press, 1980] 79). However, as this chapter moves on, I will insist that our character is shaped not only "under the eyes of God" but "before and with God"—and not only in relationship to God but also before and with each other. Our "theological self" is our character before God *and* neighbor in Word *and* Spirit. Once again we can see how crucial it is to read the Pastoral Constitution's chapter on the individual (whence this quote is taken) in relationship to its chapter on the community (pt. 1, ch. 2) and human activity throughout the cosmos (pt. 1, ch. 3).

[15]I think (for example) of the American Catholic Bishops' effort to teach on behalf of a community that can embrace certain kinds of Christian pacifists *and* certain kinds of just war theorists; see (for the second draft and final version) *Origins, NC Documentary Service* 12 (no. 20, 28 October 1982) and 13 (no. 1, 19 May 1983). I think that this position is theoretically and practically incoherent, but perhaps this is the best a pilgrim community can do at this moment in its history.

[16]See Friedrich Nietzsche, *Ecce Homo: How One Becomes What One Is*, trans. R. J. Hollingdale (London: Penguin Books, 1979) where Nietzsche recommends "in a cheerful and affable way" (p. 33) that we follow Zarathustra's advice: "I now go away alone, my disciples! You too now go away and be alone!" (p. 36).

[17]Or (as Charles Taylor prefers to say) distinguishing between "internal" and "external" is only one way of talking about our "self"; I prefer to say that talk of our "self" is a peculiarly modern way of talking about our "character." See Charles Taylor, *Sources of the Self: The Making of the Modern Identity* (Cambridge: Harvard University Press, 1989). For the "moral topography" of internal-external, others might substitute private-public, individual-commu-

nity, subject-object, or numerous other signs of our fragmented times. For example, Karl Rahner's distinction between "the transcendental" and "the categorical" does work analogous to my distinction between "internal" and "external" joys and griefs. However, when Rahner argues that questioning is our inescapable background because we cannot challenge it without contradicting ourselves, he seems to presume that questioning is self-grounding; see, for example, Karl Rahner *Foundations of the Christian Faith: An Introduction to the Idea of Christianity,* trans. William V. Dych (New York: The Seabury Press, 1978) 11. Bultmann and Tillich make similar moves, although they claim that questioning arises out of systematic *angst* rather than out of the self-transcendence of a good creature. But to get ourselves into a position of conducting an experiment with pure questioning, we would have to devote ourselves *solely* to inquiry; see Bernard Williams, *Descartes: The Project of Pure Enquiry* (New Jersey: Humanities Press, 1978) 467. Aquinas is more correct in proposing that our deliberations ought to be highly tuned to context and subject matter (although there are notorious problems in Aquinas's way of relating our "natural" inquiries and our inquiry into revelation); see, for example, Aquinas's treatment of *consilium* in *Summa Theologiae,* 1a2ae. 14.

[18]William James, *Pragmatism* (Indianapolis, Indiana: Hackett Publishing Company, Inc., 1981) lecture 4 (The One and the Many), especially p. 67. The point is important, for if there is only one thing (for example, God or the World or Us or Me), any relations will have to be *internal* to that thing; on the other hand, if there are no internal relations, we would live in a world of isolated particulars..

[19]I should emphasize that this systematically comprehensive aim might include "internal" as well as "external" joys and griefs. Thus, Aquinas offers a systematic account of our physical, affective, intellectual, and other powers; others might argue that a focus on our *powers* (including those perfected powers Aquinas calls our virtues) risks the (masculine?) mistake of neglecting our needs—particularly our *needs* before God.

[20]See William A. Christian, Sr., *Doctrines of Religious Communities,* 177–186.

[21]See George A. Lindbeck, *The Nature of Doctrine: Religion and Theology in a Postliberal Age* (Philadelphia: Fortress Press, 1984) 84–88 as well as doctrinal rules developed as a choice "between two alternatives, both of which are bad, but one of which is worse than the other" (p. 98).

[22]For two appreciative theological critics of "character," see Gilbert C. Meilaender, *The Theory and Practice of Virtue* (South Bend, Ind.: University of Notre Dame Press, 1984) especially ch. 5; Oliver O'Donovan, *Resurrection and Moral Order: An Outline for Evangelical Ethics* (Leicester, England: Inter-Varsity Press and Grand Rapids, Mich.: William B. Eerdmans Publishing Co., 1986) ch. 10.

[23]I have benefitted here from L. Gregory Jones's argument that we need to locate formation of character in the context of discipleship lived in friendship with the triune God—including his account of how such formation takes place in relationship to worship and sacraments, Scripture, and the Church; see L. Gregory Jones, *Transformed Judgment: Toward a Trinitarian Account of the Moral Life* (South Bend, Ind.: University of Notre Dame Press, 1990). My ac-

count here seeks to suggest why our character "before and with" each other can be Christianly enacted only "before and with " a triune God.

[24]Once again, for promising directions with regard to the Trinity and the moral life, see Jones, *Transformed Judgment.* For the ecumenical issues, I am most sympathetic to Yves M.-J. Congar's "contribution to an agreement" among Greek and Latin Christians in *I Believe in the Holy Spirit,* trans. David Smith (New York: The Seabury Press and London: Geoffrey Chapman, 1983) 3:ch. 4. With regard to characterizations of the "immanent" Trinity, I am not satisfied with any of the current options; see my "Re-Trieving Trinitarian Teaching: A Review Discussion," *The Thomist* 48 (no. 2, April 1984) 274–296.

[25]Jaroslav Pelikan, *The Emergence of the Catholic Tradition (100–600), The Christian Tradition: A History of the Development of Doctrine,* vol. 1 (Chicago and London: University of Chicago Press, 1971) 172. Good historians like Pelikan also worry that such summaries "give the superficial impression of a greater smoothness than the facts warrant" (p. 172), but the superficial impression is useful for the point I am making.

[26]See Charles Norris Cochrane, *Christianity and Classical Culture: A Study of Thought and Action from Augustus to Augustine* (London: Oxford University Press, 1957) especially ch. 11.

[27]Irenaeus, *Against Heresies, The Writings of Irenaeus,* trans. Alexander Roberts and W. H. Rambaut (Edinburgh: T. & T. Clark, 1868), vol. 1, bk. 2, xxviii, 3 (= p. 221). See the biblical theme in Isa 48:17; 54:13; 55:1; Jer 31:33–34; Prov 9:1–6 or 1 Thess 4:9 and 1 John 2:20, 27.

[28]Augustine, *Expositions on the Book of Psalms,* ed. A. Cleveland Coxe, *A Select Library of the Nicene and Post-Nicene Fathers of the Christian Church,* ed. Philip Schaff (Reprint; Grand Rapids, Mich.: William B. Eerdmans Publishing Co., 1979) 8:521 (on Ps 105). See also "Lecture or Tractates on the Gospel According to St. John," *A Select Library of the Nicene and Post-Nicene Fathers of the Christian Church,* 8:314 (Tractate 63.1); "On the Holy Trinity," trans. Arthur West Haddan and William G. T. Shedd, *A Select Library of the Nicene and Post-Nicene Fathers of the Christian Church,* 3:122, 125, 134, 199.

[29]Gregory of Nyssa, *In Ecclesiasten,* Oratio 7, *Gregorii Nyseni Opera,* ed. Werner Jaeger (Leiden: E.J. Brill, 1962) 5:400–401 (Commenting on Eccl 3:6). Compare Lessing's Promethean choice: "If God held all truth in his right hand and in his left the everlasting striving after truth, so that I should always and everlastingly be mistaken, and said to me, 'Choose,' with humility I would pick on the left hand and say, 'Father, grant me that. Absolute truth is for thee alone'"; Henry Chadwick, "Introduction," *Lessing's Theological Writings,* Henry Chadwick, ed. (Stanford: Stanford University Press, 1956) 43. It is not that God does not offer us a choice between (*inter alia*) truth and falsehood (although there is no such thing as a single Absolute Truth that destroys particular truths). But why must "everlasting striving after truth" imply I must "everlastingly be mistaken" in *every* case?

[30]See Mitchell Dahood's discussion of the competing translations of Psalm 105:4 in *Psalms III 101–150,* The Anchor Bible, vol. 17A (Garden City, N.Y.: Doubleday and Co., 1970) 49, 52.

Name Index

I have not included names of translators or editors. I have included the biblical books identified by a proper name.

Subject Index

ACTION-GUIDES. *See* GOOD
AND GOODS; PRACTICES.
ACTS OF THE APOSTLES,
35, 63, 76, 81
AGNOSTICISM, 172
AMERICANISM, 141
ANOINTING, 25, 51, 85, 90,
124, 146, 149
APOCALYPSE, BOOK OF, 63,
66, 146, 172
APOLOGETICS, 42, 81-82, 173
ATHEISM. *See* GOD, God-
lessness.

BAPTISM, ch. 2, 56, 85, 117,
124, 148, 188 (notes 4 and 6)
continuum of practices, 28
ritual context of inquiry, 25
BEAUTY, 41, 148, 153
BISHOPS, 4, 7, 36, 89, 100,
129, 209 (note 15)
Synod of (1985), 70, 196 (note 5)
See also CHURCH, offices;
ORDERS.
BUDDHISM, 6, 14, 39, 82, 107,
112, 125, 141, 144, 146, 170

CANON LAW AND
LAWYERS, 4, 5, 182

CANTICLE OF CANTICLES,
134, 189 (note 21)
CATHOLIC PARTICULARITY,
xi-xii, 1-18, 21-24, 50, 56-57,
101-116, 134-136, 152, 180,
182, 185 (note 2), 192 (note 7)
CAUSALITY (or uniformities in
the cosmos), 35, 37, 148, 171,
187 (note 2), 190 (note 28),
206 (note 36)
CHARACTER, 28, 58, 123,
155, 165-174, 208 (note 10)
Character-traits, 138, 144, 182
Dispositions, powers and
needs, 4, 210 (note 19)
CHRONICLES, BOOKS OF, 125
CHURCH, 5, 8-11, 33-35, 74,
ch. 4, 147, 155, 157
Goods, quest for diverse, 88-91
Missionary community, 150-153
Narratives of, 60-62, 85, 105
Office, 200 (note 34). *See also*
ORDERS.
One, holy, catholic, and apos-
tolic, 1, 56, 92, 185 (note 2)
Representatives of all humanity,
102
Saints and sinners, 91-93
See also VATICAN II.